CARRIER
PILOT

An unforgettable true story of wartime flying

CARRIER PILOT

An unforgettable true story of wartime flying

Norman Hanson

 Patrick Stephens, Cambridge

First published in 1979

British Library Cataloguing in Publication Data
Hanson, Norman
  Carrier pilot
  1. Great Britain. Royal Navy   2. Illustrious, *Ship*
  3. World War, 1939–1945—Naval operations,
  British—Personal narratives   4. Aircraft carriers
  I. Title
  940.54′59′410924   D772.I/

ISBN 0 85059 349 2

Photoset in 11 on 12 pt Imprint.
Printed in Great Britain on City Supreme Antique Wove
and bound by The Garden City Press, Letchworth, Hertfordshire, SG6 1JS,
for the publishers, Patrick Stephens Limited,
Bar Hill, Cambridge, CB3 8EL, England.

Contents

To my comrades of the 15th Naval Fighter Wing—
the quick and the dead.

Here dead lie we because we did not choose
To live and shame the land from which we sprung.
Life, to be sure, is nothing much to lose;
But young men think it is, and we were young.
A. E. HOUSMAN

Acknowledgements

A number of good friends, shipmates and representatives of commercial and official bodies have been of invaluable assistance in providing information and in lending photographs for reproduction. My sincere thanks are due especially to:

John Winton, the naval author and one-time Midshipman in HMS *Illustrious*, without whose enthusiasm, guidance and encouragement this book would never have got under way. Les Retallick, old friend and shipmate, for detailed information on 1830 Squadron personnel; to my sorrow, he died in Canada in April 1977. Captain A. H. Wallis, CBE, RN (Ret), former Commander of HMS *Illustrious*, for details of ship routine which I had long since forgotten. Captain R. L. B. Cunliffe, CBE, RN (Ret), my first Captain in HMS *Illustrious*, for permission to reproduce his photograph. Les C. Wort, Lieutenant-Commander (A), DSC, RNVR, a good and true friend from early flying days, for similar permission. Lady L. Lambe for kindly allowing me to reproduce the photograph of her late husband, Admiral of the Fleet Sir Charles E. Lambe, GCB, CVO, former Captain of HMS *Illustrious*. Michael Turner, whose painting adorns the dust-cover. Mr T. Clark, Press and Information Officer, Vickers Ltd, Barrow-in-Furness, for technical details about HMS *Illustrious*. Miss L. Gilbreath, LTV Aerospace Corporation, Dallas, Texas, USA, for photographs and technical information about the Corsair. Imperial War Museum (Department of Photographs), for their ready and cheerful assistance in producing photographs from their archives.

Technical and nautical expressions and abbreviations have been kept to a minimum in the text except where authenticity demands their inclusion. However, I have provided a glossary of these on pages 253–255.

Suddenly there was gunfire . . .

The port side 4.5s cracked out with their ear-splitting clatter, soon followed by the thumping drum-beat of the Bofors. I ran to the port-holes on the port side, putting on my tin lid on the way.

I stuck out my head. There was a twin-engined Jap—a Betty—getting some rough treatment from the Fleet's guns way out on the port beam, where a Seafire from *Indefatigable* was recklessly trying to engage him at the same time. Coming up on our port quarter was another Betty, flying fast and low. He, too, was taking a lot of punishment from everybody within reach and, as I watched, his starboard engine started to belch smoke. As he came up to us, going like a train about 80 yards away, I saw flashes from his mid-upper turret. What the hell is he signalling for, I thought. Must be crazy! Then I heard the clang of shells on our hull—Christ! He's not signalling! He's *firing*! And any second now, Hanson, you stupid bastard, you'll get your bloody head blown off! I pulled my head inside—or, rather, I intended to, but the rim of my fine American helmet, only just capable of passing through the aperture, now stuck on the outer rim of the port-hole.

From my right, from the front of the island, 30 or 40 feet away, came a blinding flash. I can't remember hearing the deep clang of the explosion; there was only the concussion whose violence rattled my head inside the tin hat like a pea in a drum. My head came inside then without *any* trouble, almost pulling in the port-hole with it. As though from miles away I heard Mike shout:

'Come on, Hans! Stretchers!'

He was already running through the door, pulling one end of a stretcher. I went after him, taking up the back end. We galloped down the ladder and out on to the deck. It was a shambles. Some of the ratings of 854 Squadron had been man-handling two Avengers down the deck and had been caught abreast of the island. Both aircraft were in flames and bodies were strewn around and beneath them, in various horrible forms of death. Mike was heading for the port nets, whence came shouts and shrill screams. Halfway across the deck I dropped my end of the stretcher to stop beside a chap lying in the middle of the

11

crash barriers. He was flat on his back, spread-eagled, gazing open-eyed at the sky. He hadn't a scratch on him and there wasn't a drop of blood to be seen. I knelt down. It was 'Cock' Hardwick, the Petty Officer who operated the barriers; a fine chap and a true stanchion of the Navy.

I slapped his face, gently. I was still deaf, with my ears singing away merrily from the effects of the blast.

'Come on, Cock,' I said. 'Come on—get up. You're all right. Not a mark on you. Sit up and I'll get you a quick tot to bring you round.'

He didn't move. He was deeply unconscious. I moved round to his head. If I raise him gently, I thought, it might help to revive him faster. I put my hands under his armpits and lifted, easily and slowly.

He had no back. His shirt was gone—and his spine, his lungs and whatever else a human being has above the waist. I was looking straight at his rib cage. An iron hand of shrapnel—or a chunk of the shell casing itself—had gouged out his back. No blood—the searing hot metal had cauterised him solid as it had rubbed him out in one flashing, fleeting second. There were no guts—nothing. I dropped him and ran like hell to Mike at the nets. There seemed to be a lot of wounded, and the cries and screams were undiminished. But Mike had found another partner to help him lift his customer.

'Hans! Hans! Come over here—quick!'

It was Charlie Hobbs, the bos'n. Fire-fighting crews were already smothering the Avengers' engines in foam and Charlie was pulling the bodies from beneath the aircraft. They were in a hell of a state. All young, mostly under 20. One kid's scalp had been torn from the back of his head and his hair was covering his face like a grotesque mask. The grey sponge that was his brain was protruding from his cranium. Poor little sod, I thought; but he would never have known what hit him. In split seconds, as I looked at this fearful relic of some mother's pride and joy, I thought of the comments of wives, sweethearts, mothers, sisters: 'My, Jack! You look lovely in your uniform! How it *suits* you!' I wondered what they would think now? . . . But Charlie was bawling at me again.

'Come on, Hans, for God's sake! Move these lads up against the island!'

I caught up the legs of one body and pulled it, slowly and tenderly, to the high, grey wall of the island. I just felt sad—oddly enough, not sick. Just unbelievably sad.

'Oh! For Christ's sake, Norman!' (My Sunday name now!) 'Get a bloody jerk on, son! Those bastards'll be back any minute!' Charlie was grabbing them by the ankles and fairly hurling them across the deck. He looked up and saw my face.

'Don't let it worry you, Hans,' he said, surprisingly gently and softly, despite the rumpus that seemed to fill the deck. 'They can't feel anything now, you know. You can't hurt them any more.'

What a great man you are, Charlie, I thought. Somewhere along the years you will tell them that you were the bos'n of *Illustrious* and some smooth bastard who knew the sea only from kicking pebbles into it from Southsea beach will say 'So what?' No one but your shipmates will ever know what a sterling character you really are.

That evening Charlie was sewing those mangled kids into tarpaulin sheets.

Later, much later, as I walked down the deck to get below to my cabin, the flight-deck party was hosing down the deck. The foam, like some filthy detergent polluting a river, was tumbling reluctantly towards the round-down. In its centre, even more reluctantly, was creeping that grey, pathetic sponge. I could only say as I flopped down the ladders, desperately tired, 'Jesus! Jesus Christ!'

Euryalus, the pivot cruiser in the centre of the Fleet, on whom we all kept station, had also been firing at the aircraft which had tried in vain to blow off my head. When *Illustrious* interposed herself between *Euryalus* and the target, she had failed to check her fire. *Euryalus* hit us, fair and square, with two 5.25-inch bricks. One, 'mine' and the Captain's—for it succeeded in shattering his ear-drums—hit below the windbreak on the front of the compass platform. It was the shrapnel from this that did the damage on and beyond the flight-deck. The second shell penetrated the starboard side of the hull below the island and caused chaos and unutterable confusion there for the next six or seven hours. In all, 12 were killed and more than 20 injured.

The island is the brain of the carrier and all the electrical wiring controlling virtually the whole ship was carried down a great trunking before it spread out its tentacles throughout the vessel. The second shell smashed through this trunking; so we communicated for the next few hours as Nelson had done—by word of mouth, passed from man to man. But the Navy—and Dartmouth training—can rise above all difficulties. The ship's officers and men were magnificent and worked wonders.

One of the boys killed was an anti-aircraft gunner, who operated a twin Oerlikon 20 mm mounting from a contraption vaguely reminiscent of a motor cycle sidecar, from a position just below the compass platform. Later, when we cleared lower deck to count heads, we were one short—this gunner. He certainly wasn't in his sidecar and there was no evidence of anyone having been seen blown over the side. As a final check Harry Prior, one of our Warrant Gunners, climbed up to the Oerlikon position. He looked inside the sidecar and promptly vomited. What he saw there was a pair of legs, cut off at the thighs; a cockpit floor covered with—well, what? And hanging from the 'handle-bars' controlling the guns were two hands, still grasping the rubber grips, severed at the wrists. Nothing else.

That evening, as we cruised slowly south-eastwards, 100 miles or so from the coast of Sumatra, we buried them. Our great ship slowed down to six knots. George Fawkes read the Burial Service, standing beside that silent row of Union flags. One after another the boards were tilted and the hammock-like tarpaulins slid swiftly and quietly into the Indian Ocean. The plaintive notes of the bugle rang out over the great waste of water and they were gone. We could do no more than hope to remember them.

1

How it all started

Fun runs in families and, although my parents didn't seem to have had a great deal to laugh about in their early days, at least they had learnt to take life no more seriously than it deserves by the time I came along in 1914, followed four years later by my brother.

Fun seems to have occupied the greater part of my life—the sort of fun that comes from 'doing things'. I was never much of a spectator. 'Having a go' has driven me along for 60-odd years very pleasantly, sometimes excitingly. And although I can't honestly say that participation has provided me with cabinets bursting with silver trophies, the urge to try my hand has brought a wonderful zest to the business of living.

My pre-war experience of flying had been limited to say the least. I must have been about 18 when my brother and I walked across the grass of Carlisle's airfield with a ten-bob note clutched in my hot little hand, to clamber into one of Sir Alan Cobham's ancient Avro 504 biplanes. We sat on a plank in the rear cockpit—an open 'bath-tub' about the size of a garden tool-shed. There was no safety harness and certainly no nonsense about parachutes. Flight-Lieutenant Tyson took us over the city. The Norman castle, the cathedral, our school, my cricket club, the great railway network—all these were laid out below us, amazing and beautiful. The thrill was unforgettable and for a cash outlay of five bob a whole new world had been opened up for me.

We made our second flight during a visit to the Rhineland in the summer of 1938; the time of Munich, when Neville Chamberlain returned from visiting Hitler, brandishing his piece of paper which he fondly imagined had bought time for us. We spent most of our holiday in Cologne, a beautiful city in those far-off days before thousand-bomber raids pulverised it into rubble. From the airfield on the city's northern boundary (not to be confused with the splendid modern airport now situated between the city and Bonn) we took off in a three-engined airliner, a Junkers Ju 52. Its austere passenger cabin gave no suggestion of the luxurious fittings to which air travellers would eventually become accustomed. There was no such thing as a pressurised cabin, no seductive lighting, no long-legged air steward-esses. It was utilitarian; and within 12 months it would have shuffled off its cloak of respectability and shown itself in its true colours, trans-porting the Wehrmacht first to Poland, then with bewildering speed to Rotterdam, Paris, Oslo, Belgrade, Athens, Tripoli, Benghazi and the Russian front. There had been a time when it seemed possible that it would land at Croydon or Northolt too! It was a regular warhorse; the German equivalent of the American Dakota.

On that sunny afternoon over the Rhine, however, the possibility of war was still remote, and we revelled in the fact that we were airborne again. To look down on that smiling city, with the great Ring arcing through the suburbs on the western side of the river, the massive Gothic cathedral and the fine Hohenzollern and Hindenburg bridges spanning Mutter Rhein, was a great thrill to impressionable young men.

However, on the following day we saw some indications of the coming conflict as we watched, in awed silence, a brigade moving up the left bank on its way to the Eifel area. Everything was there—motor-ised infantry, artillery, tanks, camp kitchens, AA guns, anti-tank weapons and ambulances; all moving on pneumatic tyres at 30 mph. My brother's only comment—he was currently engaged in building airfields in the south of England—was that our own manoeuvres on Salisbury Plain with cavalry, horse-drawn vehicles and the usual leisurely approach of peace-time Britain to matters military, seemed pretty silly by comparison.

That very morning, too, we had seen Jews scrubbing pavements in Cologne's shopping streets, supervised and encouraged with the occa-sional kick in the ribs by large, fat characters dressed in khaki. Wear-ing black jack-boots and swastika armbands, they carried cudgels in a manner which suggested that they hadn't learnt *that* sort of thing in Sunday School.

But we were young and carefree, with plenty of good, solid British pound-notes to change into cheap Reichmarks; and food and drink—everything, in fact—was cheap enough in Germany in 1938. We considered Hitler to be a rather comical character who took himself frightfully seriously and did the hell of a lot of bawling; but hardly a major contender for the European Handicap. How wrong can you be?

My brother, at 20 years of age, suddenly became a 'militiaman' in the summer of 1939. He joined a local artillery regiment and was soon busy digging holes all over the Carlisle parks in which to site 18-pounder guns; an antic which must have frightened the life out of sleepy old Carlisle. September came and the British Expeditionary Force popped across to the Continent on a late summer holiday. One of our friends, a short-service commission pilot in the RAF, was kept frantically busy flying soccer and rugby goal-posts across to France. And Hitler didn't seem to mind one little bit.

In our innocence, it didn't seem like war at all. Now, in late-middle or early-old age, I realise that war is never as one imagines it could be. My daughter and her generation—like her father at a similar age—fondly imagine that going to war immediately plunges one into a wild furore—donning uniform, grabbing a rifle, gun, tank or aeroplane and firing it without pause, night and day—which doesn't let up for one moment until someone blows a whistle and suggests an armistice. Nothing could be further from reality. Unless someone makes an unforgivable blunder, the man who enlists only for the duration of the war has a year or two to endure before it dawns on him that the war of his dreams—or nightmares—might never happen.

The Civil Service knows this; certainly *they* were in no hurry to see off Hitler when war was declared and were to the forefront in ensuring that it was kept going until we, the 'hostilities only' people, had joined. When I suggested through the usual channels that I might relinquish my 'reserved occupation'—routing papers from the 'In' tray to the 'Out' via the weird and wonderful machinations of my most un-Civil Service mind—and dash off to fight the foe, they smiled indulgently and consigned my letter to that favourite of all receptacles in the Civil Service, the 'pending tray', there to lie with correspondence from earlier keen types who had tried in vain to get in on the Ashanti or Crimean wars. By dint of writing to my headquarters once every 14 days, however, in terms which became progressively ruder and more basic in their English, I eventually won and in July 1940 volunteered for the Fleet Air Arm.

To do so, I went from Whitehaven to Carlisle one fine Saturday afternoon and presented myself at the Naval Recruiting Office.

'Well, young fellow-me-lad! And what can I do for you?'

'I want to join the Navy.'

'Well, now. Let's see. Have you registered?' (This for National Service.)

'Yes—a long time ago. But I've been in a reserved occupation and have only just been released.'

'Ah! Now, there's a snag. You see, sir, if you've registered you'll have to wait till you're called up. No other way. Don't worry, though. We'll keep it going till you get in.'

'Are you *sure*?'

'*Course* I'm sure. It's my job to be sure. Now just be patient, lad. Come and see me when you're called up and I'll see what I can do for you.'

A week later I was in Carlisle again.

'Ho! It's you again! Been called up?'

'No such luck. Have things changed at all?'

'Now don't go rushing around, spoiling a perfectly good war. You'll have to wait, like I told you. The only things you can volunteer for are the Royal Marine Commandos and the Fleet Air Arm.'

The Commandos sounded like hard work for an old man of 26. So—'I'll join the Fleet Air Arm'. I enjoyed tinkering with cars. Surely an aircraft would be something similar? Wouldn't I just enjoy being an aircraft mechanic on a carrier?

'Right. Name and address, please. No forms right now, but I'll be getting some in from Newcastle any day now. I'll post 'em on to you.'

He did, too. They arrived during breakfast a few days later. A batch of forms fell from the envelope; and each one was stamped in large capitals—PILOT OR OBSERVER. I handed them to my wife Kathleen without a word.

'You?' she said with a grin. 'You, at your age? I thought you said you were going to be a mechanic?'

I had to believe her. In my own eyes, I certainly didn't fit in at all with the image of an aircraft pilot. For one thing, I was approaching 27. I wasn't one of the eagle-eyed, dashing young daredevils who were already writing history in the skies over London. I didn't think for one moment that I was brave, heroic or the material to endure untold hardships. Nevertheless the forms were completed and posted that very day.

The weeks passed. At long last, on the day following a bad blitz on Portsmouth, I arrived by train at the Town Station to find that the line down to the Harbour Station was bombed out of existence; that the road to the harbour was impassable to traffic; and that to walk was the only means of getting down to the Gosport Ferry. It was quite an experience. Demolition workers were flattening houses, shops and blocks of flats which, in their broken, smouldering and drunken-looking state, were a menace. The gentle thumps of the dynamite going to work punctuated the shouts of the firemen and workmen who were going about their jobs. Fire hoses wriggling like worms crossed the roadways in their scores. Baths and washbasins dangled tenuously from exposed walls, suspended only by their piping. Wardens were gently dissuading householders from entering precarious ruins—a chance they were obviously willing to accept in the forlorn hope of salvaging some cherished possessions of personal value. There were some sad faces to be seen, gazing mutely and dumb-stricken at what had been cosy homes 24 hours earlier.

At HMS *St Vincent* I presented my summoning letter to the guard and was directed to a room where some 40 or 50 of us were to await our ordeal. We were quickly divided into two parties—one for medical examination, the other for interviews. I fell to be medically examined.

It was quite a rigorous morning. Heart, lungs, blood pressure, physical stature and posture were minutely examined. But the eyesight tests were probably the most searching as far as a layman was concerned. For example, colour-blindness tests were of great import-ance. So, too, were tests for depth perception, the need for which only dawned upon me some months later when we actually started flying.

After a couple of hours it was all over, and I was delighted to find that I was accepted. So far, at any rate. The interview was to come after lunch.

Age or not, I had now firmly decided that I wanted to be a pilot, come what may. The chairman of the triumvirate I now faced, a Rear-Admiral, couldn't have been more friendly in his greetings. Then he handed me over to an Instructor Lieutenant-Commander. Forthwith he plunged into mathematics. In two minutes flat he had laid bare my ignorance and was regarding me with that leer of genial contempt which, until that moment, I had thought to be the exclusive right of my old maths master, 'Buster' Brown. With a look of 'Christ! We really get 'em!' he metaphorically threw me along the table, like a bit of scrap paper, to the Engineer Commander.

I fear that up to this point the Admiral had steadily lost interest in me. He perked up, though, when I drew for the Commander a rough sketch of a carrier both in elevation and in plan and, by way of an encore, added the arrestor wires. I was able to identify three or four aircraft recognition models. I even told him that it was necessary for a carrier to sail into wind to operate her aircraft. Things were going better.

I sat in a waiting-room while my destiny was discussed. Then I was recalled. The Admiral spoke.

'Well, Mr Hanson, you seem to be determined to fly. You would rather be a pilot than an observer?'

'Yes, if you please, sir.'

'Oh! Yes, we agree. You will be sent for as soon as arrangements can be made—and very good luck to you!'

'Thank you very much, sir!' I beamed on all three. I even grinned at the mathematical genius who had torn me to shreds. I backed out as though taking leave of royalty. I was at the door—

'Just one thing, Hanson. You know your way back to the Ports-mouth ferry?'

'Yes, thank you, sir.'

'Good. We were rather afraid that, with *your* maths, you might have found some difficulty.' His large red countenance was wreathed in smiles. He *must* have met dimmer types than me! Never mind—I could take it—I was in, wasn't I!

But it took months before 'arrangements could be made'. I lived in mortal fear that, in a weak moment, someone might thoughtlessly sign an armistice.

So Kathleen and I made the most of the weeks that were left to us. She would have to find work of some sort or other for the duration and had decided to return to her parents rather than live alone. We relinquished the tenancy of our brand-new little house, so dear to her heart, and our furniture went into storage. She was marvellous, for never once, during the whole of the war, did she complain or try to dissuade me from doing what I wanted. I never knew her to make a fuss or display any signs of emotion. She knew I might have to go to the far ends of the earth but she took it and the war in her stride—and hoped that I would live to tell her all about it.

Mother who, it seemed to me, had worried all her life that another war might come and take away 'the boys', would never have to worry about either of us, thank God. Two years earlier she had survived a heart attack. Now, in the depths of a desperately hard January, she had contracted pneumonia following months of bronchitis and her heart could take no more. Today, penicillin or a handful of antibiotics would do wonders and enable her to soldier on. In 1940 the doctors could only stand and watch her die. I, too, stood there at her bedside at ten to seven on that Friday evening and I thought my heart would break.

2

Bell bottoms—and proud of 'em!

After much impatient waiting I eventually reported to the Royal Naval Air Station, Lee-on-Solent, in company with 100 or so other raw recruits. The atmosphere was one of great *camaraderie*. We had good, airy quarters and excellent food. We were virtually at the water's edge, it was fine spring weather and we couldn't have been happier. We were kitted out with commendable rapidity, although the habit of carrying off with an easy nonchalance the wearing of a sailor cap and a bell-bottom suit came much more slowly. Life at Lee was settling down to a pleasurable existence when—true to form, as we were to discover throughout the war—we were abruptly moved off to Gosport: to HMS *St Vincent*, that old stone frigate dating from the early part of the 19th century. Now we were formed into courses—observers even numbers, pilots odd numbers. Mine was Rodney 27. We lived on the first floor of G Block, a gaunt, forbidding-looking building. I suppose it was prison-like and the food was pretty horrible. The straw palliasses were a shade different from Kathleen's bed. The cockroaches in the galley were large, numerous and at least as hungry as we were. But I loved every minute of it.

Having so recently convinced the Navy of the excellent states of our several healths, we now set about trying to smoke and drink ourselves to death. Needless to say, this we continued to do until the end of the conflict, including injury time.

St Vincent was a naval barracks of the old style—gloomy, forbidding and ceding not an inch to comfort or reasonably gracious living. The regular officers were fine chaps but the RNVRs, with one or two exceptions, seemed to me—in my brief acquaintance of six short weeks—to be a fairly bloody-minded lot who probably resented the fate which had found them a seemingly thankless task in pushing through an endless procession of birds of passage.

The Chiefs and Petty Officers, on the other hand, were an entirely different cup of tea. They were inured to discipline and knew all about the Navy from the age of 14 onwards. I am fairly sure, in retrospect, that they saw a nine-to-five job, coping with genial, responsive young men who couldn't wait to shake hands with Death himself, as infinitely preferable to the cramped conditions of crowded quarters, the cold, the wet and the misery of life in general aboard a frigate or a destroyer out in the wilds of the North Atlantic, where any number of keen young National-Socialists were just itching to put a torpedo through them. In the main they were more than friendly and anxious to teach; although the older ones found it difficult to believe that our eyes should sparkle more brightly at the thought of learning to fly than at the dubious advantages to be gained from pulling a bloody heavy cutter around Clarence Dock or mastering an endless list of bends and hitches.

Now we were at Gosport it became necessary, in order to survive, to learn to live with CPO Willmott, whose unprepossessing face and enigmatic expression, not to mention the accompanying harsh, barking voice, must surely be imprinted forever in the minds of all Fleet Air Arm officers. More easily assimilated was a taste for PO Oliver, who in six weeks transformed me from a desk-bound Civil Servant into something more closely resembling a man. Dear Olly! I can see him now, striding across the parade ground to start his day, tall, erect and immaculate in his uniform, for all the world as though he might just have stepped out of Gieves' window.

From his opening remarks onwards, Olly taught me a lot about the Navy. The overture was traditional.

'Well! You look a right shower o' berks and no mistake! Christ! The officer who wished you lot on me deserves to be shot—well, transferred anyway. You won't look like this when I've finished wiv yer, I'm tellin' yer! Smart? Yer'll look in the bleedin' mirrer and say, "Jesus! *E's* a good-looking bugger! Wonder who *'e* is?" Then yer'll look at yer watch card and say "Christ! It's *me*! Nah then, 'ow did *that* 'appen?" 'Ere's where I show yer. You, Shortarse' (this to a pale youth about six feet four), 'where the 'ell did you get that jumper? You look like a nursin' mother! Get it changed! Never mind the bleedin' Navy, yer a disgrace to *me*!'

He was a marvel, a genius.

One morning as we sat in a circle on the grass he told us the mysteries of the Vickers gas-operated machine-gun. He showed us, beneath the barrel, a similar tube through which the gas generated by the exploding cartridge was carried, its energy then being used to eject the spent round and to put the next 'up the spout'.

There is a special type in every class; and Guthrie was ours. He was an artist at day-dreaming and on this particular morning he was doing just that. Olly had stripped down the gun, describing the function of each part in turn.

'Nah then,' said PO Oliver, holding up the gas tube for all to see. 'Nah then, Guffrie, wot's this, then?'

Guthrie awoke with a jerk. He could only hope to flannel his way out of trouble.

'Er—a tube, sir.'

'That's right, Guffrie. A tube. An' wot's it for? 'Ere, grab it.' He threw the tube across. Guthrie caught it, stared at it, turned it over. He hadn't been listening and hadn't a clue.

'Well, Guffrie, stick yer bleedin' finger inside it.'

'It's black, sir,' Guthrie replied, surveying his right index finger.

'*Course* it's black! Black as the inside of a sweep's arse, Guffrie! Nah why should that be?'

No one heard what he put forward as an explanation, for the rest of us had collapsed in roars of laughter.

Oliver was the last person one would accuse of malice or vindictiveness. But he had a strong sense of humour which reacted quickly to Guthrie's peccadilloes.

We were drilling on the large parade ground in sweltering heat. Olly was standing by the barrack blocks on the long side of the square. Guthrie was drilling the squad, standing to attention by his side. I was standing behind them, awaiting my turn. The squad had just passed us, executed a right wheel and were now halfway up the left-hand side of the square. It needed a strong pair of lungs to reach them.

'RI-I-GHT W-H-E-E-L!' yelled Guthrie. The squad turned, heading across the full width of the parade ground.

Below the centre of the square was a large air-raid shelter, with flights of steps leading down to it from both ends. The right-hand man of the leading file told me later that it required only a slight adjustment on his part to steer the squad directly for the steps—which he did. Guthrie didn't notice. He had turned the squad and now needn't worry until they hit the wall on the far side. Suddenly the leading files disappeared down the steps.

'Well, Guffrie! Nah yer've gone an' done it proper! Poor fuckers, gropin' abaht in the bleedin' dark! Really, yer fuckin' lucky, mate, I'll tell yer! Wiv a bit o' luck they might come back!' (Just then the leading files *did* re-appear up the far steps.) 'What if it 'ad bin a bleedin' dock? Wot then, Guffrie? Christ! Fink of all the fuckin' explainin' yer'd 'ave 'ad to do!'

Just before I took over with the squad standing to attention in front of us, Olly marched, with all his Whale Island swagger and polish, to the marker, where he stood facing him, stiffly to attention.

'Funny bugger!' he said, then executed a smart About Turn and rejoined me. Not a muscle of his face had moved.

But we began to make progress. Soon we could march like sailors. We were learning navigation, morse, semaphore, meteorology. In a matter of a few weeks, we would sit examinations to qualify us for the next stage—elementary flying training at either Luton or Elmdon; or to be cast into outer darkness.

And then one morning, 30 of us were told we had been selected to go for training to Pensacola, with the American Navy. I rang Kathleen that evening.

'Go', she said. 'It's an opportunity you shouldn't miss. Some people have all the luck!'

A few days later, bright and early in the morning, we left *St Vincent*. We marched to the ferry and a Navy duty boat ran us to Portsmouth Harbour Station. Halfway across the harbour we met a public ferry and there, standing on the after deck, resplendent in his tiddly No 1s, was Olly.

'Three cheers for Olly!' someone shouted. We roared out our farewell to him and he blushingly waved back to us. He wasn't accustomed to adoration and obviously realised that the object of our cheers was now being admired by the typists, crossing to the dockyard, standing all round him.

Eventually, we boarded the liner *Stratheden,* converted into a troopship, off Gourock in company with what appeared to be thousands of RAF types. As we hit the deck, each man was thrown a hammock and told to report to a certain deck. Few of the RAF boys knew the purpose of this large canvas sausage with which they were suddenly presented and it fell to the 30 of us to show them how to sling them. Having organised them satisfactorily, we then found ourselves without a foot of space in which to sling our own. In the Stygian darkness of a hold abreast of H Deck, we eventually found a corner where we could make ourselves reasonably comfortable. So fantastically has the world changed in 40 years that I have no hesitation in saying that few young men in the civilised world would now dream for one moment of accepting conditions such as those for 11 nights and days. I don't suppose we enjoyed it; but we accepted it without demur—there was a war on!

We sailed along at a cracking speed in company with another trooper, the French *Pasteur* and two destroyers. Somewhere south of Iceland we parted company with *Pasteur* in the teeth of a howling gale, during which we were horrified to see a Petty Officer swept to his death from the fo'c's'le of one of the destroyers. Her captain gallantly dived into the boiling sea in a vain attempt to rescue him; and he himself was pulled back only with the utmost difficulty.

Two or three days later we landed at Halifax, Nova Scotia, which we were assured was a backwater as far as the rest of Canada was concerned. Locals told us that during World War 1 an ammunition ship had blown up in the harbour and that Halifax had never recovered from it. It certainly wasn't a raving metropolis.

BELL BOTTOMS—AND PROUD OF 'EM!

The naval barracks, though, were a joy to behold after Gosport. The buildings were modern affairs with bags of green lawns in all directions. The food, too, was superb and the few days we spent there were wonderful. I can remember two incidents during our short stay.

I had chummed up with John Barker, a Manchester lad, and spent a wonderful Sunday serving as crew for a well-to-do young man, a casual acquaintance who picked us up at St Catherine's Bay and invited us aboard his 40-foot Bermuda-rigged sloop. We had a marvellous day's sailing. He entertained us to dinner ashore in the evening, provided us with bunks on board for the night and drove us into Halifax next morning in time for the parade at 0800. When he had driven away—and only then—I discovered the ulterior motive behind all this lavish hospitality. Whilst I, isolated in a tiny cabin up in the fore-peak, slept the sleep of the just with a profundity which only a depth charge could have interrupted, this young man had spent the night making non-stop onslaughts upon the virginity of my friend Barker. Instead of yelping for assistance, which I, twice as big as our yachting friend, would readily have given by bending a Navy boot over his left ear, he had suffered in silence—apparently successfully.

The night before we entrained for Toronto, five or six of us went out to a local pub for a few beers. Well—the original intention was for a few, but somebody lost count.

The New Zealanders were determined to make a night of it, none more so than Des Fyffe, who set about the local brew as though it was going out of fashion. If, indeed, there was a last bus, we missed it; and reluctantly trudged off the three miles or so back to RCN barracks. We were at last in the dormitory, counting-down for the swift drop into our beds, when Des announced himself to be *sans* teeth. Somewhere near the pub it had become essential for him to heave to for a while to be violently ill. This had seemed to rejuvenate him for a while, for he had set off again at a merry pace. Now, alas! He was back again in a condition of stupor, with rolling eyes, garbled Kiwi speech and a cavernous mouth full of gums and tongue. We sighed, found a torch and five of us set out on the road again.

About an hour and a half later, after a fruitless search, we crawled back into our dormitory, calling blasphemously upon our several gods and more dead than alive. Someone saw fit to shake the snoring cause of our midnight forced march. At last he succeeded in awakening him. Des grimaced at the bright light, then smiled stupidly.

'Thanks, fellers!' he said, displaying a blinding array of porcelain. 'They were inside my flannel all the time! Nice of you, though!'

We cried ourselves to sleep.

Under a scheme originated by Admiral Towers of the US Navy, his Service had recently undertaken to accept 30 Naval and 100 RAF cadets per month, to augment the flying training programmes in the United Kingdom. Our party was the second to arrive at the Naval Air Station at Pensacola, a city within itself seven or eight miles from the town of that name. To the US Navy, Pensacola was known as 'the Annapolis of the Air'. Sixteen thousand men, together with a great number of families in married quarters, were stationed there. The site included two churches, shops, bowling alleys and facilities for sport of every kind. There was a wonderful auditorium capable of holding 2,000 people. It possessed a stage with curtain and lighting sets which any West End theatre would have been proud to own. Being air-conditioned, it was the most comfortable place on the station.

The living quarters were luxurious by British standards of that time. We lived eight to a room in spacious, well-equipped dormitories. The dining-rooms were spotlessly clean, airy and light, with Negro stewards on duty. The whole set-up was highly organised. The famous A. C. Reed, who had made history by flying one of the four NC–4 seaplanes across the Atlantic to the Azores in 1919, was the captain.

We Naval cadets were destined for fighters, the RAF contingent for flying boats. This arrangement—known as the Towers scheme—took a great deal of weight from airfields in the UK, where the demand for fully operational fields was forever increasing. It also meant that training could be carried out without the destruction and interference of air raids or their threat.

All of us were integrated into classes of US Naval and Marine cadets. We had our own liaison officers—in our case, Lieutenant-Commander 'Dago' Kennedy—who took no part in our training but were on tap to represent our interests should any friction arise.

For the first six weeks we did nothing but attend ground school. Officially we saw no aircraft at all other than in workshops, although in our spare time we hung around them like children. We studied alongside American cadets, working at their peacetime curriculum—navigation, celestial navigation, meteorology, theory of flight, fuel, oil and hydraulic systems. We attended lectures and instructional films in the auditorium and each day there was a compulsory period of two hours of physical training. Every Friday afternoon we underwent written tests on all school subjects.

Pensacola possessed a decompression chamber through which all of us had to pass during our ground school training. For some reason or other I was a bit under the weather when my own class endured the ordeal. Some days later I joined a company of US Marine Sergeants—trainee pilots—to see what it was all about.

A Surgeon-Commander opened the ball with a short talk on the effects of lack of oxygen at altitude, which we would not fail to notice once the test began; lips and finger-nails turning blue, decreasing ability to concentrate, drumming in the ears and so on. When oxygen was restored to us, we would feel the improvement immediately. Doctors would observe us through port-holes throughout the run, ready to apply first-aid and, if necessary, to remove us from the chamber in case of serious trouble. We would be given three written tests during the 'flight', the first at ground level, the second immediately after a simulated flight to 18,000 feet without oxygen. At this stage we would don oxygen masks and ascend still higher to a simulated height of 30,000 feet, where we would complete the last test.

Tastes vary, I know; and this was no place for those with tendencies towards claustrophobia. I imagine the panic-stricken expression 'Let me out!!' originated here. The chamber was a cylinder with a flat wooden floor. At the entrance end was a small compartment about eight feet long by six feet high, entered through an airtight door. Beyond that, through another airtight door, was the main chamber—of similar height but about 20 feet long. There was an all-pervading hiss of compressed air around the place which did absolutely nothing to encourage tranquillity. Great fun.

So we trooped in, surrounded by nervous gulps and the odd sick joke—but not too many. The American sense of humour, so different from our own, doesn't normally extend to such situations. We sat down at small individual desks, whereupon a marine promptly fainted and was carried out even before the airtight door was locked. We did the first test—a foolscap sheet filled, single-spaced, with capital letters from which we had to delete every 'R' preceded by 'A' and followed by 'S'. This wasn't as easy as it sounds. There were hundreds of 'R's, but very few meeting the requirements. And it was all against the clock. The airtight doors were locked with a heavy clang, we handed in our papers and off we went to 18,000 feet. The hissing suggested that the air was now being decompressed in earnest!

The doc was right. My nails did turn blue and I was fascinated to see that the lips of my neighbour took on a similar livid appearance. Obviously mine did, too, for he took only one short peek at me before he fainted. A doctor at the rear of the compartment came forward and clamped an oxygen mask over his mouth.

At 18,000 feet the hiss of the compressor died away. Almost immediately two characters were carried through into the air-lock to be resuscitated. The test was on similar lines to the first. This time, though, I found it tricky. I had to force my reluctant brain to move from one line to the next. It persisted with a surprising obstinacy in reading over and over again the line I had just completed. The clock was stopped only a second or two after I had finished.

Now we were fitted with masks. At once all became normal. We galloped off gaily to 30,000 feet, did our last test, then descended slowly to ground level.

The doctor now took us into the adjoining classroom for another short chat, mainly designed, I realised later, to give his CPO time to mark our papers. At some stage during the talk the Chief emerged from his caboose to show one of the papers to the Commander. There was a whispered discussion, rounding off with his being told to 'get back in there and check it out again'. Finally he returned with all the papers. There was another secret huddle. Then—

'Hanson? Which is Hanson? Stand up!'

'Sir.' I stood.

'Ah! The Limey!'

'Yes, sir.'

'You been through this apparatus before, Hanson?'

'No, sir.'

'You know anybody in the duplicating department? You had a chance to see these papers, Hanson?'

'No, sir.'

He stood for a moment, pensively stroking his chin.

'Gentlemen, I want you to look at this guy. He looks human but he ain't. He's the first man to beat the system. The *only* guy—yessir, the ONLY GUY in 10,000 to pass through this and get maximum marks in all three tests. Hanson! Just how in hell did you do it?'

I told him I hadn't the faintest idea. I even apologised, his only response to which was a very old-fashioned look. Against a maximum 240 for each test, the results averaged out at something in the region of 200 for the first, 40 to 50 for the second and 130 or 140 for the third. I departed feeling as though I had contracted a terminal disease.

Most of us had seen only a matter of weeks in the service of the Royal Navy. Nevertheless, a month or two with the US Navy showed us some of the wide disparities between the two. There was no doubt that 'on parade' to the RN officer demanded considerably more from us than did similar situations in the US Navy. On the other hand, matters which, where the RN were concerned, seemed to be treated superficially and with good-natured indifference and humour were looked upon with the utmost severity and beetling eyebrows by the young men from Annapolis.

Our living quarters at Pensacola were in Block 624, a spacious, good-looking, two-storey building of great length. At each end of both floors was a desk and a wooden armchair at which sat a Mate of the Deck, a duty we all fulfilled in rotation, standing a two-hour watch. The Mates of the Deck were distinguished from their fellows by the wearing of a khaki webbing belt.

The drill for taking over the watch was laid down explicitly in standing orders issued to us through the almighty duplicator, without which, it seemed, their Navy could never have functioned. At the appointed hour for change of watch, the new incumbent was obliged to approach the desk and stand to attention before his predecessor, announcing loud and clear:

'Sir, you are relieved.'

At this, the outgoing Mate would leap to attention and reply:

'Sir, you have the watch,' at the same time unbuckling and handing over the belt of office.

This drill was rigorously adhered to by the American cadets, whether or not an officer was present. Not without good cause, either, for America was still at peace. Pensacola was the prerogative of the best of Yale and Harvard; competition was fierce and cadets could be fired at the drop of a hat. Naturally, they were appalled at the slap-happy change-over performed by the British.

Five to ten minutes late, the oncoming Mate would saunter along the passage towards the desk. The man to be relieved would hail him at a range of 20 yards:

'And where the fucking hell have *you* been, you lazy sod? Had your bloody head down, have you?'

The response was equally officer-like and gentlemanly.

'Go and get stuffed, you moaning bastard! Give me the sodding belt and stop bitching!'

Thus was the take-over satisfactorily achieved, although not without a fair amount of eyebrow-raising from any Americans who happened to be passing.

To square matters, however, it must be said that in other respects we showed up well. Our salutes to American officers were punctilious and correct to a degree; and our marching around the station was a model to both American sailors and marines alike. Not for one moment would one of us have let down PO Oliver and his beloved Whale Island!

Those six weeks seemed to last for ever, sitting day after day in ground school. Then we started to fly. In those days, Pensacola possessed many small emergency strips and four main airfields: Chevalier, on the station itself, where instrument flying was taught; Curry, between the station and the town; Saufley, some ten miles inland; and Ellyson, at a similar distance to the north-east. I was allocated to Saufley and, together with two more cadets, placed under the care of Lieutenant (Junior Grade) Charles Culp, USNR.

The basic aircraft—our trainer—was the N3N–3, a 235 hp dual-controlled biplane, built by the US Navy. It was remarkably uncluttered and had fixed undercarriage and no flaps. There was a throttle lever; a joystick whose fore-and-aft movements controlled the elevators which caused the machine to dive or to climb, and whose lateral movements controlled the ailerons, the hinged sections at the outward end of the trailing edges of the wings. 'Left stick' produced a banking effect to the left; 'right stick' a similar effect to the right. Finally there was the rudder bar, slight pressure on which turned the aircraft—in conjunction with a little 'bank' to prevent skidding or yawing—to right or left, according to which foot was doing the pressing.

The instrumentation was simple enough. A 'needle-and-ball'—an Americanism for a turn-and-bank indicator; a 'rate of climb', in feet per minute; an altimeter; an instrument which showed how much power the engine was exerting, calibrated in inches of mercury; a simple compass; an oil pressure gauge; and, probably from our point of view, the most important, an airspeed indicator. To stay alive, you must keep an aircraft flying above its stalling speed. If you drop below that danger mark the aircraft will, with a degree of rapidity which varies according to the particular type of aeroplane, go into a spin. You will then be in lots of trouble and all you can do is to call on your experience. The snag is that, as a learner, you haven't got any.

The instructor occupied the front seat where he had a duplicate set of controls and instruments. He had a rear-view mirror—and a good instructor spends most of his time, in the initial stages, watching you through it. He wants to see that you are enjoying flying. If you don't, there is no point in carrying on. You either love it or you don't—there are no half-measures. And if you don't fall in love with it at the very outset you are wasting your time and everybody else's in trying to get used to the idea. The only sensible thing to do is to walk away from it and take up embroidery or flower arranging. You will be much happier and you won't kill either yourself or anyone else.

The instructor also had a speaking tube, known in the US Navy as a Gosport, for all the world like a length of flexible gas-tubing, with a mask and mouthpiece for him to speak through and a pair of earphones at your end. He could, therefore, chat to you until he was blue in the face in the comfortable knowledge that you couldn't argue. In the business of learning to fly, there is only one guy who should be doing the talking—and he shouldn't do any more than is strictly necessary.

I hadn't been at Saufley more than a few days before death struck—and in a particularly nasty form. Charlie Culp and I were walking down the line of planes at 0800 one morning, with N3Ns on all sides running-up their engines preparatory to take-off. A young Captain of US Marines, Phillips, came towards us. Charlie and he, yelling above the infernal racket of the aircraft, shouted greetings. Charlie made signs to me that I should carry on to our plane while he spoke to his friend.

Culp had not yet rejoined when some mechanics, gesticulating vigorously, compelled me to turn round. Aircraft ground-crews—and Charlie—were running like mad from all directions to—well, something that was lying off the taxi track, between the aircraft. It was all that was left of Phillips. He had taken his leave of Culp and turned—straight into a propeller, busily rotating at 1,000 revs a minute. Only his uniform provided any identification.

My N3N took on a different appearance that morning. Like all other aircraft, it could be a killer—if you were fool enough to give it the chance.

I embarked on the great adventure with an hour and a half's flying around the local countryside, Charlie Culp up front flying smoothly and uneventfully, myself sitting behind him, purring like a cat. The cockpits of those days, of course, were open; and flying hasn't been the same since lids were put over them. The beating roar of the engine and the rush of the slipstream from 120 knots were music to my ears. After a while Culp told me to place hands and feet lightly on the controls and to 'follow him through' several gentle manoeuvres: straight climbs and glides, level turns, turning climbs and glides. He then told me to try some myself. The results were most ham-fisted. As in learning to drive a car, everyone over-controls to begin with. Then the period was up. Learning to fly is a mentally exhausting business in the early stages and a little goes the hell of a long way. But no sooner are you down than you itch to be off again. It becomes an obsession.

So we went on for nine hours spread over a number of days. When we climbed down after the last flight, Culp told me in a matter-of-fact way that I would be seeing another instructor on the following day. Next morning, I saw the name 'Payne' against mine on the flight board. I met him at the aircraft.

'OK. Let's go. Start her up; take off; fly down the lane' (this was a corridor marked by high wooden pylons leading from the airfield into the outlying country), 'then we'll talk some more.'

I was then put through my paces, rounding off with one or two landings and take-offs on a quiet satellite grass field. When I landed back at Saufley and taxied to the apron, we descended to the tarmac.

'I've only one question,' he said. 'Can you get this thing off the ground and put it back again without killing anyone? You're entitled to kill yourself but'—this with a smile—'killing anybody else is against the rules. Can you?'

'Yes, sir. I think so.'

'Don't think. I want to know.'

'Then I can. Yes, sir.'

'OK. There ain't more than a dozen good reasons why you shouldn't. Good luck!'

31

He was gone.

Next morning, for the first time, my name stood alone against an aircraft number. I climbed into my N3N—and there was a yawning gap in the front seat where Charlie should have been sitting. (There was also a yawning gap, for the first time, where my intestines should have been. It was probably just as well I didn't know it that morning, but that gap was going to re-appear time after time over the next few years!). I rumbled out to take off, flew out to a small field and landed and took off until the end of the period: round and round, and round and round again. Then I came back to Saufley Field and made it. And no one was killed.

I think it would be generally agreed that to land an aircraft is probably the aspect which causes more heartache than anything else to the pilot under training. There is an oppressive feeling of uncertainty about the business of landing a heavier-than-air machine on *terra firma* without breaking something—and his neck in particular. In the initial stages, at least, he sees the matter of landing as one fraught with immense difficulties.

Had we trained in the UK at that time, our elementary flying would have been carried out on grass airfields, without runways. Saufley Field, like the other three large training airfields at Pensacola, was one enormous expanse of tarmac, on which landings were made directly into the wind as indicated by the windsock. Our elementary training aircraft were not fitted with R/T, so there was no instruction from the control tower. One joined the queue approaching the field and landed in strict rotation. The approach was made at an altitude of 500 feet, flying downwind with the field some 400 yards away on one's left-hand side. On reaching a point abreast of the downwind end of the field, one cut the throttle and promptly entered upon a 180 degree turn to port, gliding across wind and finally turning into wind to a landing on the tarmac.

A 'three-point' landing was the aim; in other words, a landing where all three wheels touched the tarmac simultaneously. After his final turn into the field, the pilot lined up the nose of the aircraft on some point on the distant upwind end of the field—and fixed his eyes steadfastly on that point until the landing was completed. *Never* looking at the ground, he judged its proximity purely from the attitude of the aircraft's nose in relation to the far horizon. As the horizon appeared to 'flatten', he 'flared out' for landing by easing back the joystick, thereby changing the aircraft's attitude gently from a glide to level flight; and from that point steadily continued to ease back still further on the stick until the machine stalled and sank to the ground. As the wheels touched, the joystick should then have been pulled back all the way to his stomach. Still with his eyes glued to 'the point', he then juggled the rudder bars with his feet to keep the aircraft running straight; and applied brakes gently and evenly only when it became necessary. Brakes were applied alternately—first right foot, then left, quite rapidly—so as to avoid putting the aircraft on its nose.

Despite their success in surviving the rigorous medical examination which was undergone before acceptance, several of our group faded out soon after flying training commenced and were returned, defeated and disconsolate, to the UK. There were various reasons, of which one was persistent airsickness, diagnosed by the US Navy instructors *not* as something which would disappear in the fullness of time, but rather as a firm indication that the sufferer had a subconscious phobia about flying which would prevent him from 'making the grade'. The other was 'depth perception', that aspect of eyesight examination which I had not fully appreciated when being medically checked. It is the quality and breadth of depth perception, apparently, which enables one to judge one's height from the ground whilst steadfastly watching the horizon; and now a number of our friends were dismayed to find that their eyesight was lamentably lacking in that quality. One of our boys persistently attempted to carry out three-point landings whilst still 50 to 60 feet above the runway, a manoeuvre which did absolutely nothing for the peace of mind of his instructor sitting in the front cockpit. It was decided that he would be much safer standing on his own two feet in the UK.

It will be appreciated that before the advent of the 'tricycle' under-carriage, the extreme 'nose-up' attitude of an aircraft on the ground precluded any forward visibility for the pilot. Taxiing, therefore, was always carried out in zig-zag fashion in order to enable the pilot to see where he was going.

For a long time, we weren't exactly *persona grata* with the Americans, servicemen or civilians. It took some time for the reason to dawn on us. There wasn't, though, the slightest suggestion of anti-British feeling about Captain Reed.

It wasn't long before some of the boys acquired motor cars—second-hand 'jalopies' which could be bought quite cheaply; and run even more cheaply with petrol at 11 cents a gallon. Pat Reynolds, one of our group, ran a noisy though efficient Chevrolet; and one evening at about 6.30 he departed for Pensacola town and his lady-love.

The main gate of the station was guarded by US Marines and every car was examined, boot and all, on leaving the station. Apart from US Navy personnel, 2,000 civilians were employed in the large air repair workshops, most of whom commuted by car. There was a lot of valuable material in those workshops and the Marines were taking no chances.

After working hours, however, things quietened down considerably, and when Pat reached the main gate in the early evening there wasn't a marine to be seen. At this time, Pat's love for the Americans was no greater than their love for him, and he was damned if he was going to dismount to go and look for a guard. He drove gaily through the gate.

Seconds later he was surprised to see part of his dashboard disintegrate before his very eyes. He stopped. From the bench seat on which he sat protruded a mass of fluffy horse-hair—and the rear seat was in a similar state. He ran to the back of the car and found a neat hole drilled through the metal. There was a whistle.

Standing at the gate was a marine, waving him back to the gate. Pat reversed down and jumped out again. The marine in question was standing, feet apart, ejecting an empty cartridge from his .45 revolver and was reloading the empty chamber.

'Why didn't you stop?'

Pat could hardly believe his eyes or ears.

'Did you fire that thing at *me*?'

'Yeah! You know the rules. Why didn't you stop?'

'Because there was nobody there. What the hell do you mean by firing a revolver at me?'

'You broke the rules, buddy. So I fired. OK?'

'Let me see that thing.' Pat held out his hand for the revolver, which the marine handed to him without protest.

'Why! You . . .' and promptly landed a beauty of a right on the marine's chin which, with the marine still attached to it, smartly hit the concrete. Pat was a big boy.

There was a sudden eruption of marines from the guardroom and, before he knew what was going on, Pat found himself carried bodily into the jailhouse at the back of the guardroom, where he was left for the night to cogitate.

Next morning he was hauled before the Captain. The charges were laid—driving through the main gate without stopping and striking a sentry who was performing his normal duties. All the evidence was heard. Finally the Captain, in friendly tones and with no hint of rancour or displeasure, asked Reynolds if there was anything he wanted to say before being sentenced.

Pat was renowned as a gabber. He was not in the least backward in coming forward. He told the Captain quite frankly that he had taken a chance on driving straight through the gate because he was in a hurry. After the Captain's explanation, he even went so far as to agree that the sentry was only doing his duty in firing his revolver—'though the idea in England is that we should reserve our bullets for Germans'.

'But, sir, there *is* one thing which seems to me to be very strange.

With all due respect, I don't go much on a United States Marine who allows me to take his revolver from him—and then stands there while I hit him with a straight right.'

There was a silence—a long one, while the Captain thought hard. 'Reynolds,' he said. 'Reynolds, you got something there, my boy!'

Pat was released from durance vile. The unfortunate marine went to cells for a number of days. Somewhere or other there's a moral.

We found cars very useful in enabling us to explore our own little bit of Florida—which, by the way, was not the glamorous part. We were to see that later! Distances appeared to be no object. Mobile, Alabama, lay 60-odd miles away; and we thought nothing of buzzing out there on Saturday evenings for a drink or to see a film.

After a quiet drinking session one night at the Battle House Hotel in Mobile, we decided at midnight that it was time we started to wend our way back to the station, using the method by which we had come—hitch-hiking. The four of us stood on the pavement of the main street, in the direction of Pensacola, and waved our thumbs. A big open Oldsmobile cruised to a standstill.

'Pensacola, boys? OK, climb aboard!'

The driver, a man of about 45 years of age, was cheerful—nay, downright jovial. This was not surprising considering the amount of alcohol he seemed to have put away. His joviality was somewhat blurred and his driving slightly erratic. He crawled along for a minute or two, then stopped again.

'Hey! Any o' you fellers want a piece of ass before we get going? On me, boys—my treat. How's about it?'

What on earth was a 'piece of ass'? We looked dumb—he thought so, too.

'You Limeys don't know what a piece of ass is? You don't want a jump? Hell! You know! A woman! A good whore! How's about it?'

To a man we declined. His opinion of Limeys had hit an all-time low. What sort of fellers were these?

'Well, I'm having me a blow-through before I leave town. Only keep you waiting ten minutes, boys. Hey! Officer!' (This to a policeman, patrolling the street.) 'Hey! Officer! Where's the nearest whore-house?'

The policeman wasn't at all put out by the request, the inflammable breath or the bleary bloodshot eyes.

'Second left, third house on the left. Good house, too. OK?'

We drove down. He pulled up the car with a screech of brakes outside the brothel; a good-looking three-storey house in a nice enough district.

'Sure you won't join me in a piece of ass, boys? Round your evening off nicely.' He leered. Then he stood up in the car.

'Hey! Mother! Bring out your whores! Bring out your whores!' He was bawling at the top of his voice. 'Goddammit! Woman! Bring out them whores, for Chrissake!!'

I wondered how much longer he would create a disturbance before someone did something about it. Then suddenly a first-floor window opened. A middle-aged woman, hair in curlers, stuck out her head. Her voice was equally refined.

'Now you just git the hell out o' this. My girls have had a long, hard day and they're all tuckered out! Git the hell out of it!'

'Ah! The hell! You just git them whores o' yours down again and open this goddam door! I've bin pinin' for a piece of ass for the last two hours and I just ain't goin' home!'

'Mister, you can just fuck off. All my gals are in bed and you ain't gonna see one of 'em!'

Our friend drove away. For the next half-hour he was sullen and morose and never uttered a word. All at once he brightened up. He was reasonably sober now and had a merry smile on his face.

'Well, goddammit, boys! If I ain't just remembered! There's a whorehouse open all night long just outside Pens'cola! You're *sure* you won't come with me?'

We were sure. He dropped us at the main gate of the station with cheery shouts of farewell and drove off about 1.30 in the morning to 'round off his evening'.

We were soon to learn that certain 'Southern gentlemen' dropped in to the local brothel with the easy nonchalance Englishmen pop into their local pub—but without their wives, of course!

Generally speaking, it was rare for us to leave the station other than at weekends. Our working hours were long and our leisure hours short; so we had to find our entertainment within the station.

However, almost every day we found time to swim in the lagoon which separates the mainland from Santa Rosa Island, where the big flying-boats taxied in and out, the deep rumble of their Pratt and Whitneys music to our ears. We became expert with surf-boards—rectangles of wood about the size of a large tea-tray with a pair of rope reins, towed behind a fast motor-boat. Was it the fore-runner of water-skis? The technique seems to have been virtually the same.

But, whatever one's leisure activities, life revolved around flying. We seemed to talk of nothing else. The progress of our friends, indeed, was just as important to us as our own.

Elementary training only begins with one's first solo flight. I carried on for another 60 hours under Charlie Culp. He would take me out for a morning, teach me new 'tricks' and give me two periods of solo in which to practice them. After that, more dual and more practice. Each stage was checked; and, in the event of a failure, that particular stage had to be worked again and rechecked after that.

I am sure that every flying career is punctuated by 'incidents'. Unfortunately for some, the first incident is the last. Lucky indeed is the pilot who lives to count his incidents! He remembers them—and bores his friends with them—for the rest of his life!

Number one for me came when I had done 20 hours solo. Charlie had recently been initiating me into the mysteries of aerobatics (*not* taught, I may say, to qualify the pupil to star in some future air display! The whole purpose is to accustom him to flying in what are known as 'unusual positions'; and to enable him to recover from them into normal flight with a minimum of fuss and danger) and here I was, on this particular morning, out in the country busily doing my homework. I was practising loops—a highly satisfying pastime for, in order to do a good loop, it is essential that the aircraft, on its dive out of the manoeuvre, passes through the 'column' of disturbed air it has created on the upward zoom. The jolt is both noticeable and exhilarating.

Now the N3N–3 possessed a carburettor of the normal motor car type; in other words, it had a chamber and a float. When the aircraft was in inverted flight at the top of the loop, the float was apt to fall from the bottom of the chamber to the top; the supply of petrol to the cylinders was accordingly interrupted and the engine cut out. When the aircraft recovered its normal right-side-up attitude, the float fell again to its normal position and the engine cut in. You were in business again.

There was the odd occasion, however, when the float *didn't* fall back into position—and on my ninth or tenth loop this happened. Well, you can't get out of the thing and kick it or belt it with a hammer; so you're in trouble. First, height. I looked at the altimeter—8,000 feet. All the height in the world. Next—where to put it down? About two miles away I saw an emergency grass field. I glided down to it and flew a circuit. The windsock indicated there was a good breeze. Warily watching the altimeter and air-speed indicator, I crept cat-like around the field for another couple of circuits. I could bear the strain no longer; I just had to go in. It was now or never. I might not make another full circuit, in which case the end would be disastrous; something I did not dare to contemplate. So here goes.

Of course, I came in far, far too high; but luckily Culp had taught me to sideslip (plenty of left rudder and the stick well over to the right and slightly forward) and I practically tore the wings off the poor thing in slipping off a lot of height. I touched down in the middle of the field and rumbled to a standstill. God! How quiet it was! Birds and things chirping and rustling all around me. Then I remembered the drill. If in trouble, a pilot had to remove his parachute and place it on the top wing of the aircraft, to be seen by any passing instructor. This I did, then descended to the grass, walked a safe distance away and sat down to await developments. I lit a cigarette. At least I tried to; but my hand was trembling to such an extent that I was considerably exercised to get the match into the same parish as the cigarette. Eventually I made it. I was alive. I had pulled off my first forced landing and was now living it over again, wallowing in a sea of smug complacency. Hanson, what a bright sod you really are, I thought. What will Charlie say about *that*?

Another N3N came winging over, heading south towards Saufley. I watched him droning steadily across at about 5,000 feet. I thought he had missed me when he suddenly went into a steep bank, cut his engine and glided to a perfect three-pointer alongside my aircraft. The instructor bounced down, full of beans.

'Trouble, son?' (He was about three years younger than I.)

I told him.

'How many hours solo you got?'

He whistled. 'Why the hell didn't you bale out?'

I told him the idea hadn't occurred to me. He gave me a long, cool look. Then—

'OK. Sit tight. I'll be right back.'

He returned in half an hour with a mechanic in the back seat nursing a carburettor. The fitter sauntered over to the business end of my N3N, withdrawing from the rear pocket of his overalls a wooden mallet. He delivered a sharp tap to the side of the carburettor. The instructor jumped in and started her up; then switched off again. I made to climb up myself.

'No you don't, son. Not today. Climb into mine. We'll pick this up later.'

Next morning Charlie Culp opened the day's proceedings with a quiet 'I hear you did OK yesterday. Let's go.' And that was that.

Culp was probably a shade younger than I and came from Baltimore, Maryland. Although we never reached the stage of becoming bosom pals, at least we found the odd evening together when we would go out to the San Carlos Hotel—the social and alcoholic centre of Pensacola—for a drink or two. He was quiet, reserved and gentlemanly. I liked him a lot.

He was also a very good instructor. One of his colleagues had long assured me that I was fortunate in having one of the best. In the air he was as quiet as he was on solid ground. He spoke to me only when he found it strictly necessary and, long after I had left his tender care, he explained to me why an instructor who nattered unceasingly (as some did) was of no use to anyone.

'You see, if I checked you or ticked you off the instant you started to do something wrong, you would never be given the chance to develop that mistake. You would never know what the hell you had been letting yourself in for. The only way is to let you do whatever the hell you were going to do; to let you go on, getting deeper and deeper into trouble until it dawns on you that you have gotten yourself into something you just *can't* get out of. Then—and *only* then—I'm there to dig you out. You'll sure remember never to do *that* again. See?'

One morning we were practising emergency landings into a short grass field—not an easy manoeuvre in the early stages of flying. The instructor flies the aircraft in circles around the perimeter of the field and, at any moment and at any position on the circle, cuts the throttle. At that point the pupil takes over. Without any further assistance from the engine, he has to judge height and distance and, with the down-wind end of the field uppermost in his mind, glide to a dead-stick landing.

So Charlie, up front, suddenly cut the throttle. Now it was all mine. I looked back to the downwind end of the field—NOW! I banked over steeply and glided downwind, past the end of the field, then into a left-hand 180 degree turn. I was far, far too high. I put the N3N into a screaming sideslip—hopeless; yet in my keenness and obstinacy I persisted. Charlie's quiet voice came through my earphones.

'If you get *this* one in, I'll kiss your ass in the San Carlos Bar.'

Suddenly I was in a jam; and I hadn't the faintest idea how to extricate myself. *Jesus!!*

'OK, OK,' said Culp. 'OK, I got it.'

And he had.

I wasn't the only one to do odd things. An RAF pupil, taking off at night from Curry Field, flew into a tall metal chimney, red warning light and all. The aircraft wrapped itself tightly round the chimney and slithered softly to the ground. No bones broken.

Another RAF pupil, out on emergency landing practice, dozed serenely in the luxury of his postbreakfast somnolence as his instructor flew the aircraft. Then something registered. Yes! That was it! The instructor had closed the throttle! Once awake, his reactions were faultless. Grabbing the stick with his right hand, he shoved it firmly forward. (Rule 1: if your engine dies on you, put the aircraft into a gliding attitude to maintain flying speed.)

He was always rather vague as to what happened next. One thing *was* certain—he hadn't maintained his grip on the stick, for the next moment he was cavorting freely around the sky; and his N3N, with a very empty rear cockpit, was cruising along towards Pensacola, 100 feet below him. At this point his reflexes entered a short period of lethargy, for he admitted that it was fully five seconds before he realised what had happened. More importantly, what was *going* to happen if he didn't pull his ripcord pretty quickly.

He parachuted safely into a ploughed field where he sat for an hour awaiting a pick-up truck, wondering why the hell he hadn't rigged his safety harness.

The instructor had felt the jerk on his Gosport tube, the violence of which had almost removed his head. He looked into the rear-view mirror preparatory to delivering a blast to the pupil—but no pupil. Searching above and below for him, he finally located him above and some distance astern, with his parachute just blossoming. Having seen him land safely, he high-tailed it back to Curry Field.

Charlie Culp was in the CFI's office when this instructor strode in. He was of Teutonic extraction and, at the time, hardly the type to be a pro-British raver. To the CFI:

'Chief, you know that fuckin' Limey you sent out with me?'

'What of it?'

'Well, you gotta believe it, but this is all I got left of the sonofabitch.'

Before the CFI's face he dangled his face-mask and mouth-piece—but no Gosport tube.

An evolution which figured largely in all our lives was that known as circle-shooting. On a grass satellite field was marked in white a circle, 100 feet in diameter. At what was obviously regarded as a safe distance, even for us, was a tall mast carrying a windsock. Around this circle Charlie Culp would order me to fly for a couple of circuits. Then, on a down-wind leg, abreast of the centre of the circle, he told me to cut the throttle and, with no further assistance from the engine, to land, touching down inside the circle. Even the dumbest of us realised that this was our apprenticeship to accurate flying, intelligent gliding and judging of distance. It was permissible to use sideslipping, a technique which had recently been taught to us.

Most of us surmounted this stage without much trouble. There were others, however, to whom it came more slowly; and one of these was a room-mate of mine, a cheery New Zealander called Jack Sisley. Each evening on our return to Pensacola I would find Jack (who was training at Curry) inveighing against circle-shooting and describing his apparent inability to 'get the word' on this manoeuvre in language which, coming from the son of a Methodist minister, was more than a little surprising.

'I'll get that bastard tomorrow and no mistake, you see! I'll put the sonofabitch inside that fucking circle if I have to *crash* the bastard into it!'

Jack, if nothing else, was a man of his word. Finding himself, as usual, far too high as he glided nearer and nearer to the circle, he put his N3N into a powerful sideslip which he held until the port wing was

18 inches *below* ground level. His instructor, watching with a tutorial eye from a safe distance outside the circle, sighed deeply and pondered on the idea of farming as an alternative occupation. Jack walked away from it—something for which most of us, at some time or other, were grateful to be able to do.

We sweated for hours and hours under the hood of a ground-based Link trainer, practising 'flying' on radio beams, making timed approaches to 'airfields' and controlled let-downs in simulated bad weather. Then we were off in a Harvard dual trainer, sitting in the rear cockpit with a hood over us, preventing even a chink of light from reaching us. The instructor, acting also as safety pilot, sat in front. He flew the aircraft until we were within radio distance of a small civil airfield; then turned on our radio and left us to it. We had to find the beam, track down it at the right altitude and speed; and finally to put the aircraft in an exact position to let down on to the duty runway. Our ears had to make sense of the radio signals flowing in to them. We had to read our instruments and stop-watch intelligently. And our hands and feet had to transmit all this correlated information to the aircraft controls. This time we were listening to real live radio and aiming for a real live airfield. No Link trainer nonsense!

Flying blind made great demands on concentration; keeping at steady heights on steady courses at set speeds; listening, listening all the time to the high-pitched drone of the beam; losing it, finding it again. Then doing the let-down, feverishly watching the stopwatch, trying to keep an even rate of descent; getting the correct beam for final approach, crossing the 'cone of silence'. Now! Airfield ahead! Waggle your wings!

The instructor snapped up the blind-flying hood. *Is* the airfield ahead?

Sometimes it was, sometimes it wasn't. This time, nothing but the Gulf of Mexico as far as the eye could see. Last time it had been a forest. Christ! Where did I go wrong?

'OK, OK, I got it. We'll go out north again and have another crack at it.'

Then it was good-bye to Saufley and across to Ellyson, where we took on something heftier for an hour or two in the shape of an 03U–1, an ancient Vought Sikorsky biplane, reminiscent of a Swordfish. Its rear cockpit reminded me forcibly of brother Ray, for it was almost identical to the one in which we had first become airborne those many, many years ago. After that we moved on to a more sophisticated model, the OS2U–3, known as the Kingfisher, an aircraft which, fitted with floats, the US Navy employed aboard its cruisers and battleships. Our model had an undercarriage and was now used solely as an advanced trainer. At this stage we were introduced to landing flaps and constant-speed propellers, and training was confined mainly to formation flying. We were making progress.

So the flying hours droned on and on, and more and more pages of our log books were filled. We now felt ready to tackle what we were pleased to refer to, in rather a blasé manner, as 'real' aircraft.

One of the final 'tricks of the trade' in which we had to be checked out before leaving Pensacola was the inverted spin. If you feel that life is becoming a bore, that you are fed up to the back teeth with politicians and that the daily grind offers nothing by way of relief, excitement or novelty, try your hand at recovering from an inverted spin.

A spin in the 'right-side-up' position is exhilarating, to say the least, and would consign the average layman to a nursing-home for neurotics for the best part of a month. When a spin occurs out of the blue, so to speak, one is too busy recovering from it to devote much time to thinking of its violence and dangers. But to put the aircraft deliberately into a spin is much more exciting. One pulls back the throttle until the aircraft sighs from lack of forward impulsion. The stick, too, is eased back until the aircraft loses flying speed and stalls. At that moment, the average aircraft will 'drop a wing'. If it doesn't, a firm kick on one of the rudder pedals will certainly cause the wing on that side to fall smartly—and you are away in a spin. The nose of the machine is pointing towards earth at an attitude of some 60 or 70 degrees and the aircraft is milling around in a circle, with its nose in the centre of that circle, at an ever-increasing rate. The more spins it completes, the more violent the motion and the more difficult it becomes to recover. The faster and more sophisticated the aircraft and the higher its wing-loading, the faster and more violent its spin.

The classic method of recovery is to kick on full opposite rudder to stop the spin, centre the ailerons with the joystick and then to ease forward on the stick to regain flying speed. (The main thing is to remain cool!) Provided you are not close to Mother earth, all you have to do after that is to ease back gently on the stick until you level out from the resultant dive. On the other hand, if you are too close to those green fields you will quite rapidly and altogether too noisily cease to take any further interest in the proceedings and will henceforth be nothing more than a shovel-and-wheelbarrow job.

But an *inverted* spin . . . ! Ah! Just like the other but more so—decidedly. For everything is happening in the 'upside-down' position which adds considerable quantities of relish to the operation.

I took off one morning with an instructor who, until that moment, was a complete stranger to me. He was what the Air Arm called a short-arsed little bastard, about five feet three in his regulation socks.

Unlike Charlie Culp, he was a great talker who beat my eardrums to pulp all the way up to 8,000 feet. At that altitude he uttered something intelligible for the first time.

'Well, this is how she goes, son!' he confided to me in a bellow down the voice-pipe. 'No need to be afraid. Just listen to every goddam word I say.'

I had little option.

'And here we go, Limey! Keep your ass in one piece and hold on!'

Flying straight and level, he than half-rolled to invert the N3N; and we were hanging on our safety harness. I heard the engine die and saw the nose climb away from me. Then came the jerk as he kicked the right rudder bar—and we were flung into an inverted spin.

The immediate sensation was of someone trying—with the utmost determination—to pull my eyeballs from their roots. The whole weight of my body was straining against the safety harness, accentuated every time we passed '12 o'clock' on each spin. With my head flung back by centrifugal force, I could see far below us the coastline and the blue, blue water gyrating madly. The aircraft was buffeting roughly in the disturbed air from the stall bouncing over its wings. I felt like Dante romping around in his Inferno. To add to it all, our friend up front was screaming his head off. He was almost hysterical and no sense whatsoever came through to me. Eventually, over the tumult, I interpreted what he was bawling about.

'Kick the ass off the goddam rudder, for Chrissake!'

So I kicked port rudder hard to the fullest extent of my long left leg. The spinning stopped. The noisy one in the front cockpit pulled back the stick and, after a second or two, half-rolled into the normal position. He opened up to cruising revs and flew straight and level. It was a pleasant change.

'Hey! You! When I tell you to kick that goddam rudder, you just stop fuckin' about there and kick the sonofabitch! How the hell do you think *I* can reach the goddam thing with *my* legs?' (Ah! So that was it!) There was a pause while he lifted his goggles and wiped away the perspiration from his brow.

'Shit! How I hate these fuckin' spins! They scare the shit out of me, that's for sure!'

We did three more and I duly kicked the goddam rudder as soon as the urgent invitation was extended. At least, that's what I assumed he wanted, for I still couldn't hear a word he said as soon as we hurtled off on the merry-go-round.

He was all smiles, all talk and all cigar as we walked back to the hangar.

'You see, son, I got the shortest legs in the whole state o' Texas, that's for sure.' Then he leered quite charmingly. 'But don't you go thinkin' the rest of my anatomy is on the same scale, boy! Christ! No! I'm really something when the pants are down!' There was a slight pause. 'Anyway, you did OK. You know what's wanted. Good luck, sailor!'

He passed out of my life.

3

. . . And then came Pearl Harbor

We were still—but only just—at Pensacola when the Japanese attacked Pearl Harbor on December 7 1941. This earth-shaking event caught the United States by surprise, to say the least, and the whole country took off in an explosion of war fever. Up to this point, as I have said, some of the residents had only reluctantly accepted our presence on the naval air station and in Pensacola town itself. Others were downright inimical towards us, so convinced were they that Churchill was directing all his efforts towards persuading Roosevelt to bring America into the conflict. We were freely catcalled and booed as we marched around the station on our various duties.

Now, with broken warships sitting on the bottom of Pearl Harbor, all was forgiven. We were natives of a country which had already endured over two years of war and, although most of us had yet to look a German in the face, we basked in the reflected glory of men who had been at Dunkirk and the boys who were slugging it out in the Mediterranean and Western Desert.

The impact of Pearl Harbor was by no means confined to military establishments. From coast to coast, America fell under a spell of war hysteria. Signs burst forth like a rash over main gates, barracks and canteen doors—'Through these portals pass the world's finest (sailors) (soldiers) (marines) (aviators)'. If advertising was as powerful as alleged, then there was no doubt who would win the war! US mail vans could be seen dashing on their errands throughout the land bearing banners—'YOU are an American! Isn't it GRAND to be an American!' The word just had to be put over!

I was told by Commander Davies that the programme at the auditorium for the following Sunday evening would be devoted solely to readings by a lady whose name I have long since forgotten. She had suggested that her address, or whatever, would benefit greatly from a soft background of typical English music. (Most things British are referred to in the States as 'English'. The word 'Welsh', for instance, is used when speaking of ladies wearing tall, tapering black bonnets. 'Scotch' [*never* Scottish!] refers to kilts, whisky, 'locks' [see 'lochs!'] and ancestors, in that order. 'Irish' is associated only with callous

IN REPLY REFER TO
NO. ....

U. S. NAVAL AIR STATION
PENSACOLA, FLORIDA
U. S. A.

January 30, 1942

The Commandant, Officers, Cadets, enlisted personnel
and their families extend sincere appreciation to Sub
Lieut. Norman S. Hanson, R. N. V. R. (A), for his most
generous and efficient services in performing at the con-
sole of the Hammond Organ in the Auditorium of this Station.

During your training here at Pensacola you have
contributed a great deal to the contentment and entertainment of all personnel at this Station. The musical
programs have been enjoyed very much by all of us, through
which you have not only proved yourself an artist but
a good shipmate.

As you now depart from our midst and go your way
we will miss you and herewith adieu, Good Luck and God
speed. "THUMBS UP AND KEEP 'EM SAILING"

Edgar W. Davis

Commander Edgar W. Davis, (Ch.C.)USN

Chairman Entertainment Committee

A 'cockpit' of a different kind — but still calling for co-ordination of eyes, hands and feet.

subjugation by the English, poverty, leprechauns and toothless old peasants sucking empty clay pipes.) England, unless more closely defined, always implies London. If you live in England, you must live in London. If you don't, you are an object of amazement and are immediately invited to explain to the assembled company exactly how many miles from London you are unfortunate enough to live; more especially, *why*.

Knowing that I could play the organ, Commander Davies asked if I could brush up on my English 'toons' and be prepared.

About 6.30 pm on Sunday I approached the lady of the evening. She was, I suppose, in her early forties; tall, charming and obviously itching to scatter buckets of emotion to all parts of the house. She held a fistful of foolscap paper which in itself boded ill for the audience. She grasped my forearm and told me what sterling chaps 'you English boys' were, how she prayed night and day for us and that, with America's declaration of war now delivered unequivocally, her prayers had been answered.

We sang one or two patriotic soul-stirrers. Then Commander Davies introduced our *diseuse*. The houselights were dimmed and Hanson moved into a tear-jerking, ultra-pianissimo *On the bonny, bonny banks of Loch Lomond*, with disc-brakes well applied. Madame turned to Page One.

Ten days earlier, it would have been difficult to find more than a couple of hundred true Anglophiles throughout the smiling state of Florida. But here we had the mother and father of them all. Every time she uttered the word 'England'—about once every ten or 12 seconds—her throat became choked with emotion. She read everything from Browning to Wordsworth, from Rupert Brooke to Henry Newbolt, and never missed a trick. She read, with a wealth of emotion—a highly-expendable commodity with her—things which I had never heard; and the audience was treated to a fully detailed description of the white cliffs of Dover with the blue birds aviating over them in swarms.

It was all very moving.

God knows how long it went on. Long before we had reached Dover I had run out of music relating to the British Isles—even that written by Americans, which accounts for most of it—and had resorted in desperation to variations on original themes. I then decided to compose a few 'first performances', thinking deeply the while of unemployed miners, the slums of Leeds and Liverpool and the State Management pubs in Carlisle. I just daren't dwell on honey for tea at Grantchester or those confounded blue birds.

At last she finished. I don't remember what time it was. When the thunderous applause had died down Commander Davies rose to move a vote of thanks. He looked slightly stunned. I can only think he was busy wondering what sort of country these RN and RAF students had sprung from.

On the very evening of Pearl Harbor Sunday I was having a drink with Culp at the San Carlos Bar. For the first time the British were now allowed off the station in uniform; until then we had been offically in a neutral country. So here I was, wearing bell bottoms as a true ally.

In a small lounge bar was a solitary customer—an Army Major. War had apparently not been included in his terms of reference when he had joined up, for he was now fully occupied in removing every syllable of the dreadful tidings by replacing them with booze. He was working very hard.

As we moved to the bar he put down his glass very, very carefully; stared at me for what seemed to be an eternity; then slowly and with great deliberation recited to me—six inches from my face—every obscenity and filthy expletive to which he could lay his tongue, rounding off, of course, with 'fucking Limey'. Still perched perilously on his high stool, he began methodically to remove his uniform blouse in preparation, it seemed, to obliterate at least one hated Englishman. (Churchill! What have I done to deserve this?)

I thought about our pocket manual on being 'a good ambassador to Britain whilst in the US'. I looked around at Culp. What do I do? I asked with my eyes. Do I slug a helpless man? Or allow him to carry on making a fool of himself?

Culp's wordless reply clearly said 'No action.' Instead:

'Let's go drink some place else. Good-night, Major!'

With that, he delivered a smart kick to one leg of the major's stool. As I closed the door behind me there came the music of a thundering crash.

Then quite suddenly our days at Pensacola were over. Having coped successfully with the elementary and advanced stages of flying training, we now moved to Miami, the home of the US Naval Air Corps' fighter training school. We were elevated to the dizzy rank of Sub-Lieutenant and our left sleeves wore the magic pair of pilot's wings.

Some 14 miles north of Miami lay the Navy's airfield at Opa Locka, its fighter training station. So far, our progress had brought us to the stage where we could fly an aircraft. Now we were to learn to use it as a lethal weapon of war. We trained hard, too; eight days without a break, and with a fine disregard for Sundays. At the end of eight days, peace descended for a while with one full night of liberty and the whole of the following day until 9.30 pm.

The North American Harvard—SNJ-3 in US Navy terminology—was the first aircraft we used for this fighter course. We liked this modern advanced trainer; all-metal, dual-controlled and highly manoeuvrable. It was fully equipped with retractable undercarriage, constant-speed propeller and flaps. The 700 hp engine pulled the Harvard along in great style and in fully fine pitch for take-off it gave a screaming whine which no one could fail to recognise.

It should be said at this stage that, in a matter of a week or two, our flying had rapidly become more sophisticated. For one thing, with heavier and more powerful aircraft, whose higher wing-loading would not permit them to maintain a glide with the same ease or for anything like the distance of a lighter aircraft with lower wing-loading, it became necessary to make powered approaches and landings. Instead of cutting the throttle as the final crosswind turn was made, engine power was maintained, propeller pitch was adjusted to give increased revolutions and flaps were lowered by ever-increasing degrees until the 'flare-out' point was reached. The throttle was cut only when contact between the landing wheels and the runway was imminent. No longer was a three-point landing the height of one's ambition. After we left training airfields, in fact, landings on runways tended to be of the 'transport' type, in which, with the aircraft still at low flying speed, the main undercarriage was 'run' into the runway and the tailwheel was finally dropped only when the aircraft lost forward impulsion and was fully stalled. Whatever else, this saved a lot of wear and tear on tail-wheel tyres!

Now, too, we were flying aircraft equipped with radio; and in addition to the visual aids displayed on the airfield we were informed by the control tower as to when to join the landing pattern and which runway was in use. The cockpits were more elaborate, the dials, switches and levers were multiplying, there was more to listen to and more information to transmit. But we were young; we had not a worry in the world; and all this was assimilated with an easy nonchalance which only young manhood can produce.

Formation flying occupied a sizeable proportion of our time in the air and for the first time we essayed night formation. This was great fun provided you could put out of your mind the nature of the ground below you. From the outskirts of Miami City for 60 miles to the far west and for 100 miles north from the southern tip of the great Florida peninsula stretch the Everglades, a wild region of swamp and scrubland, inhabited in only isolated areas. It was the home of countless birds, including a great number of waders; of snakes and alligators. In those days there was only one road worthy of the name across this great waste—the Tamiami Trail—and, with survival always lurking in the back of one's mind, one naturally kept pretty close to this whenever possible. Because of the swampy nature of the ground—from the air, something like 40 per cent seemed to be under water—a forced landing could be nasty, but the Navy had the answer.

The efficient management at Pensacola had greatly impressed all of us; and we were now to find that the Air Corps' organisation at Opa Locka was equally brilliant. All a pilot had to do after forced-landing or baling-out was to spread out his parachute in a circle; first, to make the search easier, and secondly—provided he stood or sat in its centre—to give him maximum and clear warning of the approach of the local fauna!

News of a man down in the Everglades brought swift action. Manned and equipped throughout the hours of flying were a number of 'ready planes', each for a specific job. As soon as alerted, the 'Everglades' aircraft, with a pilot, air-gunner and radioman, took off and flew on its search for the grounded man. (In many instances the aircraft reporting the incident would have given a pretty accurate position.)

In the meantime the 'swamp buggy', a wonderful vehicle equipped with both propellers and caterpillar tracks, which was also manned at all times, was despatched on its carrier; something similar to an Army tank recovery vehicle. This carrier drove off down the Tamiami Trail until, guided by radio from the ready plane above, it reached the nearest point to the man to be rescued. Here it was unloaded and from then on proceeded under its own power across the swamp, its propellers being brought into action whenever the ground was too soft to support the caterpillar tracks.

As soon as the victim of the incident had been found, the air-gunner in the ready plane dropped for him a bag of supplies—chewing-gum, chocolate, raisins, biscuits, a water-bottle and a revolver with a few rounds to despatch any inquisitive alligator or snake. Now all he had to do was to remain cool and await the arrival of the swamp buggy.

It all worked like a charm.

By day, we covered all aspects of fighter training: ground strafing on semi-submerged rocks off the coast; air-to-air firing on drogues towed over the Everglades; gun camera attacks on individual aircraft or on simulated bomber formations, flown by our own classmates. We persevered more and more with formation flying, but now in much more open formation, giving us time and space to search for 'enemy' aircraft. Close formation is pretty and impressive at air displays, but hopeless for fighters avidly looking for enemies.

Then we started the course all over again. We graduated to Brewster Buffaloes (F2A), fighters which had lately been discarded by the US fleets as obsolete. They were short, chunky machines with a 1,200 hp Wright Cyclone engine. At this stage, too, we dropped our American instructors and Charles Evans took over. He was then a Lieutenant-Commander, one of the war's great fighter pilots, eventually to become

Vice-Admiral Sir Charles Evans. He had a great flair for teaching and was determined that we should leave Miami with some of his experience in combat well ingrained into us. He would demonstrate how to shake off enemy fighters. He would set us patrolling on a certain course and then himself appear out of the blue, streaking in with all the menace of a true enemy. It was up to us to turn towards him at the right time to parry the attack. At other times he would set a similar exercise but, instead of attacking himself, he would send in individual pupils whilst he sat high above, watching, assessing and criticising our ability in both attack and defence.

My nearest approach to a crash whilst at Miami came when I was landing a Buffalo one afternoon. Everything was checked and in order as I approached touch-down. She sighed as I cut the throttle, flared out and touched down on three points. As she ran down the runway at something like 70 mph the port wing dropped slightly. Despite a touch of 'right-stick' it went on falling until it eventually touched the tarmac. Then I screamed off to port into the sand, where I endured a long ground-loop, raising clouds of dust and sand until at length it stopped. All I could hear was the scream of the fire tender and the ambulance. I took off my helmet and climbed down. The port undercarriage had partially retracted.

'You OK?' It was the doctor from the ambulance.

'Yes. Fine, thanks.'

'OK. Get in the wagon.'

'I'm fine, sir. I'll just walk over to my hangar there,' I said, pointing to our flight a matter of 200 yards away.

'The hell you will! You'll get in the goddam wagon when I say! GET IN!'

So I got in. We roared off at speed, siren whining, and fetched up at the sick bay. The duty doctor gave me innumerable tests, rounding off with:

'You're OK? Feel OK? Go to the chief flying instructor's office.'

Lieutenant-Commander Sharp received me as a regular officer might be expected to; brisk and to the point.

'You OK?' Wasn't it just great that everybody was so interested in my well-being?

'Yes, thank you, sir.'

'What happened?'

I told him. Undercarriage indicator lights checked and re-checked. Operating lever untouched after that.

'You *sure* both those lights showed green?'

'Yessir. Absolutely certain.'

'OK. You'll be hearing from me.'

I was called to him two days later. With him stood an Engineer Lieutenant-Commander.

'Sub-Lieutenant Hanson. I have to tell you that your F2A was thoroughly checked after the accident. This officer's findings are that the locking mechanism on that undercarriage leg was malfunctioning, but it allowed the indicator to show green when, in fact, the lock was not engaged. You are therefore exonerated from all blame.'

'Thank you, sir.' I saluted and departed.

They couldn't be fairer than that!

Some weren't so lucky. One morning I was indulging in a late breakfast, not due to take off until 1000. Paul Tyler, on the course ahead of me, was just rising from the table as I entered the mess. He was carrying a photograph album.

'Didn't know you were a photographer, Paul. May I have a look?'

He passed it across. 'Sure! Will you bring it down to the hangar with you?'

About an hour later, on my way down to the flight office, I had to stop to allow a 'Queen Mary'—a heavy aircraft transporter vehicle—to go slowly past. It bore all that was left of a Buffalo—and I recognised that only by its number on the fuselage. It looked as though it had passed through a steel rolling mill. It had to be one of ours, for the American boys flew Grumman F3Fs.

I met Dudley Leamon in the hangar.

'Whose was that, Dud?'

'Paul Tyler's.'

'Is he all right?'

'Christ! No! He never got out. What's left of him is crushed inside that lot.'

I stood, open-mouthed, looking like a fool.

'It can't be, Dudley! I just left him at breakfast, only—what?—just over an hour or so ago. It can't be him! Look, this is his album.'

'It's him all right. Better give that to me, Norman. His room's next to mine. He won't be needing that again...'

It could happen at the most alarming speed.

We made the most of our leisure. During our working week, when shore leave ended at 9.30 pm, there was little point in going to Miami, 14 miles away. In any case, there was always plenty of entertainment on the station. The Captain, G. F. Bogan, was a great socialite. Miami in winter is full of celebrities and he never failed to entice some personality or other up to Opa Locka to entertain us. Betty Grable, sweet and charming—possibly even more attractive in a quiet, good-looking suit than in her normal Hollywood sequins and spangles—raised the roof with a scintillating song-and-dance act. 'Show us your legs, Betty!' shouted the American sailors. Dutifully she stood before the footlights and demurely raised her skirt halfway up her shapely thighs. Louis Kentner played a recital for us. Larry Adler entranced us with his harmonica. Jack Benny and Jack Oakie had us helpless with laughter.

We went to night-clubs of course. One evening we were sitting at the bar of a club with Tex and Easton, two wealthy middle-aged Americans who had generously become sugar-daddies to Jim Pettigrew and myself. To my right was a gentleman of mid-European Semitic origin with a beautiful girl of 19 or 20. She was a dazzler. There was a nudge in my ribs.

'You a Limey?'

I nodded.

'Is that the uniform of the English Navy?'

I nodded again.

'Hey! Tell you what! My li'l girl wants one o' them fancy buttons on your jacket. How's about it?'

Fancy buttons indeed! The proud symbols on my Sub-Lieutenant's uniform! I knew precisely what to say but I had to remember the bit about being 'our country's ambassadors in a foreign country'.

'Sorry,' I said politely. 'No can do.'

'It's worth five bucks—interested?'

I was interested only in kicking him in the teeth.

'No—I'm sorry. She'll just have to be disappointed.'

'OK, sailor,' he said, removing the cigar from his mouth. 'So you're gonna play hard to get. 20 bucks.'

Again I shook my head.

'25—and that's my last offer.'

Five pounds or so was a lot of money to a Sub-Lieutenant; but I was pretty sure that Their Lordships hadn't so recently seen fit to grant me a commission to enable me to go around Miami night-clubs selling bits and pieces of uniform.

'I'm afraid you don't understand. It isn't the money. We don't give—or sell—pieces of uniform to *anybody*. All this stuff has come from Britain the hard way and I'm not parting with it to you or your sugar baby.'

Tex's head interposed between us. He wasn't a visitor and, accordingly, didn't feel as inhibited as I did.

'You heard what my friend said, Fatso,' he growled. 'His uniform ain't for sale. I'm sure you wouldn't want him to press the point. This guy's all of six feet standing up.'

Little by little we were increasing our knowledge of the American way of life. Pettigrew and I were at the Villa Venice, one of the better night-clubs on the Beach, with a very good, well-dressed floor show. We had sat through two shows but Jim, whose whole world revolved round girlies, insisted on seeing the third and last performance. He had established—in 'shop' talk—visual contact with a young lady in the second rank of the chorus. Having already made a fair guess at her vital statistics, he was determined to know more. The last show gave him his chance, for the girls appeared clad only in wonderful head-dresses, gauntlets, high-heeled shoes and G-strings.

Jim shook me back to life.

'They're on.'

So they were. And Jim was right—she *was* a honey. Blonde, about 19; and everything came out and went back again in exactly the right places. She smiled at him and made his day.

We were cold and shivering outside, despite our greatcoats. We had a long way to go back to the station—and it was nearly three o'clock. At the lamp-post at the corner Jim stopped.

'What's the matter?'

He was looking up the avenue on the side of the club; gazing towards the stage door.

'I'm waiting for her—you just carry on.'

'Don't be a bloody fool, Jim. You'll never make first base with her.'

'Just watch, boy. You just watch!'

He was an incurable optimist with a fine conceit where women were concerned. Eventually she emerged, looking lovely enough to eat. Her hair under the lamplight was beautiful. She wore a mink coat which she must have earned the hard way. Her legs beneath it were the pride of Florida. As Jim moved towards her, she declaimed—from 20 yards, in a rasping voice which can't have done a thing for Jim's ego:

'It'll cost you 30 bucks!'

It must have been a hard life for a high-kicker in Miami.

'Thirty bucks?' said Jim, incredulously. 'Thirty bucks? Jesus! I only want to borrow it, not buy it!'

She swept past us with a look of contempt. Her perfume and the swish of her mink wafted over me. Strange things, girls, I thought. And how bloody awful to be so hard at 19! Already she must be sick to death of men. She isn't young any more. Boys, young men, have been left far behind, and the wallets of the well-to-do—men of any age, shape or colour—are her only interest.

We started to walk. Opa Locka felt a long way away. We were halfway across the causeway bridging Biscayne Bay when a cab slowed to a halt by my side.

'Going to Opa Locka, boys?'

When a taxi pulls up beside you at three o'clock in the morning in Miami, you watch your step. However, the jockey was alone and looked reasonably harmless.

'How much?' I asked with Yorkshire canniness.

'Twenty bucks,' he said.

'Bollocks!' retorted Jim, his recent encounter having set the iron in his soul a-clanking against all Americans. 'Bollocks! I'd rather walk!'

We settled for 14, a very good buy from our point of view. We got in and started rolling. As we were approaching the end of the causeway, the driver said over his shoulder:

'You boys ever been to the Boulevard Club?'

'No. Where is it?'

'On the Boulevard, 'bout 19th Street. Tell you what.' (We already knew! He got a rake-off for the customers he brought.) 'I'll drop you in for an hour and wait—no extra charge.'

All I wanted was my bed—my own bed. But Jim had tasted blood and there was no holding him. I resigned myself to a no-sleep night.

The club was a fairly big L-shaped job with a stage at the end of the long leg of the L. It was reasonably furnished and decorated, but the bartenders looked ugly customers; and they set the tone. We were shown to a table. Before we could sit down, a couple of broads flopped into the other two chairs, a little blonde and a big, big brunette. Both chewed frantically.

'Buy us a drink, boys? OK? Scotch and water.'

A waiter brought the drinks. There was no conversation; the hell with it. I wished I was asleep. Come to think of it, I wasn't very far away. Jim set the drinks up again. When the waiter arrived, he removed our two beers and, turning to the waiter, said:

'And you can take that horse-water away and bring Scotch. When I order Scotch, I *want* Scotch.'

The waiter gave us a studied look and glanced at the bar. We were marked men.

Blondie was the first to leave. She reappeared on the stage in a matter of minutes and did a fast strip, to loud cheers and deafening applause. Most of the patrons seemed to be of the 'see Miami and die' variety. Our big brunette followed her. She stripped slowly to the strains of *Temptation*, as far as her bra and a G-string. The band played it well, too. But, then, all bands in Miami were good. A short and total black-out followed. Up came the lights again. Now she stood naked, holding across the front of her well-built body a large black chiffon square. She left the stage and disappeared from our view to the other arm of the L-shaped room to our right. There were regular bursts of laughter, shrieks of ecstasy and drunken catcalls. Eventually she gravitated to our table, weaving her black chiffon to and fro in what she hoped was a highly seductive manner. She was with the Limeys and a hush fell upon our neighbours.

'Five bucks to see my pussy, boys,' she announced loud and clear. I shook my head.

'My friend is asleep, honey,' said Jim, 'and I've seen all I want to for this week.'

He flicked a coin at her. She caught it with an adroitness that comes of long practice, looked at it and flung it back with an outburst of obscenity.

All hell broke loose. The holiday-makers from Pittsburgh roared with anti-British sentiments, the barmen prepared for action, hurriedly removing their dentures. I thought we were in for a rough trip and stood up, now thoroughly wide-awake and ready for trouble. Jim did the same.

'OK, fellers—relax. This your first time here?' Round the corner of the L appeared nine US Marines, a tough-looking young Sergeant in the lead. 'Here's the drill. Grab a chair.'

His chums already held chairs at the 'high port' and had formed a defensive circle. We joined them. The barmen hung around, waiting for a straggler. We moved slowly and evenly towards the door, then threw the chairs at them and beat it. We were laughing and shook hands all round.

Our cab-driver was standing outside, shaking with silent laughter. As we climbed back into the taxi:

'The guys I see comin' out like that! Say, you were great—*great*!'

Oddly enough, it was Jim who had to be awakened when we reached the station.

One morning, as we flew a patrol up the coast over Fort Lauderdale, the faint radio natter of an American exercise group some miles away, which had been in the background for some time, suddenly erupted into excitement:

'Bale out, Pete! Bale out, for Chrissake!'

'Jesus, Pete! Get out! Get out! Bale out, quick!' Then mumbo-jumbo and bags of hysterical yelling.

After lunch Derek Forbes and I went along to our room for a short siesta. I had just flaked out on my bed when I heard the sound of a woman sobbing.

'Where's that, Norman? Some crafty sod has worked a woman into the block! Bachelor Officers' Quarters, no less! How do you like that? And now she wishes she wasn't here!'

He jumped off the bed and crept across the floor-boards in his socks. He eased open the door.

'These bloody Americans don't know how to handle women. She needs a bit of comfort from New Zealand!'

I snorted.

'I know what she'll get from New Zealand—and it won't be frozen lamb!' Then he was out of the door. A few seconds elapsed before he returned.

'Next door. Those two American boys. Crafty sods!'

I went over to the wall myself. Listening acutely, I thought it didn't sound like a girl now. I went to their door and knocked.

'Anything I can do to help?'

'Get the hell out of it!' It was a boy's voice—shrill and hysterical. 'Leave me alone! Leave me alone, can't you?'

I was still standing there, wondering what to do, when an American cadet came along. I told him.

'Oh! Just let him be. His room-mate—his buddy—was killed over the Everglades this morning. Leave him be—he'll be OK.'

They had been firing at a drogue. 'Pete' had apparently gone in on a high-side run, had lost the drogue from his gunsight and had flown slap into it. The heavy cast-iron ring which forms the open circle at the leading end had smashed through his windscreen and decapitated him. From 10,000 feet and at full bore he had dived into the swamps; and what was left of him wasn't worth collecting.

I was glad I wasn't still his room-mate when Derek Forbes plunged headlong into Scapa Flow a year later. He was too nice a kid to die like that.

Segregation between whites and blacks had astonished most of us during our time in Florida and in such places outside as we had visited. Later on in the war we were to see plenty of evidence of apartheid in South Africa but, for the life of me, I saw little or no difference from attitudes in the southern States.

We boarded a bus in Pensacola town one afternoon—five or six of us—to go out to some beauty spot on the coast. We clambered in, saw the back seat—right across the full width of the bus—completely unoccupied and, naturally enough, parked ourselves in it. Departure time came and went. No activity. Then one of us asked a passenger in front of us what was the cause of the hold-up.

'The driver's waiting for you to get off that seat,' said the lady addressed.

'This seat? Why? What's wrong with it?'

'That seat's for black folks.'

'Well—there aren't any on board.'

'Don't matter. That seat's for black folks and that driver ain't gonna go 'til you boys gets off it.'

Sure enough, as soon as we stood, the bus departed. We called that just plain bloody ridiculous!

Now, in Miami, we found things even more droll. Blacks had to clear the streets of the Beach by a certain time each evening and get off to their shanty town outside Miami City—a curfew, if you like. The segregation wasn't confined to blacks and whites either. Miami provided visible signs of segregation between Jews and Gentiles, which surprised us even more. The first sign I saw was a black-and-white painted noticeboard outside the main entrance to a fashionable golf club on Miami Beach where I was invited to play. It read, starkly and uncompromisingly, GENTILES ONLY ALLOWED HERE. There were night clubs and restaurants similarly labelled. Maybe England wasn't such a funny old country after all.

At the end of our course we were given a couple of days leave before departing from Miami. Les Wort, Johnny Adams and I hired a wonderful Oldsmobile—about four litres—for the amazing sum of £1 per day and decided to see Key West.

The Florida Keys are a pendant of small islands stretching in an unbelievably beautiful chain for 100 miles from the foot of the Florida peninsula into the Gulf of Mexico. The highway of those days connected the keys by a series of bridges, some wooden, some steel. The weather in April was gorgeous; and on both sides was the calm, turquoise water of the Gulf. Its clarity—less than ten fathoms deep—was incredible.

I had driven the whole of the outward journey. On the way back, Les was to try his hand. We must have covered something like half of the return trip when he looked at me:

'What d'you think this thing will do?'

'Dunno. But I reckon it's bloody fast.'

'A hundred?'

'Wouldn't surprise me.'

With that he put down his foot. There was no traffic, no danger. The needle flickered to 100 mph and Les, with a satisfied chuckle, eased her down. We must still have been around 70–80 when a black Stutz overtook us, going like smoke. Half a mile later he flashed on his 'POLICE-STOP' lights and led us into a lay-by.

We sat.

From the nearside of the police car emerged a gentleman clad in a Stetson, a khaki shirt and riding-breeches and high boots. He also sported a large piece of artillery on his right hip. He strolled leisurely down to us, withdrawing his note-book from his shirt pocket. With never a glance at us:

'Licence.' Les handed it over.

'Insurance.' Again the document was produced. For the first time, he noticed the RNVR gold braid—wavy—on Les' sleeve. He looked up and waited a moment.

'Say! You guys Limeys?'

'Yes.'

'Well, goddammit! Hi! Charlie!' (This to his companion.) 'Hey! *Charlie*! We got some Limeys here! C'mon! Quick! We heard there were some Limeys at Opa Locka! Well, I'll go to hell! So you're Limeys! Pleased to meet you, boys! I'm Joe, this 'ere's Charlie.'

We reciprocated; and got out for a leg-stretch.

'So you're at Opa Locka? Great! Are they givin' you a good time?

Great! Plenty o' broads in Miami, ain't that right? You bin down to Key West, boys? Ain't that somethin'? You guys flyin', huh?'

So it went on. Our homes, our families, the war, London (England), the goddam Krauts, even more so the goddam lousy Jap bastards. All these we discussed at length. Finally we were allowed to re-embark.

'Just one thing, boys. Watch your speed, fellers. The limit on this highway is 25. (*25*, for God's sake!) Apart from that, you ain't even got a permit to go down to Key West—it's a restricted area, see, bein' a naval base an' all. It's OK though; we're buddies.

'Tell you what, though. When you're leaving Key Largo, could be you'll see another car like ours—two buddies of ours called Harry and Duke are on duty. If they stop you, you just tell 'em you bin talkin' to Joe and Charlie. It'll be OK. Honest. They won't give you no trouble.

'Sure bin swell meetin' up with you boys! Enjoy yourselves and git them Krauts! S'long!'

Then it was homeward bound. Eight months had passed remarkably quickly, during which we had learnt a lot about Americans and about the US Navy who had very kindly and very efficiently taught me to fly a fighter aircraft without, as they put it so picturesquely, 'bustin' my ass'. We had met untold people and made a lot of good friends. We had enjoyed unprecedented hospitality from wonderful people who just naturally exuded generosity. I had found my way around New York. I had seen Toscanini, Duke Ellington, Arthur Fiedler, Benny Goodman, Jack Dempsey, Tommy Dorsey, Jack Benny and Betty Grable. I had emerged from Miami night-clubs as the dawn came up over Biscayne Bay, to seek bacon and eggs. I had sailed up the Mississippi in a stern-wheeler under a Christmas moon whose size I just didn't believe. I had surf-boarded in the Gulf of Mexico and flown, by night and day, over the Floridan Everglades and the Mobile and Swanee Rivers, so dear to the hearts of barber-shop quartets.

It had all been fun—well, most of it.

4

First shots at the flight-deck

We sailed home as passengers in *Avenger,* one of the early escort carriers built on a merchant ship hull. She was a good ship for the job but alas!, was to die from a torpedo in the North African landings in November 1942.

After a short leave, the recent arrivals from the USA foregathered again at Greenwich Royal Naval College. This was a fortnight's course designed to turn us into officers and gentlemen, popularly known to the RNVR as the 'knife and fork' course.

The College buildings might have seemed a bit on the ancient side after Block 624 at Pensacola, but there was no denying their elegance and aura of gracious living. The Painted Hall in particular, where we had our meals, and the beautiful chapel were more than buildings; they were an experience in one's life. After them, the lack of running hot and cold water in the cabins didn't seem to matter!

We attended a host of lectures, mainly on naval and general British history, naval traditions and the wartime role of warships of every category. Professor Michael Lewis, probably the most celebrated naval historian of our age, captivated us completely with his charm and consummate knowledge of his subject. We were taught unarmed combat and gaily threw one another around the spacious lawns. An instructor warned us darkly of the perils of gas and bacteriological warfare. He was unanimously written down as something of a queer when he went to great lengths to impress upon us that these deadly weapons could penetrate all orifices of the human body. Our women-folk especially were to be well guarded for they were equipped with an extra orifice which we didn't possess.

'Dirty old bastard! Fancy talking like that when there are men dying in China!' was Johnny Johnson's summing up of this surprising lecture.

We left Greenwich having, we hoped, been duly elevated. We had recently become acquainted with the saying:

The RN are gentlemen trying to be sailors;
The RNR are sailors trying to be gentlemen;
The RNVR are neither trying to be both.

Whatever was happening to us, we were all mad keen and trying like hell.

After that we made the long journey by train to Padstow in north Cornwall and by Navy transport for the few miles to St Merryn, a Royal Naval Air Station where we were temporarily attached to a training squadron, No 762. The countryside in which it was situated could hardly be described as entrancing, but the coves and beaches—some of them within easy walking distance—more than compensated for it.

The station was pleasant enough, its only drawback being that neither of its two runways was ever into wind. Station gossip said that when Government Met men had come down with their charts dating from around the Crimean War, the mean wind directions over the years had said X and Y; and the runways had been plotted accordingly. It seems that local farmers, watching what was going on with great interest, could hardly control their mirth when they were told what had been decided, for never in history had the wind blown in either of those two directions. Government charts, however, knew better and the runways were duly put in. So we never took off or landed into wind!

The Fairey Fulmar, an obsolete two-seater Fleet fighter with a Rolls-Royce Merlin XXX engine, was a lovely aircraft to fly. Although somewhat underpowered, she more than made up for this deficiency by her complete lack of vices. She had to be kicked into a spin and, when it came, it was a leisurely sensation which was easily controlled. If she was involved in any incidents, they were certainly man-made, for the Fulmar, bless her, was the most gentle of aircraft and would never dream of embarrassing you.

After training on American aircraft, it was now necessary to make a few minor adjustments to the mechanics of flying. Instead of applying hydraulic brakes with the upper part of the rudder pedals, we now operated air brakes with a lever incorporated in the joystick. The engine power gauge was no longer calibrated in 'inches of mercury'; on British aircraft the measurement was in 'pounds of boost'. (Both systems, incidentally, gave an indication of the pressure of the combustible air/petrol mixture being forced through the carburettor venturi.) The 'turn-and-bank' indicator was no longer 'needle-and-ball'. Now it comprised two needles.

One sunny morning I was out over the sea off Newquay, doing gun camera attacks on a Fulmar flown by an instructor called Henderson, a friendly Scotsman with a good reputation as a pilot. On one of my downhill runs to attack him from astern, I felt a cool spray in my face. Coolant, I thought. (The Merlin engine was liquid-cooled with glycol, something akin to anti-freeze. It had great penetrative powers and most engines suffered from minor leaks.) I told myself that I must report it on my return.

On my next run-in to Henderson I had to dive fairly steeply to drop to his altitude. I was immediately deluged in petrol. It flowed over me in great waves from the main tank behind me. The enclosed deck of the cockpit was soon awash, four or five inches deep in the stuff. Christ! I flapped like a schoolgirl! Fire! Any minute! Hood open, off safety harness. I was climbing out on to the wing when I discovered, in the nick of time, that in my panic I had removed my parachute harness—stupid bastard! I just had to climb back into the cockpit, fire or no, and fly the thing. Needless to say, in my flap I forgot all about Henderson and the exercise and headed hotfoot for the airfield.

Sammy Hall, our black-bearded squadron commander who could be a bit terse when on duty, strode purposefully across to meet me as a I descended from the cockpit, 45 minutes early.

'What the hell do you think . . . Where's the petrol? H'm? Where's the petrol?'

'All over me, sir.' I was shivering, too. Petrol is damned cold stuff.

He walked right up to me and pushed his beard into my uniform.

'Christ! You're drowned in the bloody stuff! What the hell have you been doing?'

I told him what had happened. 'Must be a leak.'

'That's no bloody leak! Chief! Chief! Come here a minute! Check the petrol cap, please.'

The CPO of our flight mounted the wing and unclipped the fairing covering the tank. No cap there. Sammy Hall looked grim.

'Dip the tank, Chief.' A few moments passed. Chief looked at me.

'How long have you been up?' Sammy answered before I could.

'He's been up about 15 minutes.'

'Then he's lost 30 or 40 gallons, sir.'

The wretched mechanic responsible went to the 'glasshouse' for a spell. A few weeks of unpleasantness for him, another of my nine lives gone.

I was sent one morning to do an 'oxygen climb' to 20,000 feet. The dear old Fulmar took her time to get up there but I was in no hurry, having nothing better to do. The morning was crisp and clear and I was captivated to see the whole of Cornwall lying below me like a great relief map. What was more, visibility was so good that the north French coast could be seen quite clearly. It was my first experience of seeing part of Europe as it looks on a map.

We flew a few hours on Grumman Martlets, handy little American fighters used with great effect on escort carriers. Their only drawback was the manually operated undercarriage, which was hell to wind up

or down since the handle was on the right side of the cockpit, neces-
sitating a change of hands on the joystick just at the crucial moments of
take-off or landing. It was common knowledge that at least one pilot
had wound himself straight into the ground.

One of our ex-Pensacola boys was Dennis Hillyard who, when we
first joined up, had seemed little more than a child, having come into
the Service straight from Ampleforth. I like to think that I was in some
small way responsible for his growing up for, whilst we were at
Pensacola, I seemed to spend a fair amount of time rousing him from
his bed, forcibly making him wash and shave and make his bed before
breakfast; generally keeping him out of trouble. He must have paid a
fair bit of attention to 'Uncle Norman' for he was now a smart young
man, looking every inch the dashing young naval officer in his brand-
new Midshipman's uniform. Alas! He was all too soon to die a tragic
death in the North African landings and I still bemoan the loss of a
good friend.

He was, thank God, still full of fun, life and vigour on the morning
he first took up a Martlet. The small wheel which controlled the rudder
trimming tab had, under its perspex cover, an indicator showing the
number of degrees of rudder trim in use. The snag was that, as the
wheel was turned to the right, the indicator turned to the left—all very
confusing. And you certainly needed a rudder trim on the Martlet for,
as its engine surged on to full power, the torque to the left hit you like a
brick.

So Dennis carefully put on six degrees of right rudder trim. But
when the indicator turned to the left, he was scathing in his thoughts
about the Grumman Aircraft Company of Bethpage, Long Island. So
he turned the wheel back until the indicator showed—or appeared to
show—six degrees of right rudder trim.

Off he went down the runway. As the power built up, no mortal
man could have withstood the pressure. The aircraft, just clear of the
ground, did an acute turn to port of about 130 degrees and came
tearing back across the airfield at about 20 feet. Hillyard, understand-
ably, was still in the 'office', busily winding up that infernal undercarriage. I doubt if at this juncture he had noticed anything untoward.

Now a certain young man—and I sincerely hope he has long since
recovered and is now fit and well in his old age—was driving across the
grass a petrol bowser which was adorned with a wooden mast bearing a
large yellow flag, specifically designed to warn off people like Dennis.
The pilot, however, was still trying to work things out and wasn't
paricularly worried about ground obstacles. The aircraft roared over
the petrol bowser, almost decapitating the driver and removing mast
and flag with the still partially-extended undercarriage. The staff in
the control tower, looking down from their lofty eminence on this

amazing scene, unanimously agreed that they had never seen the likes of it.

Neither had Sammy Hall. He said as much to Hillyard a short time later, though probably not in the same words.

Before we left the West Country we had a short spell at Yeovilton in Somerset. For the few days we spent there we flew Martlets, practising ADDLs (assisted dummy deck-landings), formation flying and doing a little night flying. 'Dicing' at night in Somerset was distinctly different from Miami! To fly over a countryside solidly blacked-out, under a sky with neither moon nor stars, was quite a challenge after the Miami coastline which illuminated the sky for miles around. The only lights which the station showed were sector runway lights—small dim affairs in a chain set out along the port side of the duty runway; and visible only to one approaching in the direction for landing. One night I flogged back and forth across Somerset trying in vain to catch a glimpse of those confounded candles. Chesil Beach, which I knew lay a point or two east of south of Yeovilton, was only dimly to be seen on that night; and from that point I started my endless trips up to the Bristol Channel and back. Someone on the ground must have become pretty bored with my performance for, after 20 minutes or so, a kindly AA Regimental soul obligingly illuminated three searchlights and 'threw' the column of light in the direction of the station. Then I *did* find them!

For the first time in our flying careers, concentrated practice was put in on ADDLs preparatory to making our first attempts at proper deck-landing. An instructor equipped with 'bats' stood at the end of the duty runway, where he 'batted us in' to landings as we flew interminable circuits of the field, touched down and promptly opened up again for yet another take-off.

A deck-landing must be safe, slow and in a 'nose-up, tail-down' attitude, primarily to ensure a slow approach and also to facilitate the picking-up of an arrestor wire by the aircraft's arrestor hook. Approaching to land in this attitude calls for a considerable amount of engine power, maintained until the last moment when the batting officer gives the mandatory signal—CUT!—by crossing the bats before his face.

There were, of course, no arrestor wires on the runways on which we practised; but there was an area marked approximately to the length of a carrier's flight-deck on which landings are made. Into this area the instructor aimed to bring us to touch-down. His signals were simple enough to follow:

Bats held horizontally: 'You're doing fine—just keep it like that.'

Bats held upwards in a V pattern: 'You're too low—put on more throttle to gain height.'

Bats held downwards in an inverted V: 'Now you're too high —reduce throttle a bit.'

Both bats rotated: 'You're becoming too slow—put on more urge!'

One bat held out, the other concealed behind his back: 'You're too fast—go easy on the throttle!'

Left arm raised 45 degrees above the horizontal, right arm lowered: 'You're not lined up on the deck—come to port!'

Right arm raised 45 degrees above the horizontal, left arm lowered: 'You're too far to port—come to starboard!'

Bats crossed before the face: 'Cut the throttle!'

It was all a matter of practice.

Once more we were sent on a short leave. (When the Navy hasn't the faintest idea what to do with you, they send you on leave!) The next time we would meet would be aboard *Argus,* the training carrier, there to try our skill—and our luck—at deck-landing.

Argus was at anchor in Lamlash Bay, Isle of Arran, when we climbed aboard late one afternoon. At that stage of the war the whole of the training staff was still RN; and one of them collected us in the wardroom after dinner to explain the drill for the following day. Apparently the morning was to be devoted to Swordfish landings. Our appearance would take place in the afternoon. There were ten of us including Jimmy Floyd, a Lieutenant RNVR, one of our instructors at St Merryn. We had no idea how *he* felt, but we were singularly unenthusiastic. So far in our young lives, all our landings had been made on runways which seemed to stretch as far as eternity. It would shake us to the tits to land on a carrier—and especially on *Argus*, whose deck looked to us to be about as big as two tennis courts. Still, other people had made it, so why shouldn't we? Some encouraging soul, of course, just had to point out that other people had *died* on or around *Argus*—so why shouldn't we? This was received with a chilling silence and shaking knees.

'Who's going first?' asked the training officer.

No one spoke.

'I thought as much. Each of you write your name on a slip of paper.' He tore a sheet of foolscap into strips. When we had written our names, he rolled the strips up and borrowed a cap.

'Robertson. Laidlaw. Adams. Hanson . . .' Someone wrote them down as he reeled them off. Finally he came to Jimmy Floyd, tenth to go.

The great day dawned—real summer. The Clyde looked wonderful under a clear blue sky. Beneath us was a picture-book sea, with only a slight breeze gently nipping off the wave-tops into spray. We spent the morning watching the TBR boys perform in a Swordfish. Some of the landings were a bit on the dodgy side, but there were no prangs. We were thus encouraged to eat some lunch and to indulge in a little mutual moral support.

The drill was quite simple. *Argus* had six arrestor wires strung across the after end of the deck. She had no 'island' in the accepted sense, only a rather comical structure somewhat reminiscent of a submarine's conning tower at the forward port side of the deck, which could be raised or lowered at will. She had no crash barriers. Instead, standing near the island was a very brave young officer who vigorously waved a red flag if an aircraft failed to engage any of the wires with its arrestor hook. The pilot was thus energetically exhorted to open the throttle and take off again, to make another circuit and another approach to the deck. We were each to do six landings, preceded by two dummy runs with the wires in the down position and with arrestor hooks up. The batsman would bring us on as though for a normal landing and, at the last moment, would then wave us off. After the second of these dummy runs, if satisfied with his performance, the pilot would waggle his wings. Thus he signified that his next approach would be 'for real' with hook down, to be batted into the wires for a landing.

Jimmy Robertson and Bill Laidlaw duly did their six in copy-book style without any trouble. Then Johnny Adams climbed out of the 'nets' and walked across to the Fulmar, where a fitter was reloading the magazine with starter cartridges. Johnny was resplendent in a new suit of flying overalls—black, with Royal Navy buttons. It was very much the 'in' thing at the time and had been duly admired as it was the first one we had seen. He climbed into the cockpit.

His two dummy runs were classic. He waggled his wings as he went over the bows for the third time and we saw him drop his hook as he came down wind on his circuit. He had less than two minutes to live. In the last 200 yards to the deck, he drifted to port ever so slightly. The batsman slanted his bats to correct him, more and more energetically as Johnny failed to react. As the aircraft came in over the side of the deck and supported only by fresh air, the batsman dropped for his life—and we, standing in the nets, dropped with him. The port wheel went into the nets, and the Fulmar, at about 65 knots, slewed to port and fell into the sea. As she went, we could see Johnny making the greatest and last mistake of his life; he was casting off his harness and climbing out of the cockpit. Then he and the Fulmar were gone. An attendant corvette came up at the rush and hove-to over the spot. Only Johnny's helmet rose to the surface—nothing else.

He had been married just three days earlier.

Our only Fulmar had gone, so we waited three-quarters of an hour for another to be flown from Machrihanish. It duly arrived, piloted by a most capable instructor who touched down on the flight-deck with a panache and verve that left us speechless; and with a damned sight less fuss than a secretary parking her Mini for lunch. Unfortunately during this time I had suffered a thousand-and-one deaths. I had wished the *Argus* sunk. I had yearned to be in a sanatorium suffering from galloping consumption. I had even wished myself in the Army. Alas! All in vain! Nemesis stood before me on the deck and the training officer, well inured to what we had just witnessed with strangled breath and twisting intestines, was already shouting 'Right! Who's next?'

I climbed into the cockpit like a decrepit invalid. There I sat, being helped into my harness by a cheerful, whistling mechanic—'All right, sir?' I nodded, with glazed eyes. I was beyond articulate speech. I was in a blue funk. If Johnny, 'above average' all the way through his training, could be killed so peremptorily, what chance did *I* stand? I was about to switch on and start up when an officer dashed down the deck and leapt up on the wing.

'OK. Take off now but circle the ship until we give you a green Very. The Rear-Admiral and his staff are landing aboard in two Swordfish. When we have struck them below we'll tell you to start. OK?'

I circled for 20 minutes before the two lumbering old Swordfish arrived, landed and disappeared into the hangar. That breathing space was sufficient to bring back to me the feel of the Fulmar, an aircraft I liked enormously, and the confidence I so sorely needed. I did the best six landings of my life.

That evening Dick Harvey and I made an inventory of Johnny's gear and packed it up for return to his widow. I felt bloody awful, although not half as bad, I imagine, as Dick, who was going to break the news to her. Another buddy had gone and what had appalled me was the suddeness of death in the air. I found it difficult to understand and wholly terrifying.

5

Digression in Egypt

In June 1942 I took my leave again of Kathleen and sailed as a passenger aboard the motor vessel *Penrith Castle,* bound for the Royal Naval Air Station at Dekheila, some 15 miles west of Alexandria, just on the edge of the Western Desert. I had arrived at Swansea at about eight in the morning and had found a hotel near the railway station, still miraculously standing after the recent blitz, where the manager was affably ready to supply breakfast to a ravenous traveller. In the dining-room, already well stuck into his bacon and egg, was Les Wort, an old friend from Pensacola and, more recently, another successful decklander on *Argus.*

We were eight passengers in all—and two of them didn't like the war at all. At 28 years of age I was revelling in the Great Adventure and up to date had encountered nothing to get particularly steamed up about. But here were two characters who were afraid of the war and made no bones about showing it. One was a Government accountant whose chief claim to fame was a torpedoing on his way home from Accra some months earlier, which had left him decidedly jumpy about the cruel sea. He possessed the most wonderful escape and evasion suit I was ever to see. This one-piece garment, exclusively designed and made of lightweight drill, was one mass of pockets which came in various sizes and contained everything from cigarettes to fishing lines. All the contents were most carefully watertighted into contraceptives, a contract which must have put Durex on to overtime. The suit when fully laden must have weighed a ton and how on earth the owner staggered around in it in tropical latitudes I can't imagine. He donned this apparatus at sun-down and discarded it only when the sun was a couple of feet up.

He had a natural ally in an RFA Chief Engineer, and this particular chap's fear of the ship he was ordained to join—an aviation spirit tanker, bound to attract every torpedo in the Mediterranean—seemed now to include the voyage to Egypt. Each of them acquired a bottle of whisky every 24 hours which, together with the odd beer at intervals throughout the day, ensured that by nightfall they would be in such a condition that the impact of a torpedo in the night watches would be neither here nor there. To get things under way, the engineer started the day well with two bottles of beer for breakfast. This struck me as rank heresy, for the food in the ship was first-class. Obviously I had never run into serious drinkers before!

We sailed from Milford Haven in a small convoy which, as we rounded Northern Ireland and headed out into the Atlantic, was augmented by other ships until we were something in the order of 36 merchantmen, escorted by several destroyers and corvettes. I am glad to say that the famous survival suit was put at readiness only once during the voyage. We were playing cards in the saloon when all hell broke loose in the vicinity. We rushed out on deck to find ourselves bathed in the light of scores of parachute flares. A U-boat alarm had been sounded and, to make matters worse, this wicked German was reported to be on the surface in the convoy lanes. One feels singularly naked and unprotected when, on a pitch-dark night, it is possible to read a copy of *Men Only* held by an off-watch officer on the next ship in line. What our accountant friend thought about it I don't know. He emerged on to the deck, miraculously torn from the arms of a very drunken Morpheus and flapped around in his tailored shroud like a stupefied duck, wanting to know what was going on. As a matter of fact, *nothing* was going on. There was no U-boat and no cause for panic, but the escort had a jolly romp up and down the lanes which must have been a refreshing change for them from the dull monotony of zig-zag escorting.

The voyage was full of interest. At Freetown we broke up the convoy and, alone in the great open spaces, we plugged down the South Atlantic at 13 knots and eventually anchored in Table Bay, Cape Town. For the first time I looked upon Table Mountain, surely one of the most imposing rocks in the world. She even sported her famous 'table-cloth' in our honour. The captain went ashore alone and that only for his orders. But how the lights of the city beckoned us! After over a month at sea, an hour or two of the pavements and bright lights would have been more than welcome. In the morning we weighed anchor and were off again.

We fed well. We had excellent company. During the day, Les and I were Assistant Officers of the Watch, and in the evening we read or played chess or bridge. And always there was the sea, the great rolling, endless, blue ocean, incredibly alive with all its creatures. The glorious albatross with his skimming flight, his love of company, his beating up from astern with never a flicker from his great wings; then, as he reached the bridge, his soaring wheel out to starboard as he glided off downwind again, to reappear half an hour later, low-flying at nought feet over the waves. There was a great whale who joined us one afternoon in the Mozambique Channel to play with us for three

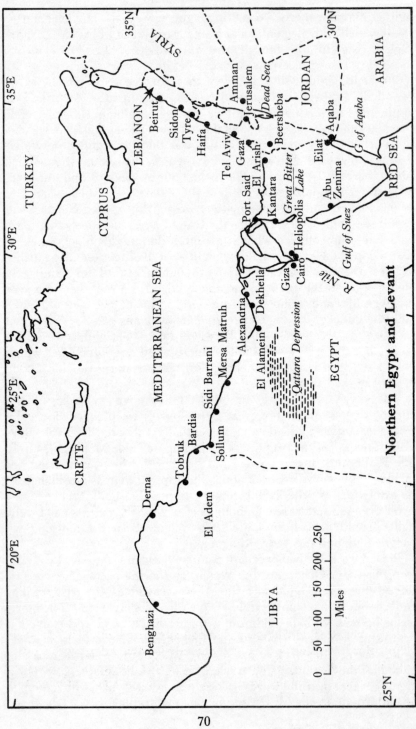

Northern Egypt and Levant

hours, crossing and re-crossing our bows, blowing and sounding at regular intervals to show us what a clever fellow he was. There were sharks who came to look at us, or to pick up some garbage, but who never stayed for long, for our speed was too much for them to keep up with us. Flying fish were there in their hundreds, rising in clouds under our pressing bows, darting forward like silver arrows for 20 yards before diving back into their other element. Schools of porpoise, keeping pace with us on either beam, rose and fell like steeplechasers.

It was a world of fantasy. And we were brought back to reality only when we sailed one fine morning up the Gulf of Suez and saw, rising from a small airfield on the Sinai coast—Abu Zenima—a Fulmar, no less! That evening we anchored in the roads off Port Tewfik and next morning, having embarked a Canal pilot, we joined a convoy for the passage through to Port Said.

It took eight hours; and all I remember is soldiers. Hundreds, thousands of soldiers swimming, sitting on the Canal banks, waving, giving V-signs, with all their tented camps stretching behind them as far as the eye could see. We passed through the Bitter Lakes, past Ismailia, past Kantara with its great camel stockade on the Asian shore and finally into Port Said. All this was one long dream. I was fascinated. Until now, these far-away spots had been names in an atlas. Now here they were—and I wasn't disappointed. I am without doubt one of the people Thomas Cook had uppermost in mind when he opened up his business. I am a born sucker for exotic places.

Next morning Les Wort and I took our leave of *Penrith Castle* and our fellow-voyagers. We took a hot, dusty train which was covered with Arabs like locusts on a tree, their 'nighties' flapping madly in the breeze. Back up the Canal to Ismailia, across the Desert to Zagazig, Benha, just north of the great Nile barrage to the north of Cairo; Tanta, Damanhur and finally, after eight long, weary hours, into Alexandria. As we came out of the station there was the roar of aircraft overhead. Searchlights pierced the black Egyptian night sky. 'God!' I said to myself. 'We'll be at it tomorrow morning!'

There was a good-looking young Leading Seaman standing at our side.

'You for Dekheila, sir?'

'Yes, thank you,' said Les, as the sailor picked up our gear and led the way to a small van parked nearby. He enjoined us to get into the cab alongside him on the big bench seat.

'Keep yer eyes on that gear if I stop at traffic lights, sir,' he said. 'These thievin' bastards'll have the bloody lot if you don't watch out.'

We hung upon every word. Here was a man of experience and we were two green Subbies, green as grass, who had never thought of Egyptians as 'thievin' bastards'.

'Do you have air raids *every* night?' I asked, amazed at once at the lack of gunfire and his airy nonchalance.

'Air raids, sir?' His sailor cap, now flat aback, shook with mirth. 'Air raids? Ain't no air raids 'ere, sir—well, bar the odd one or two now and again. Bloody sight safer 'ere than in London, believe me! If yer gonna get killed 'ere, sir, if you don't mind me sayin' so, it'll be clap, not Jerry!'

Bang went another illusion. Never mind. At least they had 'kept it going' for us while we had been sunning ourselves round the Cape. We reached Dekheila when most people had gone off to bed, just in time for a sandwich and a beer. That evening we knew no one. We were ignored. We were a couple of white-kneed sprogs just out from UK and we would have to find our own feet. I had a second somewhat depressing beer and trudged off to bed, in a cabin which I was to inhabit for a year. For the first time in my life I tucked a mosquito net under my mattress. Someone had just told me that the 'mosquitoes were worse than the Wogs'. No one mentioned the Germans sitting at El Alamein, 35 miles away.

We had hoped to join a Hurricane squadron, then stationed up in the desert. The next morning we were dismayed to learn that this was to be disbanded in a matter of days and to our chagrin we were allocated to a stooge, or non-operational, squadron—Les to the Fleet Requirements Unit, myself to the Communications Flight of 775 Squadron.

So, despite my disappointment and some untimely bitching to Commander (Flying), who briskly cut me down to size in the space of one short minute, I embarked on one of the most enjoyable years of my life.

Dekheila was a happy station. Looking back on it, I recall it as a genial, friendly flying club rather than a Naval Air Station. Captain C. L. Howe was a quiet, gentlemanly type who administered the place without fuss or commotion. His Commander, 'Jumbo' Jackson, maintained discipline with a light hand and allowed no jarring notes to creep into the informal, relaxed manner in which we were sent about our duties. 'Wally' Wallington was our Air Engineering Officer, Peter Bagley the Air Gunnery Officer and Jimmy Waddell, ex-Jersey Airways, our Lieutenant Commander (Flying). The pilots were a good crowd with whom to live and work. Peter Snow, an RN Lieutenant who, as a Midshipman, had been to Dunkirk in a destroyer; Mick Powell; Geoff Symonds; and not least Jim Pettigrew, my old Miami buddy. There, too, I found again Sammy Langdon, a friend from St Merryn, probably one of the finest pilots I ever knew. Sammy looked like a saint. Certainly a halo wouldn't have seemed out of place encircling his flaxen-fair hair and pale, aesthetic-looking face. Yet he was full of fun and one of the most engaging characters you could wish to meet. A new friend was Arthur (Speedy) Craven, a clever electrical boffin who completely baffled us by building his own radar set from parts picked up here and there, particularly from RAF acquaintances. One or two of us lent a modest hand by spending Sunday afternoons in flying set patterns for him from which he was able to calibrate his equipment. It worked, too!

Life was most uncomplicated, and we had a lot of fun. Off duty, our day time relaxation was swimming, for the blue waters of the Mediterranean lapped the shore only 50 yards from my cabin window. In the evenings we drank—sometimes modestly, more seriously at other times. Now and again we would see a film in Alexandria as a pleasant change from Shafto's horrible cinema on the station, where the comfort was non-existent, the projector erratic and the screen unmentionable. The building had a corrugated iron roof. When the heavy autumn rains were upon us, the drumming on this made it completely impossible to hear a word being uttered by the speakers. There was an abundance of good restaurants in the city where we could enjoy decent food when station meals palled.

A 'dim-out' was imposed in Alexandria during the hours of darkness, though nothing on the scale of a British-type black-out. Walking the streets at night, even in the city centre, was an exercise calling for great caution. Numbers of careless Servicemen awoke at dawn in some squalid back alley with nothing more than a thick head and, if they were lucky, their underwear. Taxi-drivers took on board a mate after dark and it was asking for trouble to take a cab—alone—from the city centre to the harbour or the suburbs. Safety lay only in numbers.

The quarters at Dekheila, whilst by no means palatial, were reasonably civilised considering there was a war on and that they had been bequeathed to us by the Egyptian Air Force. Nothing so pansy as running hot and cold water was laid on to our cabins. Our Egyptian stewards arrived each morning with a large enamelled jug of hot water for shaving and washing. Near by was an imposing row of 'thunderboxes'. Whatever else, the wardroom and dining-mess were comfortable enough. The entrance hall was usually enhanced by a number of potted plants and several ornamental trees, anything up to six feet high, which had been removed from Alexandrian night-clubs. At one time they were in such profusion that our hall porter was heard to grumble that, if we insisted on introducing all this greenery, the least we could do was to 'kidnap a bloody Wog to water the bastards'! He had a point.

The airfield was good and safe. Although most of the runways were on the short side, even by 1942 standards, at least the approaches to them were clear and uncomplicated. The largest hangar abutted on to the sea; and the seaward doors were forever shut. I was at a loss to understand this, for I would have thought that the additional light afforded had they been open would have been a great boon to the fitters working there. I mentioned it to our Chief.

'You're right, sir. We could do with the light, no mistake. Trouble is, when the doors were open, the pilots kept flyin' through the bloody hangar!'

Apparently it was true and after that I looked at the hangar in a new light.

In addition to all the fun there was, of course, the flying. Under the threat of Rommel, catching his breath at El Alamein after a stream of successes in the desert, half of the Navy had scurried off to Port Said, some 150 miles to the east. The division caused endless problems for there was no direct road or rail link between the two across the Nile delta; and, as I have said, the journey by way of the Delta barrage took eight hours, however it was done. In an endeavour to cope with the problems, our station was providing an air mail service flown by Fulmars from our flight. There was in Port Said an hotel room booked permanently for the duty pilot, who left Dekheila at 1500 every day, taking urgent mail and, if necessary, a couple of passengers, luxuriously seated on carpet stools. After staying the night in Port Said, he was picked up at 0630 by a Navy car and driven out to Gamil airfield (an RAF Spitfire field). There he took on mail and any passengers, took off at 0700, dropped his cargo at Lake Marryut, immediately to the south of Alexandria city; and finally reached Dekheila about 0750, just in time for breakfast. This pleasant duty fell upon two or three of us in rotation.

One of my regular passengers on this run was Commander Allen, RN, a charming man approaching middle age who had been pulled out of retirement for war service in the DEMS branch—defensively equipped merchant ships. He was genial and friendly and never failed, on arrival at Port Said, to entertain me to tea or dinner. It was he who introduced me to one of the best 'sticky cake' shops I ever gorged in—Gianola's, a Swiss bakery-cum-tea-shop not far from Simon Arzt's famous emporium. I have been an addict of that food of the gods ever since. He used to stay at the Casino Palace Hotel, higher up the street, where we would have dinner. After that we could sit outside, drink and watch the world go by; or sometimes go to the movies. This invariably ended with the playing of the Egyptian National Anthem, loudly chanted by hundreds of sailors, standing rigidly and commendably to attention, singing their own translation which was horrifyingly obscene!

Commander Allen's untimely death brought great sorrow to me. He had been to Malta on a duty trip and had been offered a 'lift home' back to Alexandria aboard the fast minelayer *Welshman*. This ship, one of the fastest in the Royal Navy, set off unescorted on a high-speed run eastwards down the Mediterranean and was unlucky enough to run into U–617. On that night in February 1943 the U-boat's captain, despite the *Welshman*'s fantastic speed, managed to get a direct hit on her. One was enough. Commander Allen, I was told, survived the sinking and got aboard a life-raft; but he was too old to survive the rigours of a freezing-cold night on the open sea and perished from exposure. He was a long, long way from his rose garden in the southern counties.

My most vivid memory of the Port Said run is the beauty of the sunrises. At 0700 in winter one took off from Gamil airfield into a sky just becoming light. I can still feel the cold in the cockpit as I sat there, waiting for the engine to warm up. Although I was grateful for an Irvine jacket, how I shivered there! The wind always seemed to come from the sea and the climb out of Gamil took one across the sand-dunes and out over the Mediterranean. A wide climbing turn to starboard covered the town; and at that moment, with increasing altitude, one 'brought up' the sun—a massive golden ball rising out of the Sinai Desert, still dark, tawny and fathomless. There was nothing, nothing at all between myself and India. At seven in the morning the earth is a beautiful sight from the air. As I looked down on the delta from 3,000 feet the irrigation canals were like pieces of silver wire. Faint wisps of smoke rose idly from the collections of wretched mud hovels scattered haphazardly among the lush green vegetation; and I thought of the fellaheen as they stirred reluctantly to face yet another day of misery and unrewarding toil. As I crossed the two arms of the Nile, the white sails of the feluccas, gliding imperceptibly beneath me, were now just catching the morning sun.

It was fun to be young and alive and a flyer. Now, with 20 minutes to go, I began to think about breakfast.

Wally, our AEO, was a romping, rumbustious fellow who kept the whole station on its toes. He had a more-than-faint desire to learn to fly; what better way to spend Sunday afternoons? Some few miles south of Dekheila, not far from the big Army transit camp at Amiriyah which thousands of soldiers of the 8th Army will remember with mixed feelings (those memories, I am sure, will consist of sand, sand and yet more sand), was a small disused airfield. Wally and I used to take one of our Tiger Moths down there and spend some happy times doing circuits and bumps until we eventually tired of the monotony. After that, it was 15 minutes' flying time back to the station for tea.

There was one afternoon when we essayed some practice in a fairly stiff northerly wind, an unusual phenomenon hardly to the taste of Wally's limited experience. We did a few touch-downs and decided to

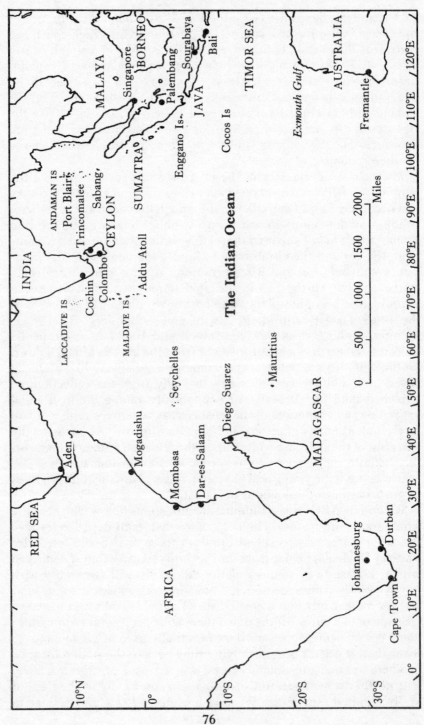

go home. No need for a compass course. The road below us led without complications to the western end of our airfield and Wally set course for the teapot. I told him to fly fairly low in an endeavour to escape the main force of the strong wind. Tiger Moths could never be described as fast aircraft, but even I was surprised when an Army staff car, heading for the coast as we were, passed us with ease and rubbed salt into the wound when its rear-seat occupants indicated by their gestures that we were welcome to a lift from them. Wally, who had been a racing driver of some repute in pre-war years, uttered comments down the voice-pipe which were certainly not meant for human ears. Needless to say, he wandered about 30 degrees off course while he was expressing his feelings.

The flying business—that is, military flying—abounds in paradoxes. Half of one's time is spent in learning how to avoid death and most of the other half in doing damn silly things, many of which would appear to be calculated expressly to attain death in one of its nastier and more messy forms. For those of us who lived, these remarkable evolutions resulted in little more than a giggle.

One of our intrepid aviators to whom I shall refer as George Smith, for obvious reasons, was a leading contributor to such merriment. Sent one fine day to Port Said in a Gladiator, one of the most beautiful flying machines ever created, there to take part in an exercise over the Fleet on its return from Malta, he entered his name on the 'Record of Bloody Silly Things To Do' with the utmost panache and verve.

He took off from Gamil airfield in that heavenly little biplane fighter, to rise out across the sand-dunes and out to sea. It is only fair to say that George, like many of us, was a flashy pilot with a thick streak of exhibitionism in his make-up. He held down the Glad's nose to build up speed and at the last moment whipped back the stick to do an awesome take-off.

It so happened that on the northern extremity of the airfield stood a wooden, single-seater, all enclosed workmen's lavatory cabin. Whether or not this was concealed from George by the Glad's engine or wing-struts I don't know. The fact remains that at the moment of pulling back the stick, he collected this object—fortunately with the indicator showing 'Vacant' at the time—with his lower starboard mainplane and took it up in one piece to 200 feet. Either the lavatory or the Gladiator took umbrage at that altitude and decided enough was enough. Still clinging intimately together, this incongruous pair (George was merely a spectator) descended abruptly and none too gracefully into the sand-dunes. Both were write-offs.

George was lucky; he got away with a scar which starts in his hair-parting and runs in a gentle, undulating line down the side of his cheerful face to just below his chin. It is the only thing that mars an otherwise handsome countenance; and should serve as a stern warning to all attendants of remotely sited public conveniences.

How cruel can one's fellows be! George was henceforth known as—and you will pardon the expression—'Shithouse Smith', which I am sure he heartily detested. But the Air Arm felt that an unkind and vulgar nickname was infinitely preferable to an epitaph on a tombstone.

Much, much later in the war he walked into *Illustrious'* wardroom; to my great surprise, for I didn't know we were even in the same hemisphere. He was with his CO and a bunch of young fighter-boys. I instinctively called out:

'Well! If it isn't old "Shithouse"!'

George's face was a picture of complicated emotions. He strode over to me with great speed and purpose.

'Shut up, you stupid bastard! This lot think the Germans did it!'

I rocked with laughter and reluctantly he joined in. After that we shook hands, put our arms round one another's shoulders and embarked on the timeless dialogue: 'Whatever happened to old . . .?'

I wish I could provide something equally scintillating from my own flying log-book. All I can find of interest is the entry: 'March 30 1943: Tiger Moth N9121. Pilot—self. Passenger—Surgeon-Lieutenant Sheehan, RN. Local flying. Duration of flight—Nil. Ran off runway on take-off and shattered lower starboard mainplane; other damage.' (I like the 'other damage'!) How laconic! What a masterpiece of understatement! The reality was a little more exciting.

Doc and I were having Sunday lunch together. I was eulogising on the raptures of flying with one's head sticking out in the fresh air when he admitted to my great surprise that he had never flown.

'*Never*, Doc? Good God! What an admission to make on a Naval air station!'

'I've often thought about it, but never got around to it. Why don't you take me up sometime?'

'Sure. What's wrong with this afternoon?'

'*Now*?'

'Why not?' I walked over to Jimmy Waddell who seemed to be skipping lunch in favour of a wee dram or two. He willingly lent me a Tiger Moth for the afternoon.

Now I must confess that up to this time I had never flown a Tiger. To be honest, if it were the last flying machine left on the planet, I would rather take a bicycle. Even after I had recovered from the shame of the prang and the torment from my chums and had mastered the little beast, I could never bring myself to admit the creature to what I regarded as the family of aircraft. It was and must forever be to me nothing more than an airborne brown paper bag. How Amy Johnson stood it all the way to Australia defeats me.

There was a fair old breeze whipping across the field as we taxied out. A rating shouted to me 'I'll come out to the duty runway with you!' and took hold of the starboard wingtip. Now the Tiger has no tail-wheel, let alone a steerable one. It has a small metal skid. Worse, it has no brakes. Without these two civilised aids I now found it extremely difficult in a strong breeze to taxi across wind without a man on the wingtip. Immediately he removed his hand, the Tiger obstinately, but quite naturally, 'weathercocked' into wind.

I reached a runway, probably some 40 degrees out of the wind, a disability that neither a Fulmar nor a Glad would have deigned to notice. I felt that the rating had walked far enough for a Sunday afternoon. I waved him away, the Tiger turned herself smartly on to the runway with no help from me and we were away.

As long as the wheels remained on the ground, progress seemed reasonably normal. As soon as they lifted, the wind from the port side drifted me off to starboard at a rate of knots. In a reasonably heavy aircraft, all one has to do to counteract this is to apply rudder and drop the port wing slightly. I might as well have sucked my thumb. Still, provided nothing got in the way, I would clear everything and climb away. Hard luck, Hanson! Pride was coming before a fall—and bloody quickly at that.

In the centre of the airfield stood a German 88 mm gun, the mainstay of our AA armament. Surrounded by a solid eight-foot wall of sandbags, it thrust its menacing barrel and flash eliminator defiantly to the sky, looking very tough and very German. I now found myself flying (for want of a better word) sideways towards this obstruction at a surprising speed. The sandbags were topped by five faces, crowned with sailors' caps, white, drawn, incredulous and frightened out of their wits. As one man they ducked out of sight like elusive targets at a fairground shooting gallery. I couldn't blame them. They were doing exactly the right thing, for with a crash—much quieter than I had expected—I careered across the top of the emplacement, shedding the complete undercarriage and half of the propeller; and shattering the struts of the lower starboard mainplane. Such bits of the aircraft as were left—including Doc and I still strapped in our seats—came to rest on the Tiger's belly, remarkably gently, facing into wind on the duty runway where I should have been all the time.

Silence after a prang is always beautiful, provided you are in a fit condition to notice. One hears things—the rustle of the wind in the grass, the song of birds, the drone of a far-away aircraft, the screech of the ambulance and the snort of the fire tender. I stepped out of the debris and glanced at Doc. He was in one piece and seemed surprisingly cool. There was scarcely a look of enquiry in his eyes.

'Come on, Doc. The party's over.' I undid his harness.

'Something wrong, Norman? Aren't we going?'

I couldn't believe it. He had noticed nothing at all! And I had damn nearly killed him. I made a vow that afternoon never again to be such a bloody fool as to endanger the life of a passenger—especially if that person happened to be a friend!

I went back to the mess. 'Wings' Waddell was still there, sitting at the bar.

'I'm sorry, sir. I've had a prang.'

'Good God, Norman! Are you all right, laddie?'

'Look, sir, you don't understand. It's a real prang and I've written the thing off, good and proper, and I'm very, very sorry. It was all my own fault.'

'Oh! The hell with that load of junk! Are you sure you're all right? Have you seen the Doc?'

Had I seen the Doc? Now that *was* funny!

The remains of the Moth were piled untidily in the corner of a hangar. So far as I know they're still there.

There were times when, either for a change of duties or because of a temporary shortage of pilots, we would do a job for the Fleet Requirements Unit. One fine day the C-in-C's office called for an exercise on cruisers and destroyers returning from their 'milk run' to Malta. What they wanted was a simulated mass torpedo attack to exercise their gunnery branches. The attack had to be done in Luftwaffe style—boring in at nought feet from miles away.

We mustered every pilot and aircraft we could lay our hands upon—Swordfish, Albacores, Fulmars, even Gladiators. Naturally, the fighter pilots amongst us hadn't the faintest idea how a torpedo should be dropped to enable it to conduct itself in an orderly manner. However, on this occasion torpedoes were out. Instead, our instructions were to fly at a ship until it looked like the Albert Hall, fire off a Very cartridge (simulating the moment of dropping the weapon) and then to get the hell out of it before we dented the hull. From the position of the aircraft and the distance and time at which the Very cartridges were fired, the gunnery officers of the Fleet could calculate how many—if any—of the torpedoes would have struck.

Today I was lucky enough to grab a Gladiator, an aircraft I dearly loved to fly. Our strange armada batted out at nought feet, at varying speeds, until we saw the Fleet in all its grandeur, pressing on for Alex. I picked out a cruiser, opened my hood and checked my Very pistol, suspended round my neck on a bit of string. At the last moment, when my lovely *Orion* seemed to me to be as long as Euston Station and as high as Nelson's Column, I raised my right hand and fired off the cartridge. I then shot at a rate of knots over 'B' turret, giving her captain and myself a full house of peptic ulcers.

One of our chaps, Gore-Langton, had a much more interesting time as navigator of a Swordfish. G-L approached all aspects of life in a highly nonchalant manner. When his pilot yelled 'Now!' for his observer to shoot off the Very light, G-L coolly lowered the pistol over the side of the cockpit and fired. To his surprise—but to nobody else's—the Very light passed through the lower starboard wing of the aircraft, setting on fire the doped fabric—highly inflammable stuff. His pilot now found himself in a somewhat embarrassing situation, flying (if you can call the contortions of a 'Stringbag' flying) over the rear or blunt end of a cruiser, yelling blue murder and fanning at the fire, figuratively speaking, with his hat. Faireys, however, knew what they were building when they produced that old warhorse; and G-L and his pilot returned safely to Dekheila with only a couple of square feet of the wing fabric remaining.

Whilst the enemy caused us little or no trouble in the delta area, the same could hardly be said of our own side. Our mess at Dekheila was Liberty Hall, with 'welcome' written all over it. Thanks to its situation on the coast, our airfield remained open when most other fields were closed down by sandstorms and forlorn souls in their scores dropped in for the odd night. They were genuinely made welcome, wined, dined and bedded down—and I doubt if any of them ever saw a mess bill.

By awful comparison, it befell a number of us to have to stay overnight at RAF Heliopolis on rare occasions. The difference was unbelievable. In my own experience, not one person ever uttered a word to me. No one offered a drink. When one approached the bar as a non-resident, drinks had to be paid for there and then. To eat in the mess, one first had to pay for a chit without which entry into the dining-mess was impossible. I used to wonder whose side I was on. I could only draw the conclusion that they must have had a fair number of welshers through their hands.

Even favours, granted by the Dekheila boys as a matter of common courtesy, were rarely accepted with grace. I flew early one morning to Fayid, a large airfield on the shore of the Great Bitter Lake ruled by a consortium of RAF, RN and USAAF, to drop a passenger. As I prepared to taxi away from the control tower, I received a steady 'Red' on the Aldis lamp. An RAF rating ran down the steps of the tower and climbed on to the wing of my Fulmar.

'Going back to Dekheila, sir?'

I nodded.

'There's an Army Captain here, sir. Wants a lift to Alex. Can you take him?'

I nodded again, switched off and descended to the tarmac. The Captain walked across, very much the desert warrior, bush jacket, knotted silk scarf and suede half-boots. He was carrying a small grip.

'How far is your base from Alex?'

'Fifteen miles, sir. I can organise a lift into town for you.'

'Right. Let's be off.'

I climbed on the wing again, opened the hood of the rear cockpit and brought out a harness for an observer type parachute. I held it open for him to insert his arms.

'What the hell's this?'

'Parachute harness, sir. The chute's inside the cockpit. I'll show you how to clip it on in case the worst should happen.'

'Don't be so bloody stupid! What the hell's going on in the Navy? Never heard anything so ridiculous in my life! I've flown thousands of bloody miles with the RAF and never once have I had to wear one of these bloody things!'

'This isn't the RAF, sir. Our rules are: no parachute, no ride. Sorry if I appear awkward, but those are my orders.' I stood fat, dumb and happy, waiting for him to accept the inevitable. Anyway, what the hell was all the fuss about? I wore one all the time and *I* wasn't crying!

With remarkably ill grace he allowed me to harness him up. He got into the cockpit, I showed him the parachute and gave him a helmet and mouthpiece, connected to me by one of the old Pensacola-type 'Gosport' tubes. No fancy electronic nonsense about the old Fulmar!

I climbed to around 3,000 feet and headed out across the desert towards the delta. There were heavy rain-clouds ahead, black and menacing. You could practically hear the thump as I went into them. I climbed a few thousand feet more but there was no end to the overcast, so I came down while I still had the chance. This time I went into the rain belt at about 1,000 feet. Visibility deteriorated rapidly and soon I was scudding along at 500 feet.

The beauty of flying in lower Egypt is that there is nothing to fly into, apart from electricity pylons. The lines are carried across the two arms of the Nile on immensely high pylons whose whereabouts you have to know precisely in weather like this. Fortunately they were well to the north of my course and I had no worries. I pressed on.

We had suffered five minutes of this blinding rain when my passenger spoke up. He thought the weather was too bad. We should return to Fayid before it became worse. I told him we were all right. I was on course for Dekheila and there was nothing in the way. And I needed my breakfast.

In order to keep in visual contact with the ground (for, radar or no, we had no radio anyway) I was soon down to 300 feet—and that looks mighty low to a passenger unaccustomed to flying. The captain was soon back on the intercom. Now he was more forceful. I tried to allay his fears by assuring him that I had no intention of turning my wife into a sorrowing widow. I couldn't soothe him, though. He became a bit rough and finally ordered me, as a junior officer, to obey his instructions to turn round. I pointed out to him that we were well past halfway and might just as well force on. At this he accused me of rank insubordination, to be dealt with in due course. Whatever else he said was spoken strictly to the bottom of the cockpit, for I had now pulled out the plug.

We landed in a blinding rainstorm and a wind not far short of gale force, for I succeeded in putting her down only on my second pass; and then only by lifting the flaps as I flared out for touchdown. At the air watch office I dismounted to help him out of the rear cockpit. He was furious, white-faced and frightened.

'I see you're a Sub-Lieutenant. What is your name and the number of your squadron?'

I told him.

'And where is the office of the Captain of the station?'

I just had to stop him.

'Now look here, sir. You're doing the wrong thing if you go to see Captain Howe. *You* asked for the lift. You're here, all in one piece. We have sent for a car to take you into Alex. What more can you ask for?'

His only reply was a brief, pungent lecture, Army style, on insubordination and the dire penalties a perpetrator stood to bring down upon his head. He stalked off in the direction of the admin block.

I didn't run into the Captain until lunchtime. He told me then that my passenger had complained most forcibly about my conduct.

'Did you tell him about the facts of life, Hanson?'

'No sir. I thought it would be better coming from you.'

'All I did was to tell him that the Army should take steps to learn the rules about flying. I pointed out that if a Leading Seaman had been piloting the plane, he would still be the boss, Army Captain or no. I also assured him that, when *I* flew with you, I wouldn't have the temerity to say half the things *he* had said.' He grinned.

Flying our Captain on his regular tours of inspection was one of the rare treats that fell to the lot of Communications Flight in amongst the run-of-the-mill duties. Apart from his command of our station, he was also in charge of all the other FAA establishments in the Near East. Flying to Beirut with him was a graphic lesson in history apart from the pleasure of his company. Like so many other RN officers, his knowledge of the Bible was boundless and, to please us both, we invariably transformed the return flight into a conducted tour.

We climbed out of Beirut, heading south. To our port side, towards Damascus, stood massive Mount Hermon, over 9,000 feet high, wearing its winter snow-cap. Soon we were passing over Sidon at 2,000 feet. Then—very quickly—Tyre stretched out from the land

into the Mediterranean, still connected to the mainland by the causeway Alexander's men built when he besieged and reduced the city in
332 BC. So far, I knew what it was all about, but from now onwards my
passenger took over.

'Go inland now, Hanson,' spoke the intercom. 'Keep going east
until we hit the river.'

In a matter of moments we came up to the Jordan and I now turned
to starboard to follow its course south. Very quickly we reached the
Sea of Galilee—probably better known now as Lake Tiberias. I circled
over the lake while the Captain kept up his absorbing commentary—Capernaum, down the screes of which had tumbled the
Gadarene swine. A slight detour to the west brought us to Nazareth,
its white adobe and tawny, sandy habitations strewn over a great
hillside.

Then we were back to the Jordan which, down to Allenby Bridge,
was now transformed into a madly rushing torrent, diving through dark
narrow gorges. Over on the east bank stretched the scrub desert of
Jordan and the mountains of Amman—nothing, nothing to see.

I was told to circle. We were over the ruins of Jericho and I
could hear the shrill blast of the trumpets as Joshua's men summoned
the city to surrender. No doubt when the mighty walls tumbled
down before him he was as surprised as the next man. What a
fanfare!

Then we climbed the hill to Jerusalem, sitting astride the backbone
of the mountains that reach north and south. More commentaries,
more photographs: the Temple, the old city, the Mount of Olives, the
Garden of Gethsemane. Down the road now, along the ridge to
Bethlehem, where it broods from its rocky eminence over the Dead
Sea to the east, that great, mysterious, placid lake, 1,300 feet below
the level of the Mediterranean.

From this point we could make our way home by two routes:
straight out to the west, to the land of the Philistines at Gaza, thence
'round the corner' to El Arish and Port Said. The second, further
south over the undulating scrub and sandy 'moors' to Hebron and
Beersheba, those legendary Old Testament names; and from there out
west to El Arish. The Sinai Peninsula, to our left, always seemed to
be a forbidding waste. It was rumoured that the nomads who
roamed over the area, forever striking or pitching their long,
low, black tents in their search for grazing for their goats and
sheep, were a particularly nasty crowd who disliked all strangers and
white men in particular. Certainly we were always armed when we
flew over it, in case of a forced landing; and we were adjured to keep
the last .38 shell for ourselves.

But the crisp crackle of the Merlin's exhausts never faltered, thank

God, and the Fulmar winged its way serenely to Dekheila; to a drink, a meal and a session on the pianos.

Late one afternoon, homeward bound and approaching Port Said, I looked at my petrol gauge. It was dodgy. With my Captain aboard, I plumped for safety first and landed at Gamil to fill up. After arranging with the Duty Officer for a supply of 100 octane and for my oil to be topped up, the Captain and I went for a stroll in the sand-dunes.

Some time later we returned to the aircraft. The petrol bowser had already returned to its parking place and an RAF rating was about to wheel away the small oil bowser. Some premonition prompted me to ask him if the petrol cap had been replaced safely. He gave me the look which all RAF ratings seemed to reserve exclusively for anyone in Naval uniform. When asked a second time, he deigned to climb up on the wing again and unclipped the fairing covering the petrol filler cap. The cap was there all right—but it was sitting on the tank, leaving the filler tube uncovered. He screwed on the cap, clipped down the fairing and descended to the sand without a word.

Well, now.

'And what about the oil cap? Has *that* been put back?' The Captain watched in silence.

The fairing for the oil cap was on the port wing. This he unclipped, sucking his teeth. No cap. He searched the sand below the wing—no cap. He whistled through his teeth and looked bewildered.

'What about your pockets?'

There it was, in the patch pocket on the thigh of his battledress.

I marched him across to the Duty Officer and put him in the rattle. He had certainly done enough damage for one day. God knows, the petrol was bad enough. Thirty-odd gallons of ice-cold petrol had poured over me in a Fulmar from St Merryn because of similar negligence and scared the hell out of me. But the oil was even more serious. Ten minutes out of Port Said, the oil would have boiled over from the tank, the engine would have seized solid and the Captain and I would have dug a deep hole in the delta. Sure, an Accident Investigation Department team would have discovered the reason for the crash but we would have been in no position to take any interest. I shudder to think how many crashes resulted from such lack of interest—let's not beat about the bush; criminal negligence.

There was no doubt, though, that we were learning a lot about flying. We had no maps, for flying over the Western Desert was like flying over the sea. No oxygen. No radio. But at least we had good if obsolescent aircraft. We learned to live by experience and practice, flying over the great wastes of the desert by rule of thumb, round the corner to Palestine and Syria, using such unlikely landmarks as a pranged Wellington bomber, a shattered German tank, a disused airstrip bounded by oil drums—all precisely in the middle of nowhere. When we were luckier, we used as signposts the temple of Baalbek, the Sea of Galilee, the battered nose of the Sphinx or the balloon barrage over El Adem. When we found ourselves well and truly lost, we got ourselves out of a mess without help—or never came back. The experience was invaluable and saved our lives over and over again in the years to come.

We were also learning to be Naval officers. Throughout our training we had been birds of passage; we had been scholars attending a school, with no responsibilities where the running of the air stations was concerned. For most of us, Dekheila was the first station to which we really 'belonged'. For the first time, the ratings of our squadron were lads to get to know, people who mattered to us, young men with whom we had to try to co-operate. The aircraft were *our* aircraft, not something akin to a hired car. The Commander looked upon us as *his* officers rather than a collection of odd bods who were cluttering up his station for a few weeks, learning to fly and keeping the padre and the gravediggers on their toes.

For the first time, we were officers.

Within two weeks of my arrival I made my debut as Officer of the Day. I took over at 0800 and had a wonderfully easy ride; no mutinies, no fires, no mayhem and all the boys on their best behaviour. I superintended the issue of rum at 1150 and tried to look RN, knowledgeable and interested as I strode through the dining hall calling for 'any complaints'.

In the late afternoon I inspected libertymen and sent them off to Alex for their fun and frolics. At 2100 I accompanied the Commander on 'rounds'. All that now remained was to attend Colours at 0800 on the following morning. Nothing to it! Well . . .

I was shaving at 0715 when there was a knock at the door.

'Master-at-Arms' compliments, sir, and will you please see him at the guardroom right away.'

I hurriedly finished dressing, leapt astride my trusty BMW motorbike (a present from the recently departed Wehrmacht) and romped off to the guardroom. There was all hell on. Two Marines were grappling with a large red-bearded young man—a stoker—who was apparently recovering from an all-night drinking session and wasn't enjoying the process. He was in a nasty, thoroughly homicidal temper and the appearance of a Sub-Lieutenant RNVR (he was a regular) did nothing to improve his humour. The Marines were at full stretch to prevent him from eating me.

The Master-at-Arms looked at me rather sadly. I could almost hear him. 'Christ! Another bloody rookie!' But he was a man of steel. He didn't say that at all.

'Morning, sir! Stoker Doughty, sir. Did return on board drunk and disorderly, sir.' He then closed two smart paces to the right until he was breathing down my left ear, assuming the role of a sinister prompter. In a whispered aside which Rommel might have heard, he said:

('Put him in cells, sir.')

I stared at the stoker rather like a rabbit facing a particularly hungry python.

'In your own interests, Doughty, I shall have you put into cells.'

There was a deep, seismic rumbling.

'I'm not goin' in no bloody cells!'

('Tell 'im he bloody well is, sir!')

'Doughty, you bloody well *are*.'

'I want to see a doctor.'

('He can't see a doctor, sir.')

'You can't see a doctor.'

What on earth was going on? Hadn't all this happened before, somewhere? Was it the Marx Brothers? Or Flanagan and Allan? It was pure burlesque!

'I know my fuckin' rights.'

(' 'E ain't *got* no fuckin' rights, sir.')

'You ain't got no fucking rights.'

This was becoming ridiculous! I was almost hysterical! I was in the middle—and very much a part—of a cross-talk act and could see no way out of the *impasse*. Fortunately the Master-at-Arms was a man of resource. He had met plenty of my kind in his time. He was a dapper little man, expert in his trade, smart as a row of new pins. His face, irrigated by a mass of purple veins and his tight-lipped mouth, precisely machined to accommodate the neck of a beer-bottle, bespoke his hobby. He knew all about drunks. He made an agitated sign to me.

'Christ, sir! There's the Commander's car! For Chrissake stop 'im, just 'til we sort out this little lot!'

I rushed out of the door. As I closed it behind me, I heard a quiet thud. There was no car, no Commander.

When I re-entered, the Marines had disappeared and the Master-at-Arms was bending over his desk, sorting out the morning's charge-sheets.

'It's all right, sir. He went quiet enough to cells once you went out. If you don't mind me saying so, sir, I think it was your stripes that sort o' put 'im off a bit. Made 'im restless-like, if you know what I mean. He'll be all right now, sir.'

I was learning. I was growing up. There were some things that an officer should not see. It was only by a pure fluke that I had even heard it!

One of our messmates was Reggie Brooks, truly an ace among pianists. He was a lad with a dark complexion and jet-black hair, a lean young man in his early twenties. He was a professional, and music of every type flowed from his long, lean fingers in a profusion that baffled description. He had an angel's touch and his readiness to sit down and to play whatever anyone called for made him one of the most popular fellows in the mess. (He was also a capable pilot!)

One evening after dinner, shortly after my arrival at Dekheila, I pulled over a chair, sat down at the bass end of the piano and joined in with him. We quickly found that we thought on precisely similar lines where harmony was concerned (a million-to-one shot). In a remarkably short time we were swopping and changing ends, having a lot of fun. Our tastes varied from 'pop' tunes of the times through ballads, piano transcriptions to Brahms' Waltzes and Dvorak's Slavonic Dances. Both of us had good memories and the total absence of music didn't appear to worry us. Where the bright lights and allures of Alexandria had called us most nights of the week, they now lost their attraction. So much so that, after a few weeks, a once-weekly jaunt for a change of food or to see a new film was the only thing that interrupted the regular after-dinner jollies on the piano with Reg.

Brooks, let it be said, had a weakness for Old Mother Alcohol, which he enjoyed but couldn't hold. Being inclined to over-indulge at times, he was apt to commit some act of childish exuberance when in his cups and thereby incur the wrath of our Commander, 'Jumbo' Jackson. 'Jumbo' was a genial soul and it had to be something pretty bloody stupid to make him take notice. The result was that Brooks was regularly off the team, at which times he would cunningly do a vanishing act whenever Jackson appeared.

During one of these spells, he approached me one day in a state of high excitement. Scrounging a drink in the Chiefs' and PO's mess one evening, away from 'Jumbo's' eagle eye, he had questioned one of his hosts about an upright piano standing in the corner. On finding (as he suspected) that the residents could find better things to do than play a fornicating piano, he had immediately struck up a provisional deal for its transfer. Now he was asking me to pursue it.

'You're in Jacko's good books at present. See what he says. The PO's mess will part with it for a couple of cases of Scotch.' Scotch whisky at duty-free prices was a bargain in anybody's currency. I said I would do what I could.

The Commander didn't bat an eyelid.

'Organise it, Hanson. Arrange for a removal party and I'll see to the whisky side of it. Get on with it.'

That very day we had our second piano in the mess and Brooks was on the next bus into Alexandria to lay on a piano tuner to come out to pitch the two together.

Now we were as happy as two pigs in a farmyard full of manure, if I may tidy up a famous New Zealanders' expression. With a good piano each we had infinitely more scope for our duets and our hobby now became a nightly affair. Within a short time we were amazed to find that the habits of our messmates were altering. To our surprise, they took to staying aboard instead of trailing off to Alex. The bar profits soared to unheard-of levels and to dispose of them became a real headache to our mess treasurer. Only by dint of throwing regular cocktail parties did we manage to dissipate them.

By some means or other, Brooks later made contact with the Fleet Club in Alexandria, where concerts were regularly organised for Service personnel. He quickly blackmailed the people in charge into staging a show by 'Brooks and Hanson'; and the programme included in this book is the only record I now possess of the fun we had together in those happy days.

I took the air mail to Port Said on October 23 1942 and returned as usual next morning. Most of the chaps had left the mess when I arrived for breakfast but one of the laggards said to me:

'Just come in from Port Said?'

I nodded.

'Have you heard what's going on? No? Well, all I can tell you is that there must be all hell breaking loose up the desert. At about half-past ten last night the whole place shook and every bloody door in the mess blew open. Somebody said it was an artillery barrage, but I told him to get stuffed.' He was wrong. At about ten o'clock the previous night there broke over the Alamein positions the greatest artillery barrage in history—something that would have astounded even Napoleon, the greatest master of artillery of all time. The battle was on. The concussion or shock wave, with not a blade of grass to stop it, had come 35 miles down the desert to us. Things were never quite the same again.

For a month or two we had noticed plenty of Army movement up the road that ran westwards at the back of the airfield. The attack when it came, therefore, was probably no great surprise to us. Once the balloon had ascended, there was an enormous build-up and the road was cluttered, night and day, with convoy after convoy. It wasn't long before hordes of prisoners could be seen, wearily filing down from the operational area. A sizeable camp for Italian POWs had long been established just over the fence from our field. 'For you the war is over' rapidly became a stock phrase.

There was now no shortage of jobs for Communications Flight. As the 8th Army pushed the Italians and the Afrika Korps relentlessly

Sub-Lieutenant (A) R. Brooks, RNVR, 'Taffy' Thomas (Air Fitter, 775 Squadron) and the author involved in the entertainment business in 1943!

westwards, so we followed and found ourselves taking squadron observers to Benghazi or Derna; bringing sick types back to Alexandria from Tobruk; taking operations officers up the blue to supervise flying operations between Benghazi and Malta. Flying in and out of Benghazi was pretty hazardous until such time as the RAF caught up with the Army and established themselves in that famous corner. The Luftwaffe maintained patrols over the area, fortunately at a great height and, in no position to defend ourselves (for our Fulmars had been disarmed), we had perforce to sneak in and out at ground level in the hope that we wouldn't be seen.

One of the duties of our flight entailed having aircraft at standby to take up the desert Naval Commanders who had long been appointed to take charge of harbours as and when they fell to the 8th Army. They were sorely needed, for one road and one railway line alone could not cope with the ever-increasing traffic. Supplementation by sea transport was urgently required. Now we hunted all over 'the blue' for somewhere to deposit our Commanders. We lobbed down in some strange places indeed: ex-Luftwaffe fighter strips, straight stretches of road, hard patches of sand in the middle of nowhere. We were warned off some desert strips by the Army because of mines. We landed at others, disconcerted to see a vehicle 30 yards away go up in a puff of smoke. When we reached Benghazi we found the town deserted, booby-trapped to glory and with all the water supply most thoroughly and efficiently poisoned.

Benghazi was an odd city at this juncture of the war. To a man, the Italian population had migrated to the west, leaving behind them a deserted, eerily empty town. It had been an attractive place, too; situated on a well-watered coastal strip, well cultivated with parks and gardens and with some most impressive villas, it had obviously been a good place to live. The Army had of course made a bit of a shambles of the town whilst busily 'liberating' it; but one could still get a very good impression of what it had been.

There was a fair amount of looting being done by the forces, despite the proliferation of ingeniously set booby traps, which proved to be some deterrent. We ourselves purloined three lavatory seats in an effort to raise the standard of civilisation at our outpost. We were bombed quite heartily by Ju 88s most mornings at dawn, but we were safely abed in a deep Italian airfield store with feet of concrete above us. Their greatest—and, to us, most tragic—achievement was to knock out a newly arrived merchantman, part of whose cargo, as yet unloaded, consisted of NAAFI supplies. The beer was a sad miss. We had to keep plugging away at the vino—mainly Chianti—which we discovered in a store when our local expert—Barnes, of 825 Squadron—had safely removed the wired grenades.

I had gone to Benghazi taking as a passenger a Commander (Operations) for our two Albacore squadrons which were now required in Malta. On arrival there, my Fulmar had become unserviceable and a few days elapsed before spares could be flown up from Alex. I lived with the Albacore boys and thoroughly enjoyed myself. The food was a bit limited. Every meal was the same—ship's biscuits, Australian tinned bacon and Chianti—but at least there were no unpleasant surprises. The water, pumped from local oases some miles away by Army engineers, certainly tasted as though the Army *had* had something to do with it, but the vino helped! The Luftwaffe persevered with their morning 'hate' but none of us was killed.

Young Barnes, mentioned briefly above, flaunted his mastery over the wiles of the Axis troops—and scared the hell out of us in so doing—by circumventing many of the booby traps to provide us with our few luxuries. He was a macabre soul, much engrossed in things that went off with a bang and was usually encumbered with pockets bulging with 'red jobs'—small Italian anti-personnel grenades with the nasty bits encased in bright red tin containers. He had a disconcerting habit of throwing these around the place whenever the mood came upon him and seemed to derive great pleasure from the high-speed sprints with which the rest of us covered the sand.

One of the lavatories for which the seats had been removed from various desirable residences in the town suburbs was a wooden job which stood, starkly alone, in the former Regia Aeronautica compound we had taken over. It was, for Barney, conveniently near the explosives dump from which he obtained his supply of red jobs. Coming from this dump early one morning, with pockets laden with the confounded things, he idly threw one which exploded with a rare detonation at the back of this wooden convenience. He was remarkably unrepentant when the door flew open, as if under the impact of an internal explosion, to allow his CO, Lieutenant Fairfax, RN, to emerge at full speed and to make exceedingly good time for the underground hangar in which we lived and slept. As Barney-inspired runs went it was nowhere near the world-beating class; but one can hardly expect a man fettered by trousers round his ankles to establish new records.

Our mess back at Dekheila was a great deal quieter once the Albacore squadrons had left us. They had done a good job during the months preceding the Alamein battle. It had been their hazardous duty to fly nightly over the German positions to drop flares, whilst RAF Wellingtons, flying considerably higher, bombed the enemy lines through them. A most uncomfortable role! Luckily all their bombs fell on or somewhere near the Axis troops. Certainly none hit the Albacores.

Life for the next three months continued in the usual pattern—flying the air mail run, with occasional special trips in the Near East and the odd exercise for the Fleet. Our station obtained our radio sets—such as we had—from the RAF maintenance unit near Jaffa, up in Palestine; and it was always a pleasant change to have a run up there to collect these.

One day I took Lieutenant Thorneycroft, one of our AEOs. 'Thorney' was a devil for low flying and was never happier than when the aircraft was batting across the delta at nought feet. When we had left Port Said on our return journey, he asked me to do just that. We were approaching a village, not too far from Alex, which was much the same as any other delta settlement: a collection of hovels with one significant two-storey structure which was always the headman's house. Near this were two trees, between which Thorney suggested I might just squeeze a Fulmar. I thought he was probably right—and he almost was. All I did was to clip one branch with my port wing, which transported Thorney into his seventh heaven of delight. When we reached Dekheila, we found about 80 feet of wire draped from the pitot head tube and were at a loss as to where it had come from until we found an insulator at the other end. We had, it seemed, collected the wireless aerial suspended between the trees! However, things that go wrong are made to be put right; and the following day two of our mechanics ran out to the village and replaced it, with apologies, to everybody's entire satisfaction!

And then the Lease-Lend Agreement blossomed fully and we were recalled. From the four corners of the earth, we stooge pilots were brought back to the UK, Their Lordships having raised a finger and beckoned us. In no time at all I was climbing into a BOAC aircraft—a Liberator bomber, converted into an airliner with about 16 seats—within sight of the Pyramids, and we were off.

The Captain was named Veasey and a fine chap he was, too. He was one of the old Imperial Airways' 'million-milers'. One of the passengers was Lieutenant Commander Dunsterville who, with Admiral Mountbatten, had survived the destruction of the destroyer *Kelly* in the famous withdrawal from Crete in 1941. Another passenger was an RAAF pilot called Jack Daimond and, since he and I were the lowest forms of animal life aboard, we quickly formed a friendship.

We dropped into El Adem for fuel and, after passing round the south of the Mareth Line, landed again at Algiers, where we took the opportunity to change into civvies, for Lisbon in neutral Portugal was to be our next port of call.

It was late afternoon when we landed at Lisbon; and we circled for a few minutes to allow a Ju 52 to land before us. When we eventually reached the customs shed, the occupants of the Junkers were lined up on the other side of the barrier. They were bronzed, healthy-looking chaps; and well they might be, for they were Afrika Korps men on their way to Germany for leave. In their unaccustomed civvies they looked every bit as incongruous as we, in strange, ill-fitting flannels and sports jackets, must have seemed to them. For a moment we stood, embarrassed and with averted eyes. They someone chuckled—and in a second the whole room was roaring with laughter. Here we were, the two parties of us, sworn and deadly enemies in the midst of a world war—and all we could do was to giggle!

Their Lordships might have beckoned us. The trouble was that those who had beckoned hadn't told the other types what the beckoning was for. I arrived at the office of the Naval Assistant to the Second Sea Lord, who administers all things concerning Air Arm personnel. I rushed in, breathless and all agog, the sand of the desert still gritty in my socks and shoes, and burst forth to an aristocratic young Lieutenant that I had just arrived from Egypt and what was there for me to do? I awaited his reply with bated breath. He surveyed the nails of his left hand, covered a yawn delicately with his right, and sent me on indefinite leave.

I had just settled down in Carlisle for a spell, revelling in Kathleen's company and in the heavenly cooking of my mother-in-law, when a telegram arrived urging me to report to St Merryn with all despatch. This, you will recall, was the fighter training station where I had served for a short time on my return from America. It was good to renew acquaintance with old friends and we were soon busily engaged on a fighter refresher course—this time on Hurricanes, a new type to me. In no time at all we transferred our activities to Spitfire VBs—another new type—and naturally the buzz went round that we were destined for a Seafire squadron. The buzz hadn't gone full circle before we were sent on leave yet again. Apparently our aircraft were required for another squadron with more priority than ourselves. (I wonder if they ever received them?)

So it was back to Carlisle, to my wife and our families, 18 hours in a train. They were faintly surprised to see me again so soon.

A week later I was on a train heading back to St Merryn; Carlisle to London, change for Cornwall. A Lieutenant joined my compartment at Exeter. I recognised him as an instructor from St Merryn, and after a while he laid aside his evening paper.

'Hanson, isn't it?' I said it was.

'Thought you were on your way to the States?'

'Really? It's the first *I've* heard of it.'

'That's funny. I could have sworn I saw your name as having been posted there.'

We lapsed into silence.

Later in the evening, as I left the dining-mess to get a coffee in the wardroom, Captain's Secretary came over to me.

'Is it Hanson? Yes? Can you pop in to see me about nine in the morning, old boy? Shan't keep you long.'

0900 next morning saw me in his office. He entered two minutes later.

'Ah! Hanson! Yes. You're going to the States, old boy. Got a posting for you as Senior Pilot of 1833 Squadron—new American aircraft. You have to report to Donibristle for passage. Here are your orders.'

What a bloody outfit to be with, I thought. They *really* don't know their arse from their elbow.

'And when do I go?'

'Right now, old boy. In fact—quick as you can. There's a rail warrant with your papers. Crack on! Good luck!'

Eighteen hours back to Carlisle. It's just a bit bloody thick, I grumbled to myself. I grumbled even more bloody-mindedly after standing seven hours in a train corridor from Euston to Carlisle.

I stayed overnight with Kathleen. She now wondered—as so many millions have done in their time—if the Government really knew what it was doing. There was no call for wonderment—the simple answer was that they didn't! Thanks be to God, the Third Reich managed to create the most diabolical shambles equally as skilfully as the British Empire upon which the sun never set. Otherwise I hate to think what might have happened to all of us!

6

'The bent-wing bastard from Connecticut'

We sailed from Liverpool's Prince's landing stage in RMS *Empress of Scotland,* which was conveying 1,300 Afrika Korps prisoners to the United States. They were quartered in the after part of that great ship and were allowed to emerge for several hours a day for fresh air and exercise on the after upper deck. Here they were securely caged in by wire netting and barbed wire, overlooked by Army Bren-gunners perched on the surrounding deck-houses. We weren't overdoing the precautions, for these were hard boys, bronzed and fit after their service in North Africa. One of our duties as passenger officers was to stand watches on the after bridge, keeping an eye on the Germans.

Our other major 'cargo' comprised several hundred Naval ratings going out to man landing craft and assault boats which were building in American yards ready for D-Day in a year's time. They were young, green and vulnerable and the Germans weren't slow to cotton on. They soon got around to begging cigarettes and chocolate from sailors passing their cages. Having made their acquaintance, they proceeded to frighten the living daylights out of them by confiding that they hadn't a hope in hell of ever reaching America. U-boats had been organised to intercept the ship in mid-ocean. The Africa Korps would take over the ship and any friends the Germans had made among the British would be well looked after. The impact of this war of nerves upon the young sailors—most of whom were still boys—was such that the Executive Commander was eventually obliged to make a public announcement to the effect that, in the unlikely event of U-boat intervention, the Germans would certainly *not* take over the ship. Indeed, with equal certainty, they would be the last—and he repeated the last—to leave the sinking ship. That finished it.

We eventually sailed into Newport News, Virginia, where the American army had set up a typically efficient organisation for POW reception. The tide was high and the gangway steep; and the Germans, who were disembarked first, found it difficult to keep their feet as they descended to the concrete quay, holding the gangway rail with one hand and clutching all their worldly possessions with the other. As the leading man set foot upon the soil of America and raised his eyes for the first time, he found himself confronted by an enormous 'snowball'—a large, young American negro MP, wearing a white helmet and grasping a sub-machine gun with no lack of determination. To a member of the master race this was an insult that could not be borne. He promptly sat down on the concrete, bringing the descending queue behind him to a standstill.

This was something the young American hadn't bargained for. He stood, perplexed. He had heard of Germans but had never seen one; and this chap's behaviour was beyond him. He walked slowly across to the reception huts to seek guidance from an Army Lieutenant standing by the open door. We, leaning over the ship's rails watching the fun, saw the Lieutenant gesticulating violently. The MP came back at the double. His large boot sank into the backside of the offending German.

'Come on, Joe! Let's go, eh?' he shouted, rounding off with a hefty prod of the machine-gun on the same backside.

The German uttered a sigh and slowly rose to his feet; looked round, then grudgingly walked to the huts. What on earth would the Führer have to say about this?

An hour later the nucleus of 1833 Squadron—our CO, H. A. (Eric) Monk; two other reasonably experienced pilots, Steve Starkey and 'Bod' Boddington; the Senior Pilot and 150 ratings—descended the same gangway. With us was a similar nucleus of 1834 Squadron. In the States we would join 1830 and 1831 Squadrons who had sailed a month or two earlier. Together, we would be the first four squadrons to operate the new Chance Vought Corsair in the Royal Navy.

We were destined for a US Naval Air Station at Quonset Point, Rhode Island, but apparently some hold-up in the matter of accommodation, either for us or for our aircraft, caused us to idle away a fortnight in New York.

Men vary as to their willingness or otherwise to kick their heels. But it's no joke to lounge around in the sweltering heat and humidity of high summer in New York. Fortunately I had struck up an acquaintance with Johnny Bird, a pilot in 1834 Squadron, whose father was Commander Bird, the big chief at Supermarine. Johnny came across to the States armed with a portfolio of letters of introduction to Who's Who in American aviation and invited me to string along. This made life very interesting indeed. We were given a full day at the Grumman factory on Long Island, shown Hellcats in all stages of production and entertained to lunch by Leroy Grumman himself. His chief test pilot threw a Hellcat around for our special benefit. We met the secretary of the Aviation Institute and through his influence visited several meteorological and aeronautical institutes. We were also invited to a world *première* at the Waldorf Astoria.

Up to this time, American military aviation was still sharply divided between the Naval Air Corps and the Army Air Corps; and great was the gulf between them. Seversky, the great airman and eminent authority on aeronautics, of Russian origin, had recently published his book *Victory Through Air Power;* and Walt Disney had been sufficiently impressed by it to make a movie in support. Briefly the argument was that, whilst their two air forces undoubtedly gave the necessary support to their respective arms of the fighting services, the war—and the war in the Pacific in particular—would not be won until America developed an independent striking air force. Seversky didn't actually say so in as many words but what he obviously had in mind was the Royal Air Force's Bomber Command. It was to the world *première* of this film that we were invited.

It was an evening for young men to remember. We were introduced as though we were Admirals of the Fleet. We were seated at the high table. We were plied with the Waldorf's best food and wine. We were consulted on matters relating to naval aviation as though we were an airborne Delphic oracle. I like to think that we remembered how green we were, that we didn't allow the liquor to run away with our tongues and that we didn't say anything too damn silly. But it was all fun.

Among the many notabilities we met was Mrs Mitchell, widow of General Billy Mitchell, who had shattered the entire American fighting service some years earlier by announcing that a battleship could be sunk by bombs dropped by an aircraft. He made himself damned unpopular with the Navy by saying so. So they gave him a battleship which he promptly sank, thereby making himself more unpopular still. Long after he was dead they forgave him, which wasn't a lot of use to General Billy Mitchell. Anyway, they were jolly nice to his widow, which I suppose was better than nothing.

Altogether it was quite an evening. I can recommend the Waldorf Astoria.

Each morning we heard dreadful tidings of pilots being killed in Corsairs. Then suddenly, when I felt there couldn't be any Corsairs left for us to fly, we found ourselves at Quonset Point. After supper on the first evening , the CO came across to me.

'Feel like a stroll, Hans?'

We walked up to the hangar that had been allocated to us. There was an armed sentry on guard, but Eric told him to open up and turn on the lights. For some reason or other we headed up a flight of stairs leading on to a balcony running the length of the hangar. Just then the lights came on—and there they were. Corsairs filled the hangar floor and I must say that, of all the aircraft I had seen, these were the most wicked-looking bastards. They looked truly vicious and it took little imagination to realise why so many American boys had found it difficult, if not well-nigh impossible, to master them, especially in deck-landing. We stared at them and hadn't a word to say.

'Let's look round the rest of the set-up.'

We allocated offices. We checked store-rooms, crewrooms, repair shops. Everything was in order. There were new typewriters, desks, filing cabinets—everything that we could wish for. The Americans don't mess about—they do the job properly. I tried one of the typewriters, a beautiful machine. I found a sheet of quarto and typed; and what I typed was my last will and testament. I saw no reason why a Corsair shouldn't kill me when it could obviously kill so many other lads without any trouble. It certainly wasn't going to catch me un-awares. It can't have been such a damn fool thing to do for Eric didn't laugh when I told him. He was a bit pensive himself and I think he reckoned I was employing myself much more usefully than I would have been in practising 'The quick brown fox jumps right over the lazy dog'.

The next day we collected the rest of our pilots, straight from USN flying schools: W. K. ('Bash') Munnock, Peter Builder, Reggie Shaw—all from England; Gordon Aitken from Ceylon; Johnny Baker from Toronto; and our only New Zealander, Neil Brynildsen. Now we were ten, our full complement.

K. L. ('Bod') Boddington was the first of our truly professional womanisers. As the commission wore on, we were to find we had amateurs both charming and skilful, learners and graduates; but Bod was a master and, for a young man, breathtakingly experienced. He was well-built, inclined to chubbiness, everlasting cheerful and highly competent in laying on charm to any required thickness. He first demonstrated his paces to us in New York.

One evening, suffering from a fiendish headache, he descended to the drug-store on the groundfloor of the Barbizon Plaza Hotel (two floors of this skyscraper were the compulsory home of every RN officer required to be in the city of New York) to buy some aspirin or some such before setting out on his evening's fun and games. Whilst awaiting service, he started to chat up the nearest female—a compulsive practice where he was concerned. She was, he said, about 30; and he gathered that she had a problem with her nerves for which she was now seeking something in the way of a tranquilliser. Bod 'tut-tutted' and 'dear-deared' and, as he hoped, was duly invited to her room to discuss the problem.

It seems that some ten years earlier, whilst sunning herself in Florida, she had fallen in with a Texan gentleman who had taken quite a fancy to her. They had corresponded and exchanged snapshots at long range ever since. Over the years things had progressed to the stage where matrimony had not been discussed but had

99

eventually reached probability. Finally a wedding had been arranged and she was now *en route* from her home in Vermont to Dallas, Texas, where the nuptials would be celebrated in four days' time.

Now after ten years she wondered if this Texan was in fact the man of her dreams; hence the worry. (A doubtful story.) Furthermore, her virginal state (even more doubtful) was outraged at the very idea of consummation. What did Mr Boddington think?

Mr Boddington thought hard, then decided he might think more clearly if he removed his trousers. Having done so, he gave the lady certain advice from the depths of his experience which prompted her, too, to undress.

Bod said later that the removal of her extensive and highly complicated harness was something at which his mind boggled, particularly—as he put it—when the removal of her bra, followed by two substantial thuds on the carpet, produced from his lips an involuntary 'Jesus Christ!' However, as an Old Whitgiftian he knew where his duty lay. She was apparently most grateful for his advice and especially for the dummy run. They had a few noggins together as part of the recuperative process.

Next morning even he was somewhat disinclined to believe her fanciful yarn. He was also doubtful about her age—'she could have been 40; maybe 50'—but, as he said, 'What the hell?' After that he rambled on in a vague kind of way; something about the aesthetic value of a performance of the Elgar concerto played on an extremely old Amati violin.

As far as I was concerned we had been allocated a fine bunch of lads. All of them were young, in their early twenties. One or two of them were fairly serious, introspective chaps—Steve Starkey, Reggie Shaw and Gordon Aitken. Keith Munnoch had come from the Royal Marines; somewhat sombre but with flashes of real fun. Johnny Baker, the Canadian, was old for his years but with the fresh, uninhibited outlook of a boy from the Dominions, while Brynildsen was a quiet, enigmatic New Zealander and Peter Builder, an English boy, was engagingly round the bend.

Brynildsen was a slightly built bird-like young man, quaint and with the driest of wits. There were times when he drank considerably more than was good for him and, in his cups, he was capable of doing remarkable things. It was said by his chums that on an overnight journey from Detroit to Miami, a change of trains at Jacksonville had been necessary in the early hours of the morning. When the troops were rounded up to embark for Miami, Neil could not be found. Eventually the panic stage was reached, with every man available milling around like ants searching the very large station for the absentee. With only minutes to go, one of the lads was surprised to see a

Royal Naval officer's cap badge moving up and down within a telephone kiosk, rather like a Punch and Judy show. Closer investigation
revealed Brynildsen, very much the worse for wear, leisurely and
uncertainly struggling into pyjamas. He had looked at his watch and
decided it was bedtime. They got him aboard the train in the nick of
time, smartly clad in his cap, reefer jacket, pyjama trousers and with
his shoes in his hand, whilst his chum toted the rest of his gear.

We couldn't have wished for greater variety.

All of them—with the exception of Starkey, Boddington and the
CO—had been trained with the US Navy and were therefore well
versed in American aircraft terminology and instrumentation. This
naturally helped them to find their way around the massive cockpit of
their new fighter. It contained more than enough to keep them busy
for a long time to come.

For some months, Corsairs were decidedly tricky aircraft to handle.
For one thing, they were damnably big fighters for their day. They
had a vast length of fuselage between the cockpit and the propeller
which, together with a rather low sitting position and a not-too-clever
hood (both of which were modified and greatly improved in the Mark
II version), made for very poor visibility when taxiing and landing. It
was pretty long-legged in the undercarriage department in order to
give clearance to the great propeller, said to be the biggest ever fitted
to a single-engined fighter. To increase the clearance, which undercarriage alone could never have achieved, the wings were of
'inverted-gull' format, dipping downwards for about four feet from
the wingroot at the fuselage, then rising sharply to the wingtip. Not
for nothing was it called the 'bent-wing bastard from Connecticut'.

Its armament consisted of six .5-inch Browning machine-guns,
hydraulically charged and electrically fired. The radial engine was a
Pratt and Whitney R2800, developing 2,000 hp from 18 cylinders
arranged in two banks of nine. Fuel was supplied to the engine
through a Stromberg injection carburettor, which precluded 'cutting-
out' on the top of a loop—a disconcerting feature to which aircraft
fitted with the normal carburettor were prone. A two-stage supercharger was fitted. The first stage was engaged at 10,000 feet and the
second at 19,000 feet. The aircraft was capable of producing a genuine
speed of over 400 mph at its rated altitude of around 22,000
feet.

The Corsair was a rugged machine which could take any amount of
punishment on the flight-deck and appeared to make light of it.
Everything about it was high-class and great attention to detail pro-
claimed itself wherever one looked. The cockpit was meticulously
arranged with all dials readily visible and every lever and switch
comfortably and conveniently to hand, without any need to search or

grope. (Infinitely superior, I may say, to the cockpits of British aircraft of that time which suggested, by comparison, that they had been designed by the administrative office charwoman.)

The aircraft had two built-in safety devices which were worth their weight in gold if hydraulic trouble arose. Both undercarriage and arrestor hook were hydraulically actuated. Should hydraulic pressure be lost, the hook fell automatically, ready for a deck landing. The use of the undercarriage, too, was protected. One simply had to select 'down' on the undercarriage lever and then open a CO_2 bottle which effectively 'blew down' the wheels into the 'landing-locked' position.

Rumour had it that the prototypes had been equipped with 'spin chutes' in their tails, to effect recovery from that deadly enemy the spin. Whether it was true or not, the Pilots' Handling Notes were emphatic on the point that spins should not be deliberately undertaken, for recovery was dubious if not downright impossible. (It might be mentioned that the Notes referred to were a highly important and integral part of becoming a fit and proper pilot for a single-seat aircraft in those days. They had to be studied carefully, first on the ground for two or three days and then sitting in the aircraft on the ground, learning the position of all the 'bits and pieces' in the cockpit. Nowadays manufacturers build two-seater versions of most aircraft, so that dual instruction can be given before a pilot is allowed to fly the aircraft solo.)

The fighter had originally been ordered by the US Navy for carrier use to replace the Grumman F4F, the Wildcat (Martlet to the Royal Navy); but it had proved to be such a handful in Fleet trials—particularly in deck-landing—that the new Grumman F6F—the Hellcat—had been adopted instead. The F4U—the Corsair—could now go to the shore-based squadrons of the US Marine Air Corps; and to the Royal Navy, if they wanted it. The Royal Navy accepted it willingly. The only alternatives in sight were the Seafire and Sea Hurricane—RAF production models fitted with arrestor hooks—and these just weren't carrier material. Their range were pathetically limited, even with drop tanks; and worse still, their structure, whilst perfectly adequate for airfield flying, was not up to the rough-and-tumble life of carrier decks. In both cases a heavy landing, caused either by the vessel's pitch or by the pilot's hamfistedness, often brought the undercarriage through the wings. Somehow or other the Royal Navy would see to it that the Corsair *could* be deck-landed.

Our familiarisation flights produced one or two prangs. Brynildsen put his job on to its nose on the third day and Starkey turned his aircraft on to its back when braking too enthusiastically. But the third was deadly. Just over a week after we started flying, Boddington was coming in for a landing over the James River when he inadvertently put himself into the slipstream of a Grumman Avenger landing in front of him. He was practically down to stalling speed and had neither time nor air space to recover from the incipient spin which befell him. In the early hours of the morning US Navy divers brought him up, still strapped in his Corsair, with a wound on the side of his head. Had he been killed outright, or had he drowned whilst unconscious? Whatever the reason, we had lost dear old Bod.

We were out one evening, drinking at a pub between Quonset Point and Providence when we ran into some US Army pilots, working up squadrons of Republic Thunderbolts, the Army's latest interceptors. Inevitably there ensued great argument on the relative merits of 'ours' and 'theirs'. There was extensive waving of hands all over the bar. There were loud shouts of 'Balls!' and 'Nuts!' and 'For Chrissake stop talking cock!' and similarly endearing remarks which invariably punctuate flying talk. A Lieutenant finally suggested to me that all this was getting us nowhere. Why didn't we pitch a mock battle, with gun cameras, to prove which was the better aircraft?

What a great idea! In the absence of our CO, who wasn't much of a drinking man, I committed us to a battle, six a side, for the following afternoon at 1600, at 10,000 feet over the James River Bridge. Done. Handshakes all round.

'The boss' absolutely jumped at it. His eyes sparkled and he just couldn't wait. He grinned even more as he said:

'You said 1600, Hans?'

'Yes, sir. At 10,000 feet.'

'Great! We'll show 'em!'

And we *did* show them. For Charlie Orange (CO) was an old hand and you had to be up very bright and early to put one over him. At 1545 the next day we were sitting up-sun over the bridge—not at 10,000 but at 16,000 feet. When the American boys arrived five minutes early in very tiddly formation, we fell upon them from a great height, as the Assyrians, like a wolf on the fold. In two minutes it was all over. I had learnt another lesson: war doesn't 'begin at midnight'; it starts at 2355 and gives you the drop on the sucker.

To replace Boddington, we were fortunate enough to be given Eric Rogers, a tall slim lad of 23 who hailed from Birmingham. He was to become one of the squadron's happiest assets for he was fun unlimited, with a face full of grins and a laugh that would have started a Corsair. His first remark to me about a Corsair's cockpit—'It's all tits and clocks, isn't it?'—endeared him to me. The fact that he was a competent bridge-player certainly enhanced his standing with the CO, although I doubt whether his endless gaiety and (to me) enchanting attitude of treating life as lightly as possible had the same effect! He had trained with Reggie Shaw and they quickly became firm friends.

After a few weeks we moved up to another station at Brunswick, Maine, not many miles from the coast. The whole of New England is lovely country and we had found Rhode Island to be a beautiful state. Maine, in our opinion, was even better. The coastline was sheer magic, indented with Norwegian-like fjords and thickly forested with trees now, in the autumn, turning to pastel shades of pale to rich gold and salmon-pink. Off shore there was a necklace of small islands which provide summer homes and hotels for the hot, dusty, tired—and rich—New Yorkers.

We worked like blazes at Brunswick in an attempt to attain a reasonable standard of efficiency before we returned to the UK. I started none too well! Sent by the CO on the first morning to do a 'recce' to learn the lie of the land, I set off up the coast for 20 to 30 minutes; then turned around and headed south-westwards. So engrossed was I with the beauty of the scenery that I stupidly dropped my map into the bottom of the cockpit—there was no deck as in a Fulmar—where it would remain, out of reach, until I landed.

Sure enough, I became well and truly lost. I wasn't worried. I was off the north-eastern coast of the US. If my full tank of petrol lasted the course, I would surely recognise New York in the fullness of time! Not to worry!

Suddenly, out of the heat haze below me, I found myself approaching a large city with extensive docks and no end of shipping. I was trying to picture the map when I saw an airliner—a Dakota—heading towards the coast, just lowering its undercarriage. *He* would know where he was! I followed him in; not too closely, for the airliner boys were a bit sensitive if military aircraft became too friendly. With 50 or so paying passengers aboard they were in no position to take violent evasive action. I let him land and clear the runway, then followed him in. At the end of the runway I was directed to the northern end of the field and fetched up outside a hangar bearing the words—CIVIL AIR GUARD. I switched off and jumped down.

'Sorry to drop in on you uninvited. I lost my way half an hour ago and am hopelessly lost.' At least I was honest!

'Lootenant, sir!' A hearty handshake and a very large smile. 'It's a very real pleasure and a great privilege to welcome the Royal Navy!' (My Corsair bore the magic words on the fuselage.) 'You're at Portland, Maine, sir, and we'd be glad if you would come in and accept our hospitality.'

So off we went to the operations room. I was duly introduced to everybody in sight, an opened bottle of Coke was pressed into one hand, a cigarette into the other and a lighter flashed into life before my face. You couldn't meet nicer guys.

Did I come from London? What was the bombing like? Was I

married? Aw, gee! Did my poor wife live in a shelter? How soon would it be before we gave those Kraut bastards what was coming to them?

The war in Europe satisfactorily disposed of, we got down to domestic detail. Where was I based? Were the Brunswick people nice to us? Were they finding us plenty of girls? (This is a national concern with Americans. No matter what else, visitors must never want for an adequate supply of feminine company.) What the hell was that damn big fighter standing, so to speak, at the door? Looked a bastard to fly. They sure hadn't had one of them in Portland before.

When I had signed the visitors' book (with home address CARLISLE and ROYAL NAVY, in large letters and carefully underlined, duly appended) I was allowed to leave, complete with brand-new map and gushing promises of real hospitality and plenty of girls on my next visit. They are the friendliest and kindest people in the world.

Monk flew our pants off, practising formation flying in both close and open 'patrol' formation. We did map-reading exercises over the quiet highlands towards the Canadian border. We practised low-flying well out to sea and managed, with a modicum of skill and the hell of a lot of luck, to avoid embarrassing collisions with coastal freighters, lightships and pleasure cruisers. We did thousands of circuits of the little airfield at Rockland—a delightful spot further up the coast, in one of the finest parts of New England—practising dummy deck landings. We blazed away thousands of rounds of ammunition at towed targets, taking it in turn to tow the drogue and hoping that the boys would remember that we were pulling, not pushing, the confounded thing. Early one morning young Monteith, of 1831 Squadron, pressed his trigger to produce the Shot of the Year. He was doing a high-side run on the drogue—diving on it from one side, from a height advantage of 500 or 600 feet—and failed to notice that far, far below him was one of the pretty little islands that adorn the coast of Maine, tastefully inhabited. Two of his .5-inch bullets, fair-sized chunks of armour-piercing steel, travelling at the speed of sound, tore through the outer wall of a hotel into a bathroom where a retired Colonel was leisurely bathing his middle-aged frame. Having noisily effected their entrance, the bullets then proceeded to hammer their way through the side of his bath at a downward angle of some 60 degrees, zipped across his thighs into the water and perforated the bath on the other side, thereby making completely unnecessary the removal of the plug for emptying purposes. Needless to say, such marksmanship didn't go down well.

The weeks passed and we were progressing. Our ratings were getting to know us—and one another. The pilots were gingerly experimenting with their Corsairs. And all of us were trying to understand what our new Commanding Officer expected of us. My own opinion was that he expected far too much from the boys in too short a time. Their flying experience was brief; and even briefer was their experience with the Corsair, which was proving to be a handful for even the most competent naval aviators of two nations. Apart from learning to handle their aircraft, they were still learning to be officers. Occasionally, when a suitable moment presented itself, I would remind him that they were still a long, long way from being hot-shot fighter pilots. To the young men—for I was, by years, older than the oldest of them—I tried to explain that the flurries of temper and full-strength nautical language to which they were regularly subjected were all part of the game of being a CO and that their skins would quickly become adjusted to the required thickness.

For, let's face it, Eric Monk took quite a time to adjust himself to being the boss of a squadron of RNVR pilots. He himself was RN and had served in the Royal Navy from the age of 14 until now, at his present age of 25 or 26, he had attained the rank of Lieutenant-Commander. He had enjoyed a brilliant career. From the deck of *Ark Royal* he had fought over Norway and had been awarded two DSMs within a matter of days. He had been at war on the first day—September 3 1939—when the rest of us were civilians; when some of us, in fact, had been schoolboys. Accustomed as he had been all his life to RN discipline, it was readily understandable to me that it should take him some time to assess what our sort of discipline was worth, for in its informality and 'fifth form' flavour it certainly didn't match up to his ideas.

The youngsters needed all the courage they could muster, though, for the Corsair continued to exact its toll. It was certainly no aircraft for a sprog pilot. It made no concessions to inexperience or nervousness and reacted viciously to the slightest hamfistedness on the controls. Its very size was enough to daunt the bravest and its engine power was staggering in comparison with those machines which even our experienced pilots had coped with so far in their careers. It carried a lot of 'gubbins' which were all new to us—a cockpit full of switches, levers, dials and gadgets which demanded one's undivided attention. When that attention lapsed or wandered, things happened—and happened very quickly.

A youngster called Harris from 1830 Squadron was flying high —about 23,000 feet—over Brunswick town at noon. He was tearing along at high speed with full supercharger going. (This was a small turbine of bewilderingly high revolutions positioned at the rear of the power unit, which at high altitude forced the petrol/air mixture into the engine under very high pressure.)

Quite suddenly the engine packed in through failure of the ignition system. (Both magnetos were pressurised for high-altitude flying, but

106

at this stage the pressurisation system wasn't yet perfected.) Harris glided down to around 16,000 feet, a height at which the magnetos decided to recommence operating and the engine cut in again.

The boy had already committed himself to a searing and explosive death. At this moment he had split seconds to live. When the engine cut out, he had obviously forgotten to withdraw the supercharger. Now, as the engine, from inertia, burst into life again at a high throttle setting, the thrust exerted on the bearings of the supercharger was too much. The rear of the power unit completely destroyed itself, with hardened steel tearing through fuselage, cockpit, wings—and Harris.

Down in Brunswick it was lunchtime and the main street was as busy as a bee. In the centre of the roadway stood a policeman controlling a school crossing. He looked upwards, perplexed by a strange whining. With commendable alacrity he leapt back a couple of paces as a Pratt and Whitney engine, weighing around two tons, hurtled down from a bright blue sky to bury itself in the tarmac in front of him. Nobody was hurt, but the Corsair was scattered far and wide and the young pilot had virtually disappeared.

Another dreadful accident occurred whilst we were at Brunswick. A new squadron, 1836, was practising, flying in two columns in line astern, the columns being led by the CO and the Senior Pilot. The CO decided to do a turn—in which direction we shall never know. Some faulty communication between the two of them occurred, with the result that he and his Senior Pilot turned into one another; and both were killed. It was fortunate that the rest of the pilots, inexperienced in this manoeuvre, were not flying as close to their leaders as they would have been in the months to come and had time and space to avoid doing the same thing to themselves. It was a shocking waste of good, experienced pilots that they should lose their lives in a blinding flash of carelessness or stupidity.

Being young, we weathered these hard knocks. Youth and flying survive on the easy assumption that 'it can happen to the other fellow but it will never happen to me'. Without that, most of us would never have survived the war!

At the end of September 1943 we were posted home to the UK. We were to fly to Norfolk, Virginia, for passage in *Trumpeter,* a newly-commissioned escort carrier. Despite the thousands of ADDLs that we had done, there was to be no time for initial deck-landings. We would undergo those at home.

The intention was to do the flight non-stop. However, as we flew wondrously down the length of the great man-made cliffs of Manhattan, an R/T call was made which made me laugh aloud. Our young men were really growing up!

'Red Three to Charlie Orange. I'm running out of gas. Over.'

We were flying down Fifth Avenue, so to speak, in a beautiful tight formation at the time and this urgent call was something the CO could not afford to ignore, whether or not he believed it. I could hardly see him taking a chance on one of his sprogs trying a rather fancy forced landing outside Tiffany's. The very idea must have appalled him. He called up US Naval Air Station at Floyd Bennett Field on Long Island and in two minutes we were landing. Obviously it was now too late in the day to refuel, eat and continue the flight to Virginia. When we were cordially invited to stay for the night, we snatched the offer with both hands.

Next morning it was raining cats and dogs. For two happy days and nights we trudged the streets of li'l old New York, awash with rain. Then the front cleared and off we went again.

That day produced an occasion which none of us had so far experienced and would never experience again. We landed on the Navy airfield and our Corsairs were to be hoisted by crane aboard the ship as deck cargo. To reach the docks, we had to taxi our planes through the outskirts of the town, with our wings folded, causing quite a furore amongst the street traffic! It was something our training had never envisaged when we held out our right hand to signify we intended to make a right turn, to be answered by the traffic cop with the customary wave of his hands and a big grin on his face!

Our voyage in *Trumpeter* was notable. The ship was part of the escort to an enormous convoy taking GIs to Northern Ireland, the first part of the build-up for the coming of D-Day in eight months' time. We picked up the liners transporting the personnel in New York and continued up to Halifax, Nova Scotia, to collect the merchantmen conveying their weapons and vehicles. The German High Command knew all about that convoy. Their U-boats were busy even as we ploughed northwards up the coast of New England and the packs were summoned as we set out across the wide Atlantic at 14 knots.

Off Newfoundland we ran into the dreaded fog which brought visibility down to a matter of yards. All passenger officers were put on a duty rota to stand watches on all sides of the ship to keep station on the fog buoys which all the ships in company were streaming. We carried a few Swordfish for A/S patrols and it broke our hearts when two of these, at the end of a long patrol, could not be directed through the diabolical fog to be landed aboard. Inevitably they ran out of petrol and had to ditch. Despite magnificent efforts made by Canadian aircraft operating from Newfoundland, they were never seen again. Apart from our ship, the remainder of the escort was completely American. Their destroyers, no doubt revelling in the novelty of convoying something really worth while, had the time of their lives, dashing around with the utmost gusto to throw out at regular intervals millions of dollars of taxpayers' money in the form of showers of depth charges. They were good. It speaks volumes for them that of all the U-boats which were known to be trailing us—or, rather, vectoring on us; for at our speed they couldn't possibly have kept up with us—not one was allowed to put herself into a position from which to mount a serious attack.

I was sharing a cabin, well below the waterline, with the captain's secretary. Our bunks, the upper one occupied by him, with myself in the lower, were fixed to the ship's side which, since the hull was that of a merchantman, was little more than thickish tinplate. About midnight some keen destroyer type let go a pattern of depth-charges too close to our starboard side for comfort. The underwater hull of our ship whipped under the concussion and ejected me neatly to the strip of carpet on the deck. 'Sec', for some reason or other, managed to stay firmly in his bunk!

We came into Belfast Lough on a miserable October day, groping our way through driving rain to a quayside at Sydenham airfield. It continued to rain for three days. We were billeted in a church hall, and slept on scruffy straw palliasses. We ate indifferent food; and we walked the streets of Belfast until such time as the cinemas—or the pubs—opened. The streets were full of GIs wandering around in the rain looking for something to do—strangers in a strange land. No less than three groups of them stopped us to ask if we had been part of the escort bringing them across. We said we had been—a white lie, for we had been passengers no less than they. They embarrassed us considerably by insisting on shaking our hands to thank us for a safe arrival. One young boy confided to me that the Atlantic Ocean was 'one hell of a lot of water'. He came from Missouri and had never seen the sea in his life until he sailed out of the Hudson River. I'm not surprised he was astonished!

The CO was beside himself with impatience but even he could do nothing about the weather. Then one morning he burst into the office.

'Get 'em lined up, Hans! We're going!'

I looked outside and saw, through the rain, a thin streak of light on the eastern horizon. Farewell to Belfast.

We flew across the Irish Sea in a horizontal corridor of fair weather, sandwiched between thick 'fog-cloud' beneath us and heavy nimbus above. As we entered Liverpool Bay it cleared altogether for a few miles, but things ahead looked grim. However, we would cope with that when we reached it. At that moment Eric Rogers, down on my starboard side, started yelping about his engine. I looked down at him and saw great gouts of black smoke belching from his exhaust manifold.

'Stay with him and look after him, Hans,' the CO said. I dropped down to Rog. After a minute or two:

'There's a lovely fat merchantman right below you, Eric. Ditch beside him, give him a nice kiss and he might even pick you up!'

For once, Rogers was in no mood for wisecracking. 'Sod that for a lark! I've got a load of loot in this thing and I mean to get it to Birmingham!'

The Wirral peninsula was coming up now.

'Do it your own way. Take the merchantman or, if you can hang on for a minute or two, there's a lovely beach coming up. Keep cool and you'll make it easily from this height.'

He was losing very little in the way of speed or altitude and I was now sure that he would make Cheshire safely. I left him to it and batted after the squadron who were fast disappearing. I caught up with them as they crossed the Bar Light. As we came up the Mersey, with the famous Liver birds just visible through the murk, we hit the rain-clouds which looked solid from ground level to about 30,000 feet. I could practically hear the smack as we hit them. One second we were a neat, tidy formation. The next, we were all to hell, milling around in the murk, stragglers fading out of sight. It was a dangerous moment and nasty collisions could have occurred. The CO yelled and we turned 180 degrees. Nine of us had entered the cloud. When we emerged again into comparative clear, we were only seven.

The CO now put us into line astern, dropping to 2,000 feet; and back we went into the soup. (Just then, he told me later, he lost his map, temporarily irretrievably, into the bottom of the cockpit. Quite a habit with us!) Suddenly we broke out into some sort of sketchy visibility and below us—too darned close for comfort—was a transporter bridge.

'Hans! You're a north-country man! Where the hell is that bridge? Quick!'

I remembered that there were only two such bridges in the Kingdom—and the other was at Middlesbrough. We couldn't be there!

'That's Runcorn, sir. We're all right. Just follow the river and we'll come to Warrington.'

'Where the hell is Runcorn?'

'Next door to Warrington. Press on!'

It was still raining when we landed at Stretton. Johnny Baker parked beside me and stood up in his cockpit, looking down at the rating who was bending down to put chocks under his wheels. He described, as only a Canadian can swear when he really means business, how he saw the recent performance and the CO didn't emerge too well from the monologue. When the rating stood up and showed herself to be a highly decorative girl in bell bottoms, Johnny was appalled and stumbled through some attempt at an apology. He had just met his first Wren.

Eric Rogers made it safely to a forced landing on the beach outside the Royal Liverpool Golf Course at Hoylake. Steve Starkey, dislodged from the formation somewhere over Lime Street Station, was an Ellesmere Port boy and had no trouble whatsoever in making his own way through the country lanes, as it were, to Stretton. Reggie Shaw never did remember where he had lost us or where he had been since the parting of the ways. At long last he saw an airfield and promptly landed. He taxied over to the tower where a young RAF rating ran down the outside stairs to greet him.

'Where am I?' Shaw from the cockpit.

'Weer are yer?' said the boy, fairly open-mouthed. He came from Manchester and had never heard of anyone being lost within ten miles of that northern metropolis. 'Yer at Ringway, of course!'

Reg was a South London boy and Ringway (now Manchester Airport) might just as well have been in enemy territory.

'Where's Ringway?' he retorted, rather testily.

'Weer's *Ringway*?' What on earth was going on? 'It's Manchester, of course, that's weer!'

'Then where's Stretton?'

'Weer's Stretton? Stretton's ower theer!' said the lad, holding out his arm at full stretch and pointing.

'Good lad,' said Reg. 'Now, get off the wing, keep pointing towards Stretton and don't move until I fly over you!'

So Shaw brought his Corsair to Stretton.

7

The leave-taking

In the first week of December 1943 we paraded at Stretton's village church to see Keith Munnoch take the vows of holy matrimony. Myra, a pretty lass from Hawick in the Scottish borders, was taking no chances of losing her fiancé to some girl of another colour, faith or nationality, for on that day only God knew where we would fetch up once we left the UK.

It was a marvellous occasion. Neil Brynildsen was elected to be best man and undertook to ensure that Keith remained 100 per cent sober for his arrival at the altar rail. To his great credit this was achieved (though where the difficulty came in I never really appreciated, for Munnoch was certainly not the type to blot his escutcheon) but only at Brynildsen's own expense. Whether he downed two at a time to compensate for Keith's non-participation, or was bolstering up his own courage to face the coming ordeal of appearing so prominently in the public eye, I shall never know. Whatever the reason, there is no doubt that my No 2 was hardly at his best! Apart from some breath-taking lists to port and starboard he remained fairly vertical during the service and finally made good a rather erratic course to the vestry, there to perjure himself by signing the register to the effect that he had been fully cognisant as to what had been going on. During the reception he delivered quite a homily (in Damon Runyonese) to the vicar, who was faintly surprised to hear himself being addressed every other word as 'Bish'.

A fair number of wives and sweethearts foregathered at the Victoria Hotel, Stockton Heath, there to spend with us such time as remained before the summons came. One or two modifications to the aircraft were carried out. The new VHF radio was fitted. Small scoops appeared on both sides of and below the fuselage, designed to disperse pockets of carbon monoxide which, said the boffins, were inclined to collect in the fuselage. It was thought that, because the exhaust stubs were flush with the engine cowlings, they were not throwing the expelled gases clear of the forward end of the fuselage.

Influenced to a certain degree by stories (which had preceded us across the Atlantic) of death and destruction on carrier decks, *Illustri-*

ous sent down her batsman Johnny Hastings to give us a good workout on the everlasting ADDLs. We did little else during our short stay at Stretton. Johnny was—and still is—good fun and very charming and was soon popular with the pilots. An ex-fighter boy himself, he knew most of the answers and was a man we felt we could trust to do his highly responsible job.

Our new fighter wing leader, Dicky Cork, was also sent down from the Clyde, probably to assess the quality of his two new squadrons, 1830 and 1833.

It had been decided to increase the complement of the squadrons to 14. To achieve this, 1831 was disbanded and we now acquired Monteith, our Shot of the Year friend; Ken Seebeck, a New Zealander; Alan Booth, a Cheshire boy; Alan Vickers from Southport and Stan Buchan who hailed from Dundee. Monteith was responsible for providing the only incident on the airfield. Doing a touch-down for Johnny Hastings one afternoon in a bit of a crosswind, he clipped a wingtip on the concrete runway at the moment of opening up again to do another circuit. His lack of experience—and probably a bit of panic—now proved his undoing. Instead of cutting his throttle and making the best of a bad job, in which event he would have got away with a shaking-up and a new wingtip, he pressed on. The great Corsair, under full throttle, careered across the grass bouncing on the end of the port wing, which took a very poor view of such treatment.

It so happened that the NAAFI van had just rolled up to the squadron with tea and scones. The CO and I were standing at the office window, cups in hand, when we were astonished to see a Corsair fly past—literally!—the window, busily engaged in completing a slow roll. As we looked at one another, unbelieving, there came the most monumental crash from our left. Monty had hit an earth revetment near the office which had canted his aircraft on to one side, breaking off a wing at the root. When we erupted from the office and ran across the field to a sizeable gap in the hedge, we saw the machine reclining on its belly, smoking gently amid the turnips. No wings, no prop, no undercarriage. Monty was clambering out. He looked somewhat vague. The destruction among the turnips was stupendous.

'What happened?' he asked, stumbling away with his parachute waggling behind him like a monstrous bustle. He was still saying it an hour later, sitting in an office chair to which we had led him. He hadn't a scratch. In fact, Johnny Hastings was infinitely more affected. (But then, bless him, Johnny worried about all of us.)

Keith Munnoch could spend only a short time with his bride, for all too soon it was 'good-bye' to the girls. We assured them that something would happen to make it possible to see them before we sailed from the Clyde. I must confess that, for my part, I was relying largely on past experience in arriving at this assumption! So one murky, foggy night with visibility down to ten yards, dimmed headlights, ice on the roads and a totally inadequate supply of filthy language, we ferried our ratings, our aircraft spares, bags and hammocks from the airfield to a train in Warrington Station. What with the weather, the usual last-minute chaos and one thing and another, this operation took us the best part of the night.

The next morning we flew off, in lovely weather, over Blackpool Tower, Morecambe Bay, St Bee's Head—in the distance I saw my honeymoon hotel, the Abbots Court, where the incomparable Harry Brownrigg held sway—to Machrihanish on the Mull of Kintyre.

Machrihanish was known to the Branch under several names, the most respectable of which was 'Nissen City' for obvious reasons. The most common—and only semi-respectable at that—was 'Machrifer-kin'. I should imagine that a posting to this outpost of the Empire in high summer was worth a king's ransom, for the surrounding country is beautiful beyond belief. More than that, to fly on exercises in good weather over the Firth of Clyde, Kilbrennan Sound and the Sound of Jura can have been a privilege granted only to a few.

But in late autumn or winter Machrihanish was a penance bordering upon a sentence. The weather could be and nearly always was foul. Our average evening's entertainment seemed to consist of putting extra lashings on all aircraft exposed to the fury of the gales, while we ourselves were being soaked by driving rain. Campbeltown, six miles away, was a typical small Scottish town, though somewhat dour and lamentably lacking in the amenities which might otherwise have transformed it into the Dodge City of the north.

One of the redeeming features of Machrihanish for me was that its Captain was C. L. Howe, who had been our kindly and tolerant father at Dekheila. He was the same reserved, imperturbable soul and went out of his way to smoothe out any difficulties that arose during our short stay.

Of necessity, Machriferkin became its own Dodge City. The excitement certainly revved up a bit after nightfall. If one could hear above the steady roar of the great west winds, there were sounds of revelry on all sides with many a girlish giggle. It was said—naughty, fickle rumour!—that Wrens posted to the station were hand-picked erotic types whose underwear was exclusively fitted with Robinson's Patent Disengaging Gear. I find it difficult to believe—but you take things as you find them.

I flew for only one day before my night of driving to and from Warrington Station caught up with me. The man with the red stripe said 'Bronchitis'; and within half an hour I was in hospital at South-end, at the very end of the Mull.

After four days there, I recovered from whatever had hit me and returned to the station. Within 15 minutes Dicky Cork had me airborne. For the best part of a fortnight, apart from interruptions caused by December gales, we flew exercises and ADDLs. During this time *Illustrious* was exercising in the Firth for the benefit of the crew at the commencement of a new commission as well as her two Barracuda squadrons, 810 and 847.

One wild, blustery evening the CO burst into the billiards room, accompanied by a trumpeting blast of cold air by courtesy of Greenland, followed by a liberal spattering of sleet as an encore. With a high-pitched yell he froze the shot I was about to make, demanding to know where the bloody hell the duty boy was; and would Hanson get the hell out of it and find him.

I left the 'pot black' to my partner Eric Rogers—who stood little more chance than I of making it—and went in search of Ken, that most damned elusive Pimpernel. After visiting all probable haunts I finally arriving at his cabin, the skylight of which showed it to be in darkness. Still, it was worth a try.

He was in bed. When I turned on the light, he sat up like a startled gazelle, looking most demure in white shirt, stiff collar, black tie and all. I was embarking on my opening remarks when *she* popped up on the far side of the bed—a pretty little thing with wavy blonde hair. Her neat white blouse and black tie were obviously her copulating attire.

I started again. Ken didn't wait for my closing *Nunc Dimittis*. With commendable alacrity he was out from the sheets, donning trousers, shoes, jacket and duffle coat with practised skill.

'What about her? Can you get her back to the Wrennery without getting caught? It's the rattle for the three of us if you don't make it.'

I nodded.

'You wouldn't . . . ? *Promise*, you bastard!'

'I'm a pommy, I know; but not *that* kind of a bastard. Now belt off, for God's sake. Charlie Orange wants your blood.'

I looked at the girl. Eighteen if she was a day.

'Come on, kid. Let's be getting you back.'

She slid smoothly to the modest little runner of carpet at the bedside, naked from the waist downwards—and didn't give a damn. I went to the wardrobe and found Ken's No 1 trousers. With a bit of luck they would fit her reasonably well, for Ken was on the short side. By this time she had put on pants and stockings. I gave her the trousers, dolled her up in Ken's raincoat and spare cap, and we were off.

Fortunately for us, the wind was blowing Force 7 or 8. The few bodies we met were treading warily in almost pitch darkness, bowing to the gale. We reached the Wrennery safely and without detection.

I was the worried one—*she* couldn't have cared less!

We succeeded in completing such flying as we did at Machrihanish without any prangs. I had an emergency landing on the field when, during one of my regular scans of the dials (something each pilot carries out, consciously or unconsciously, every few minutes), I saw the needle of the hydraulic pressure gauge fall hair-raisingly to zero. I headed back to the field, blowing down the undercarriage with CO_2 as I flew my circuit. With such fluid as remained in the system I was able to get about 20 degrees of flap and put her down in a pretty fast landing. When the fitter was repairing the damage, he called me to the hangar to show me the root of the trouble. He held out to me a short, highly polished steel shaft, about three inches long. One end finished in a pinion gear, the other in an uneven fracture.

'That's your trouble, sir. The drive from the power unit to the hydraulic pump. Buggered.'

'Funny that something as solid and straightforward as that should go.'

'It's called metal fatigue, sir. Something about molecules and crystallisation. Read about it somewhere.'

Metal fatigue. A new one to me, yet an expression which in post-war years was to become a household word and bring death and destruction to many a good aircraft.

8

HMS *Illustrious*

We weren't thinking of death and destruction as five or six of us walked across the Machrihanish tarmac to our Corsairs in the bright, thin November sunshine. Terence Shaw, our genial Commander (Operations), intercepted me to ask me to deliver a letter aboard the carrier. His nonchalant assumption that I should arrive in one piece, capable of handing his letter to the Commander, took a little of the wobble out of my knees.

We took off to the west, Dicky immediately going into a wide, left-hand turn to enable us to join up on him. I latched on to his port wing as we swept low over Campbeltown and out over the Firth. After a minute or two, across the fuselage of Cork's aircraft, I saw her; that great, beautiful ship, serene on a silver sea, a faint wisp of smoke above her island and only the suspicion of a feather of wake astern to belie her apparent immobility.

Dicky put us into starboard echelon. I lifted slightly and skidded over him with rudder to fall into position on No 2's starboard wing. After a sweeping turn to port, losing speed and altitude, we flew low up the ship's starboard side. Down undercarriage, down hook. About a mile ahead of the ship, Dicky broke to port, establishing the landing pattern. Seconds later, I followed No 2, carefully taking up an interval on him—a practice which in a few short months would become second nature. Now we were flying downwind, locking safety harness, locking open the hood, increasing pitch, lowering flaps; first to ten degrees, then to 20. Now I was abeam of the stern of the ship. Turn 180 degrees to port; full flaps. Already Johnny was signalling for me—'Roger' as you go. A shade faster—OK. Now come down, down, DOWN, damn you! CUT! I chopped back the throttle, held the stick steady as a rock. Three seconds, then I was on the wire. My body lunged forward against the harness with the deceleration—I was down. A red-capped director of the flight-deck party waved me back with both hands. I released the brakes to allow the wind to blow me back a couple of feet, so that the arrestor wire could be disengaged. Up hook, up flaps and taxi forward over the crash barriers. I jumped to the deck—three and a half inches of armour-plating.

The air was loud with Tannoy noise. Up there on my left, as I walked down the flight-deck, was the great island; and the whole ship, alive with men in a variety of rigs, fairly hummed with activity.

It was one of the great moments of my life.

But it hadn't all been as rosy. Whilst I had been loafing in hospital for four or five days, *Illustrious* had been suffering the onslaughts of Corsairs in their first attempts at deck-landing. There had been far too many prangs and one of them had been fatal. Brian Fiddes, CO of 1830 Squadron, despite his experience, had made a bad approach to the deck and at the last minute had been given a wave-off to go round again. In manoeuvring a shade too violently to avoid hitting the island, he had clipped the port wingtip on the deck and had crashed over the port side into the sea. Nothing had survived. He and his aircraft had sunk like a stone. Accordingly Captain Cunliffe had decided that more deck-landing training was required—particularly in the matter of the approach pattern—and this had been done aboard an escort carrier, *Ravager*. Mike Tritton, lately the CO of 1834 Squadron and another very experienced pilot, was brought to the ship to replace the unlucky Fiddes.

It should be stated here and now that the trouble with the Corsair Mark I was its built-in 'bounce'. The undercarriage legs had oleo shock-absorbers, air on top of oil. As the wheel took the weight of landing, the shock was transmitted to the oil which in turn compressed the air. Unfortunately the air expanded again all too quickly and too forcibly. The oleo leg immediately extended again and the aircraft leapt into the air like a jack rabbit. If the pilot didn't catch a wire on his first contact with the deck, the odds were that he would finish up in the barrier. This happened to far too many pilots; and how you fared in the barriers was sheer conjecture. Some boys were burned to death; some, as I have said, were thrown over the side; others didn't need even an aspirin. It was all a matter of luck.

But the matter of luck had to be eliminated and Chance Vought, of Stratford, Connecticut, eventually came up with the answer. At the top of the oleo leg an air valve was fitted. As the air was compressed by the oil, it escaped comparatively slowly through the valve which, when the aircraft next took off and allowed the legs to elongate by the sheer weight of the wheels, sucked in more air in readiness for the next landing. The expulsion of the air took the bounce out of the oleos and the wheels remained firmly on the deck. The problem was solved; but the Navy would lose lives and aircraft before it was proved how essential the modification was. The Mark II version, supplied to us when we reached Ceylon, incorporated the modification, together with a new and altogether splendid hood.

To round off the matter of the Mark II, it might be added that a third modification was incorporated—that of water injection. For those interested in technicalities the equipment was surprisingly modest and uncomplicated. It consisted of two small tanks of water under the engine cowling, containing sufficient water to give five minutes of full-bore running. The water was atomised and blown in at the carburation stage and had the effect of speeding up the atomisation of the petrol/air mixture. (You may have noticed that your car engine runs twice as briskly and sweetly on a drizzly, humid evening. The water injection produced similarly efficient running.) The throttle quadrant was fitted at its fully opened end with a microswitch, protected across the quadrant groove by a piece of wire. To actuate water injection the pilot, already flying at full throttle, merely had to hit the throttle lever hard with the palm of his hand. The wire snapped and the lever actuated the microswitch.

The result was startling. The aircraft leapt forward with an immediate jump in speed of 35 to 40 knots. It was nothing short of miraculous.

Illustrious wasn't merely an aircraft carrier. She was a legend, a ship which, in her short life, had already made history. Built by Vickers-Armstrong at Barrow-in-Furness, she was launched on April 5 1939, commissioned on April 16 1940 and joined the Fleet at Spithead six weeks later. She was a war baby.

By the time we first arrived—by various means!—she had seen a lot of war. She had fought her way through the Mediterranean with convoys for Malta and Egypt. She had taken the lion's share in the destruction of the Italian Fleet at Taranto. She had gallantly withstood all that the Luftwaffe's Ju 87 Stukas could throw at her off Pantellaria on January 10 1941, suffering incredible damage. She had struggled into Malta only to endure more attacks and suffer more damage at the hands of the dive-bombers on the 16th and 19th of that month.

After a refit in America, she had re-entered the conflict by providing air cover and attack for the invasion of Madagascar and had given off-shore support at the bloody landings at Salerno in 1943. Her motto, set in golden letters beneath the three brazen trumpets, ran 'VOX NON INCERTA'. She had already spoken in no uncertain tones. Now she had Corsairs to keep the shouting going.

This story is about flying from carriers and it must be of help to some readers if I digress long enough to give a brief description of the ship; one of three of her class. The others were *Victorious* and *Formidable*. She had a nominal displacement of 23,000 tons, although it was popularly believed that additions and modifications had brought this to something nearer 30,000 tons. Three propellers, driven by turbines each developing 37,000 hp thrust her through the water at 31 knots.

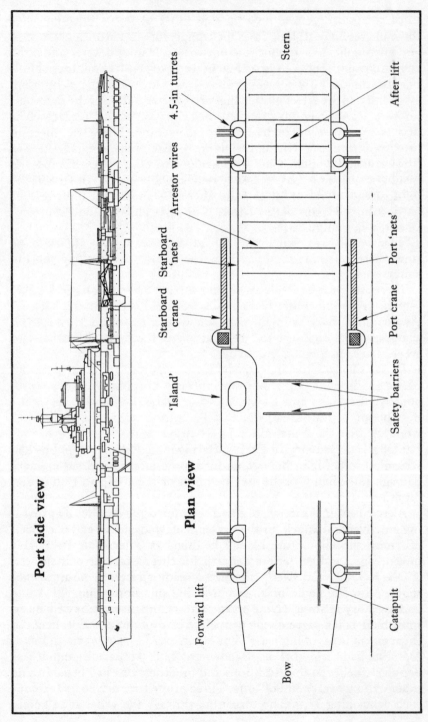

Port side view

Plan view

Stern

After lift

4.5-in turrets

Arrestor wires

Starboard 'nets'

Port 'nets'

Starboard crane

Port crane

'Island'

Safety barriers

Forward lift

Catapult

Bow

The centre propeller was situated directly forward of the rudder, whose action was thereby greatly enhanced. She could turn on a sixpence. The overall length was 740 feet, with a maximum flight-deck width of 95 feet. She was at once a mighty warship, a floating airfield and a seaborne anti-aircraft artillery regiment. Eighteen hundred officers and men lived within her steel walls.

Her great hangar, immediately below the flight-deck, ran practically the length of the ship. There were two lifts, one forward, the other aft, which conveyed aircraft with wings folded to and from the flight-deck. At the height of our commission, we carried 36 fighters and 16 bombers—52 in all. (At an earlier stage, when the Corsair squadrons were limited to 14 aircraft each, 21 Avengers had been accommodated.) A great trial and tribulation to us was a permanent deck park of 14 aircraft, rendered necessary because of the lack of hangar space. These had to be shuttled back and forth along the deck according to whether we were taking off or landing on. Alongside and above the hangar were squadron offices, stores and workshops.

To operate aircraft, the flight-deck was equipped with eight arrestor wires—strong steel hawsers stretched at intervals laterally across the deck. At each end they disappeared round pulleys through the armour-plated deck into the hangar, where they were wound round great spools on which tension, under hydraulic pressure, of varying strength according to the physical weight of aircraft being operated, could be imposed. As a wire was engaged by the aircraft's arrestor hook, so the self-centring wire was pulled from the spools, decelerating the aircraft to a standstill. The G force exerted on the pilot was between two and three, depending upon which wire was engaged.

Some 60 feet forward of the centre of the deck were two safety barriers (a euphemistic term which fooled nobody—to us they were crash barriers). These consisted of hinged steel stanchions at both sides of the deck, which were raised or lowered to allow for the passage of aircraft across them. They were connected by two steel hawsers of enormous strength, about three feet apart; and they themselves were linked together by three or four vertical hawsers, like a huge net. These hawsers, too, were capable of being stretched—though only slightly—under hydraulic tension. Six-ton aircraft at 70 knots appeared to go through No 1 barrier like a knife through butter; but it must have taken some of the way off them, for No 2 always brought them up solid.

Forward on the port side was the hydraulic catapult, capable of launching an aircraft to flying speed within a matter of 100 feet. On the starboard side of the deck, amidships, was the great 'island', which was at once the controller of the ship and the aircraft control tower.

One up from deck level was the Fighter Direction Office, from which radar and radio information was transmitted to aircraft; and from which aircraft were directed on courses to intercept the enemy. One deck up from there was the compass platform (known in circles other than naval as the bridge). Here stood the Captain, the Officer of the Watch, the Chief Yeoman of Signals and, in his own chartroom at the after end, the Navigator. On the port side a sliding door led out to a small fore-and-aft bridge, from which Commander (Flying)—'Wings'—controlled all aircraft in and around the ship. Above this level was a flat containing small cabins for senior officers when at sea; and above that again was the Admiral's bridge.

Abaft these positions were the Air Operations Room (which also served as the aircrews' ready room), the signal bridge and the Air Defence Position. There was, too, an unused area—remarkable indeed in a warship, where space is invariably used to the last square millimetre. No one knew what, if anything, had been forgotten, but the fact remains that it was put to very good use. For this was 'goofers' gallery'. It was the grandstand, like Liverpool's 'Kop'. Here gathered all those bodies whose pleasure or masochistic agony it was to watch aircraft landing. Here would collect officers and ratings off duty; those who should have been on duty and weren't; visitors; and genuine connoisseurs. All mustered here to watch the pilots dicing with death. This is no exaggeration. Most of the 'goofers', as the spectators were known, would learn in the next year or two how tragically true that was.

The ship's main defence consisted of 16 4.5-inch dual-purpose guns (they could be used against air or surface targets). They were housed in four groups at each 'corner' of the flight-deck, arranged in twin turrets in each group. Three groups were manned by Naval gunners, the fourth—X turret—traditionally by Royal Marines. Short-range AA weapons were scattered around quite liberally; in the gangways running down each side of the flight-deck (known as the 'nets') and around and on the island. There were 40 mm Bofors guns in single and double mountings; 20 mm Oerlikon cannon similarly arranged; and multiple 'pom-poms' which were rather 'old hat' by 1943. Over all, on top of the island, blossomed a great complex of radar and radio aerials.

She was quite a ship.

The ratings of both ship's company and squadrons were divided, for leave and shore liberty purposes, into port and starboard watches; and these in turn were sub-divided into first and second parts of port and starboard. Liberty could, therefore, be granted to one, two or three parts as occasion warranted.

Where duties were concerned, the ship's company—already divided into divisions: seamen, stokers, signalmen and so on—was again divided into three watches, Red, White and Blue. Confusing though it may seem, each rating was a member of two watches—one for leave and liberty purposes, the other for duties in the ship. The three-watch system embraced most sections of the ship's personnel: watch-keeping officers who, in their spell of duty, controlled the sailing of the ship and supervision of her machinery; the seaman branch; engine- and boiler-room staff; telegraphists and signallers; and engineering and electrical staff.

When the ship was at cruising stations she sailed under normal watch-keeping routine. Certain operations, however, called for more specialised activities. Entering or leaving harbour, refuelling at sea or close manoeuvring alongside another ship brought the Navigator up to con the ship and the Coxswain to the wheel. Cable-parties were required on the cable-deck and special sea-boats' crews for anchoring and mooring to or casting off from buoys.

Action stations, of course, closed up every officer and man to his appointed position. The accommodation ladders leading from the depths of the ship at each 'corner' to the hangar and flight-deck levels utilised wells whose main purpose was to provide for the hoisting of ammunition to the 4.5-inch guns. At action stations, therefore, these ladders were removed and the wells reverted to their main purpose. Personnel had no alternative but to climb up and down vertical ladders fixed to the ship's side inside the wells—a form of exercise which, with the dubious benefit of dim emergency lighting, could be highly diverting.

Living quarters in the ship were, surprisingly, not cramped, despite the fact that she was carrying 1,800 officers and men—500 more than her designed complement. The ratings—and the Royal Marines in their 'barracks'—lived on the mess-decks: open spaces of varying lengths and some 30 feet wide, divided into messes by banks of metal lockers which provided accommodation for the sailors' clothing and personal belongings. Each mess, the focal point of which was a wooden table and benches, assiduously scrubbed to unbelievable cleanliness, constituted home for 12 to 14 sailors. Life hadn't altered much since the days of Nelson. Here they ate, read, played cards and 'uckers' (ludo to you!), wrote their letters home, discussed, argued and occasionally fought. In colder and temperate climates here, too, they slept, with their hammocks slung from strong hooks fitted into the deck-head. Ventilation varied according to the situation of the mess-decks and cabins. All scuttles and port-holes below hangar level were closed at sea and only a very few senior officers were fortunate enough to breathe fresh air. The vast majority of us seemed to thrive remarkably well on forced ventilation. In the airless and windless expanses of the Indian Ocean most of us—officers and ratings alike—found space to accommodate a camp-bed in a passage or a deck open to the fresh air where we could sleep without being stifled.

Feeding was still on the general messing principle. Each mess provided two cooks-of-the-day, working in rotation. At each meal-time, these two lads galloped off to the galley and presented the 'tally' for their particular mess. In exchange they drew meals for the number of men constituting their mess. This food they then brought back to their mess at the double, for loitering, with a consequent cooling-off of a hot meal, was unpardonable. They served it with a skill born of practice under the sharp scrutiny of their messmates. Afterwards they washed the crockery and cutlery, and cleaned and rubbed down table and benches in readiness for the next meal. Tomorrow it would be somebody else's turn!

The quality of the food was as good as the catering officers and galley staff could conjure up under greatly varying circumstances. The subsistence allowance provided by the Navy covered basic needs from the ship's supply officer together with additional items, up to a certain limit, from the NAAFI's canteen manager. Any mess overdrawing from the canteen manager was subsequently charged with the excess, which was duly met from a mess fund accumulated by weekly contributions from its members.

The officers lived in comparative luxury. Lieutenant-Commanders and above occupied single cabins, the smallest of which was some 12 feet by seven feet. Junior officers lived two to a cabin, with one bunk above the other. All cabins contained a good wardrobe, adequate drawer space, a small desk and a wash-basin. We lived in four communal spaces; the wardroom, off which was a small gun-room for the use of Midshipmen; a dining-mess, containing three long mahogany tables and chairs; and a Warrant Officers' mess, which provided both dining and leisure space. The officers of ship's company and squadrons numbered about 180; and Warrant Officers some 30 or 40.

Food was on similar lines to that provided for the ratings. The officers paid monthly mess bills, which met the cost of food provided over and above the subsistence allowance allotted by the Navy.

Ratings were traditionally entitled to a daily issue of rum at 1150 every morning, under the supervision of the officer-of-the-day. The men, however, could elect not to accept the issue, in which case they became entitled to 3d per day in lieu, paid quarterly.

The officers' wardroom included a bar providing drinks at duty-free prices. Gin, for instance, at 2d per tot, whisky and brandy 3d. Beer was most expensive at 6d! An officer's wine-bill was limited to a certain monthly figure according to his rank; and the Commander, always well-informed on wardroom 'goings-on', had fairly harsh words for anyone overstepping the mark. An officer foolish enough to disregard a warning could find his wine-bill stopped completely.

The ship's and the squadrons' complements included a number of officers' stewards who served in the officers' mess and carried out certain duties for them, such as shoe-cleaning, making of beds and keeping cabins clean and tidy. In addition to their normal pay, they were usually fortunate enough to receive from their officers an additional monthly payment by private arrangement.

Although the ship possessed a laundry, the manner in which it operated was flexible to say the least. Most ratings with a deal of pride in their appearance—and most of them had—preferred to wash and iron their own clothing. Some ratings formed themselves into small 'firms' and contracted to launder for other ratings or officers. A number of stewards laundered for their own officers.

The versatility of Naval ratings never failed to provide volunteers to cut hair or repair shoes. Modest tailoring jobs, too, could be carried out without any apparent difficulty. The sailors' hobbies could provide everything we needed—models, stage scenery, cigarette lighters, boxing-rings, even toys to be sent home at Christmas. There is very little that 1,800 men can't do when they really try!

In between days of exercising in the Firth of Clyde, we lay by night at anchor off Greenock; and rumours raged through the ship like forest fires. The two short-priced favourites were the Far East (not too well received) and Norway, to attack the *Tirpitz*, anchored in a northern fjord (most popular!). When we took on board a consignment of pith helmets and other tropical gear, we unanimously decided that Their Lordships were trying to pull bags of wool over our eyes—so it *was* to be Norway!

Fully confident, I phoned Kathleen.

'Don't worry, darling,' I said. 'We'll be back in a fortnight, just you see. Then I'll give you a ring. Who knows? We may get a few days' leave.'

My next letter to her was posted in Ceylon.

Somewhere around 0745 on December 30 I awoke to find my cabin in near-darkness. Although the port-hole was wide open, not a glimmer of daylight was to be seen. How odd! I knelt on my bunk and stuck my head out of the port; there, moored within a few yards of us, was the towering cliff of *Queen Mary*'s stern. She had arrived during the night from yet another Atlantic crossing and her unbelievable bulk was completely obscuring such meagre daylight as a December morning in the Clyde can afford.

In the late afternoon we left Greenock—with *Indefatigable* lying at anchor in the stream—and made our way slowly and easily down to the 'Tail o' of the Bank', where we found a vast amount of Naval and merchant shipping, including the carrier *Unicorn,* moored and anchored.

We picked up our moorings and spent the evening putting extra lashings on the aircraft on deck, for rough weather was forecast for the middle and morning watches. At 2115 that evening we slipped our moorings and passed through the Clyde boom.

By ten o'clock the following morning we were off the coast of Northern Ireland, in company with the *Unicorn,* three destroyers and seven frigates. It was a miserable, dark December day—one of those which never really achieves daylight. Suddenly, out of the gloom to the south-east, signal flashes appeared. Fifteen minutes later we could discern the vague shapes of *Queen Elizabeth, Valiant* and *Renown.* They were pushing along in a big swell and mountainous seas were crashing over their bows, cascading green water as far as B turret. This was another moment to remember. How privileged to see such a sight! Mr Hague, our master gunner, was standing beside me on the flight deck. He scorned aircraft with all the contempt he could muster and steadfastly maintained his Whale Island precept that the 15-inch gun was the answer to every problem.

'Aye, take a good look at 'em, lad,' he said with a sigh of resignation. 'If things go the way they seem with these flying machines an' all, they could well be the last you *will* see.'

How right he was. I was glad I saw them on that dismal December day, as they appeared like wraiths out of the murk, three of the last of the 'big-gun' ships of a navy now long forgotten.

Our Fleet pressed on southwards in gloomy, damp and cheerless weather. Grey scudding clouds from the south-west maintained an unbroken ceiling, merging so precisely with a bustling sea which came at us in 20-foot rollers that it was impossible at times to discern a horizon. For the first 24 hours in open sea, some of us suffered from headaches and interminable yawning—sure precursors of sea-sickness. However, the leisurely motion of our great ship was so modest compared with that of our escorting destroyers and frigates, whose rolling hulls at times completely disappeared in the troughs, leaving only their mastheads and funnel-tops visible, that by the next morning we were back to maximum vim and vigour and in full possession of our sea-legs. In fact, at no time during the commission can I recall any of us fully succumbing to sea-sickness; though for the first day at sea following a protracted spell ashore, we generally found ourselves suffering from the slight symptoms I have described.

Heading south, the Captain and Commander (Flying) decided that the Corsairs should do no flying. The wintry weather of the North Atlantic was hardly the stuff in which to blood pilots who were still barely conversant with their aircraft and who certainly had little confidence to cope with deck-landing without suffering a sudden rush of blood to the head. The Barracudas, on the other hand, were kept busy flying searches ahead of the Fleet. One of these, returning to the carrier in the gloom of the late afternoon, had to ditch because of engine trouble; and its pilot, Morgan, was killed. I am amazed at the näiveté of the entry in my illegal diary—'Our first fatality—and the last, I hope.' And *what* a hope. Within two days of that entry I was awakened by two loud explosions, which proved to be depth-charges from a Barracuda whose engine had cut out as it went over the bows on take-off. Sub-Lieutenant Wallwork, his navigator and air-gunner were all killed. 847 Squadron was having a rough time.

A day's sailing on a south-easterly course brought us closer to land and sometime in the middle of the night of January 5 1944 we slipped through the Straits of Gibraltar into the different climatic world of the Mediterranean. Revelling in the unaccustomed warmth of January sunshine, I was standing on the flight-deck one fine morning with Johnny Hastings, amused by some of our young men ragging one another.

'Happy crowd, Hans,' said John. 'Full of beans—and it's good to see.' He nodded towards the sea, bustling past us at 18 knots. 'I wonder how many of 'em will still be with us when we pass that bloody wave again?'

I laughed at him. 'Don't be so bloody morbid, John! We'll *all* come back!'

He shook his head. 'Remember I've been here before—and I know. No—don't bother looking at them. There's no way of telling which ones. Just remember what I said, then you won't be too suprised.'

When we started flying again, it came as no surprise when things happened. Reggie Shaw knocked off his port wheel against a 4.5-inch gun and nearly killed Johnny, who was batting for us that morning. Miraculously, he managed to get his Corsair into the air again without further mishap and the ship gave him a course to steer for Maison Blanche airfield at Algiers. For some reason or other he failed to find it. He can't have been trying. After all, it was *somewhere* in Africa! After a bit of flapping around he eventually belly-landed in a ploughed field, much to the consternation of the oxen and the dusky gentlemen in attendance upon the plough. A Barracuda flew to Maison Blanche (he found it all right; navigators made all the difference!) and picked him up.

Somewhere off Mersa Matruh we came under simulated attack from RAF Beaufighters, to give us an exciting hour defending against them. In the early evening, off Alexandria, we were caught with our pants down when a German reconnaissance Ju 88 flew very high and fast over the Fleet. I cannot now remember if our radar boys had been asleep or if some blind spot in signal reception had caused us to fail to locate him. The fact remains that he was overhead when Wings scrambled the standby Corsair flight; tragically, too quickly for our young man Monteith. In his rush to become airborne, he failed to lock his wings properly in the 'spread' position, with the tragic result that, when he retracted his undercarriage as he passed over the destroyer screen, his wings folded and the aircraft plunged into the sea. He was only 20 and had become engaged, whilst at Stretton, to a charming young girl from his native Glasgow, who in that short time had captured all our hearts. It was a sad way to go.

The ship proceeded without a halt through Port Said, the Suez Canal and Port Tewfik into the Red Sea, where the heat lived up to its traditional ferocity. In mid-January we refuelled at Aden and headed out across the Indian Ocean. There would be no more flying until we reached Ceylon. Our wing leader, Dicky Cork, had laid on an exhaustive training programme which made it essential that all aircraft should be on top line by the time we reached Trincomalee. The weather was extremely hot as we sailed south-east—especially for the ratings working in the hangar, where the temperature reached astronomical heights.

As far as aircraft maintenance was concerned, it was naturally the hangar where there was most activity. In temperate latitudes this armour-plated box, capable of holding 30-odd aircraft, was a pleasant enough workshop for the boys. In the tropics it was hell upon earth. In a daytime temperature of anything up to 120–130 degrees Fahrenheit, the slightest movement produced a stream of perspiration. When an aircraft was flown regularly without mishap, its servicing was a straightforward, uncomplicated procedure. Every 30 hours it underwent an ever-increasingly rigorous overhaul culminating—if it lasted long enough!—in a truly major one which was tantamount to taking the whole thing apart and re-building it. It was also subjected to a daily check—tyre pressures, oil, hydraulic and air pressures, the correct functioning of ignition, instruments, radio and guns. If an aircrew was fortunate and their aircraft was in the right place at the right time, this daily check could conveniently be carried out on the flight-deck.

If they were not so lucky, however, the daily check had to be done in the hangar, that ill-lit, unbelievably noisy, unbearably hot dungeon where aircraft were lashed down cheek by jowl, surrounded by straining, swearing mechanics clad only in a pair of shorts—wringing wet from perspiration—and gym-shoes. Here they toiled, fuming at obstinate nuts, red-hot pipes and sparking plugs; and with the roll or pitch of the vessel calling constantly for a change of balance. Their hands never ceased to clear sweat from their eyes and within ten minutes their faces were covered in greasy filth and grime, rendering them almost unrecognisable.

They were great chaps. One of a sailor's God-given rights is that which moves him to moan like the clappers at anybody or anything at any given moment; and these lads were no exception. But when called upon to pull out all the stops they never failed us. There were times when the state of serviceability called them to slog it out in the hangar until the early hours of the morning. Yet I have found them next day, after only two or three hours' sleep, still moaning but with the hint of a smile beneath the grime, cheerful enough to say—'You'll find her OK, sir, no fear!' Over 30 years later, I still owe my life to them.

On the way out east, however, I wasn't exactly crying for them for, as squadron maintenance officer, I was spending most of my time down in the hangar with them. At moments when I began to see mirages of ice-cubes, I thought of days in Miami when Jim Pettigrew and I would emerge from a swimming-pool to reach for a heavily iced rum-and-Coke and ruminate on the hardships of war. My diary brought me back to reality: 'Another miserable day on maintenance. I feel tired out, as though the sight of that steaming, noisy hangar and the poor sweating devils working there will make me scream.' Obviously I was feeling very sorry for myself on January 26 1944! The next day seems to have brought no improvement. Again the entry is full of moans, grousing about the lack of co-operation from younger officers and even going so far as to add mutinously—'The CO has done *damn-all* this week!' The mystic East, so far, certainly held no allure for *me*!

9

First brushes with
the enemy

Our fighter wing leader in *Illustrious* was Lieutenant-Commander
(A) R. J. Cork, DSO, DSC, RN, one of the great fighter pilots of the
Fleet Air Arm who had established an enviable reputation for himself.
He had been seconded to the RAF during the Battle of Britain and had
flown with Douglas Bader. He had earned his DSO in fierce fighting
over Malta convoys. He was also very good-looking and, in addition to
shooting down a number of Luftwaffe and Italian pilots, had a lot of
very satisfied girls to his credit.

Dicky, I am sure, could have submerged us for evermore in flying
stories had he felt so inclined. Yet despite his fine record he wasn't a
line-shooter. Persuading him to open up on his exploits was like
extracting a very obstinate molar, and great perseverance was called for.

He did unbend one evening to hold us spellbound with an account
of a daylight raid carried out by the US Army Air Corps Flying
Fortresses over an engineering works on the outskirts of Paris. The
bombers were escorted by RAF Spitfires, including one flown by Cork.

As usual, German reaction was violent. Hordes of Messerchmitts
rose to meet the threat and the escort fighters were soon busily
engaged. Too many, unfortunately, were led astray by the Luftwaffe
and became involved in dog-fights far away from the bombers. Those
who had remained faithful to the B–17s found the going rough, so
much so that the strike leader, a Brigadier-General flying the lead
B–17, sized up the situation and broadcast to the fighters—'Hey! It's
getting rough out there, fellas! Come on beneath us and stay out of the
cold!'

They did as they were ordered. Cork said that the magnificent
protection given—ten .5-inch guns from each Flying Fortress—was
more than enough to keep the Bf 109s at bay whilst they enjoyed a
breather.

As soon as we were installed on the airfield at Trincomalee he set us
to work in earnest. We were roused from our beds while it was still
dark and by the crack of dawn we were out to the west coast of Ceylon,
low-flying or practising varied forms of formation flying. Then back
for breakfast. For the first time we used our Corsairs as true fighters,

throwing them round the sky, diving, climbing and turning to the outside limits. Dicky set squadron against squadron and our dog-fights seemed to fill the sky above China Bay. It was all highly exhilarating. What is more, our fighters now became a part of us, no longer a machine we were pushing about the sky.

What was it like to fly a Corsair? It is no easy matter to describe it to someone who has never handled a fast aircraft; who has never known the thrill of three-dimensional high speed. Once tasted, that thrill remains with a pilot for the rest of his life.

He climbs up on the high wing of the Corsair and lowers himself into the cockpit. The seat is a concave bowl of steel, designed to fit a packed parachute on which he sits. Between his backside and the parachute itself is a one-man dinghy, carefully stowed into a canvas case and attached to the parachute harness by a webbing lanyard. He straps himself, first, into the parachute harness, then into the safety harness. Now he dons his helmet and goggles and connects the R/T lead and oxygen pipe. He's ready to start up.

In front and to either side are ranged the controls, levers, switches, dials—in all, about 110 of them. He goes through his check-off list (or, as our tame satirist Steve Starkey so neatly parodied it, 'Chekhov-Liszt'). Magneto switches off. Control locks off; and check, too, that rudder, elevators and ailerons are all turning 'the right way' in response to movement of the controls. (They have been known to have been reversed, with dire consequences.) The wing-lock lever is in neutral and the manual lock engaged. Tail wheel unlocked. The rain cover to the pitot head, the long spear-like projection from the end of the wing which operates the airspeed indicator, has been removed. The propeller control is in fully fine pitch. The angle of attack of the blades on the air is adjustable hydraulically; fully fine pitch, offering least resistance to the air, gives maximum horsepower and is always used for take-off. Once in flight, the coarser the angle, the lower the speed, the less wear and tear on the engine and the more economical its petrol consumption. (Consumption, as a matter of interest, is about 60 gallons per hour at cruising speed and no less than 100 at operational speeds.) Mixture control to full rich, to give the engine plenty of petrol to get her started. Elevator and aileron trimming tabs in neutral. Six degrees of right rudder trim. At maximum horsepower the engine torque is enormous and will try to tear the aircraft round to port. The pilot's own strength on the rudder pedal would be insufficient to resist that force and the trimming tabs help him to overcome it. Cooling gills, round the front of the big radial engine, oil coolers and intercoolers open. Petrol cock turned on to main tank. This large container, holding 350 gallons, is surrounded by self-sealing material and is positioned immediately in front of the cockpit, behind the engine.

All this sounds quite a handful. In fact, it took only a few seconds. Now the pilot confirms to the fitter, standing to one side below him, that the magneto switches are off. The fitter grasps the propeller blade nearest to him and rotates it once or twice 'the wrong way', blowing out; tough going, this, against the compression of 18 cylinders. Now he moves back and looks towards the pilot who turns on the master electrical switch, rendering all systems 'live'. He gives the priming switch two or three short but decisive squirts, injecting a shot of neat petrol into the cylinders. Again he looks to his fitter, who signals to him that no one is standing within range of the great propeller. The pilot turns the magneto switches to 'on' and presses the starter switch, firing the Koffman starter which ignites a slowly expanding gas to hit the pistons under enormous pressure. The starter has a deep-throated tiger's cough. It jerks the propeller into life, back-fires once, then settles into the comforting roar which signifies a good, clean, fire-free start. He moves the mixture control to auto-rich and advances the throttle to give 500 revs per minute on the rpm indicator. He leaves it there until the oil pressure gauge awakens and climbs to normal. Whilst waiting, he has another look around. Hydraulic pressure is normal. Oil temperature is rising to normal. The blind-flying 'artificial horizon' is dancing around slightly, showing that it, too, is awake and healthy. He switches on the radio and the crackling and unintelligible natter from miles away tells him that the set is functioning satisfactorily.

At last the oil temperature and pressure gauges show normal. He opens up the throttle steadily to 1,000 revs and, keeping an eye on the rev counter, turns off one of the magneto switches. The revs drop by 50. He switches back to 'Both'. A pause; then he turns off the other. Now the drop is only 30. Both are acceptable, for anything up to a loss of 100 is safe. Everything is OK for him to move. He throttles back and crosses and re-crosses his hands before his face. The fitter and rigger nip below the wing and behind the lethal propeller to pull away the wheel-chocks. The fitter gives a 'thumbs-up' sign. The pilot advances the throttle a little and taxies out to the downwind end of the airfield runway.

He makes his final turn towards the runway which stretches away to the left, disappearing into the haze. He stops and looks towards the control tower. A steady red on the Aldis lamp. He looks up to the right. A Barracuda, fairly reminiscent of an airborne section of the Forth Bridge, is coming in to land. It looks as though it should have Christmas presents dangling from its wings. It thumps into the runway, its wheels leaving a spurt of blue smoke. Now the Corsair pilot closes the cooling gills. He locks his safety harness to hold him tightly against the armoured back of the seat. Then a glance at the tower. He

Above left *The author at Saufley Field, Pensacola. N3N-3s in the background.*

Above centre *Sub-Lieutenant (A) (later Lieutenant Commander (A)) L. C. Wort, DSC, RNVR. Dekheila 1942.*

Above right *The author aboard HMS* Trumpeter, *returning from the USA in October 1943* (Imperial War Museum).

Below *Training at Pensacola: with four New Zealanders. Left to right: Des Fyffe, Len Baggott, the author, 'Red' Martin and Tom Bush.*

Above *A Corsair's cockpit showing instrument panel with altimeter, compass, artificial horizon and other indicator dials. The 'throttle box' and gun switches for rendering the firing circuits 'live' are to the left of the cockpit* (Imperial War Museum).

Left *Corsairs in* Illustrious' *hangar. The narrow clearance between the deckhead and the tips of the folded wings is evident. The three small slots in the underside of the wing of the aircraft on the left are vents for ejected ammunition cartridges* (Imperial War Museum).

Above *Pilots, Chiefs and Petty Officers of 1833 Squadron, Quonset Point, Rhode Island, 1943. Left to right: Back row—CPO Maddison; Sub-Lieutenants Brynildsen, Starkey, Rogers, Shaw; and PO Geddes. Left to right: Centre row—Sub-Lieutenants Munnoch, Baker; Lieutenant Hanson; Lieutenant-Commander Monk; Sub-Lieutenants Aitken and Builder. Left to right: Front row—POs Edwardes, Coussens, Radburn, Turner, Vincent and Clifft.*

Right *Captain of* Illustrious—*R. L. B. Cunliffe, CBE, RN.*

Bottom left *15th Fighter Wing, Spring 1944. Left to right: Back row—Whelpton, Shaw, Barbour, Graham-Cann, Fullerton, Quigg, Starkey, Richardson (Wing Observer), Millard, Rogers, Maclaren, Facer, Buchan, Aitken, Pawson. Middle row—Seebeck, Baker, Booth, Munnoch, the author, Tritton, Sutton, Cole, Hadman, Brown, Retallick. Front row—Brynildsen, Clark, Ritchie, Guy.*

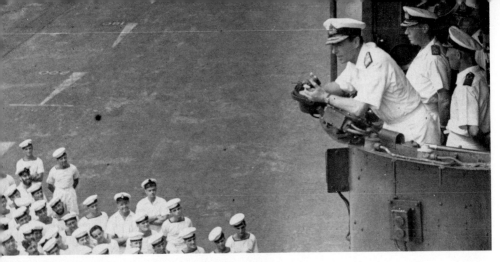

Above *Admiral Mountbatten addresses ship's company. With Rear-Admiral Moody, Captain Cunliffe and Commander Wallis.*

Left *A vivid overhead view of* Illustrious. *Both of her lifts are in the 'down' position* (Imperial War Museum).

Below *Corsairs running-up for take-off to Sourabaya.*

Top right *Corsairs taking off for Sourabaya.* Saratoga's *strike aircraft forming up*

Right *Gordon Aitken returns from Sourabaya. John Hastings batting. Note flaps and arrestor hook fully extended.*

Bottom right *At sea off the north-west coast of Australia. The Fleet is in line astern and has just been passed by* Saratoga *and her attendant destroyers (seen in the right background) bidding farewell to the Eastern Fleet as they set course for California* (Imperial War Museum).

Top left *Pilots of 1833 Squadron at RNAS Cape Town, October 1944. Left to right: Front row—Churchill, Baxter, Rogers, Munnoch, the author, Parli, James, Morgan, Booth. Back row—Lee, Shaw, Aitken, Buchan, Starkey, Heffer, Ritchie, Ayrton. (Baker missing, in hospital.)*

Left *Strafing Corsairs ready for take-off for Palembang, January 24 1945* (Imperial War Museum).

Bottom left Illustrious *entering dry dock, Sydney, February 1945.*

Above *Flight-deck activity. Corsairs under maintenance and repair during a rendezvous with the Fleet Train in the North-West Pacific, April 1945. The damage to the radar protecting screen on the front of the island was caused by the starboard wing of a Kamikaze suicide bomber, shot down a day or two earlier.*

Below *Pilots landed after a sortie against Sakishima, April 1945. Left to right: Baker, Retallick, the author, Parli and Quigg.*

Left *Captain Charles Lambe in his sea-cabin aboard HMS* Illustrious, *April 1945. (Later Admiral of the Fleet Sir Charles E. Lambe, GCB, CVO.)*

Below *A sing-song in* Illustrious' *wardroom, 1945. Resting on piano, with arms folded (from left to right): Buchan, Salmon and Doc Ellison. Author at the piano. To his right, sitting in the front row: Pawson, Hastings, Retallick, Cole and Munnoch.*

gets a rat-tatting of a green light on the Aldis, as though to say 'Come on, for Chrissake, get on with it!' The Corsair rumbles out to the centre of the runway. He trundles a yard or two to get the tail-wheel lined up; then locks it. *Now!*

He opens the throttle steadily up to the stop. It's a sticky, humid morning and great vortices of vapour fling themselves from the propeller tips. Now the 18 cylinders are developing all of their 2,000 hp and the seat hits him in the small of the back. With no assistance from him, the tail of the aircraft lifts off the runway and the Corsair is scudding along, faster and ever faster. At about 130 knots she lifts off effortlessly and the ground falls away. The pilot closes the hood and raises the undercarriage—the lever is down at his left-hand side—to lessen the drag and build up the climbing speed. He reduces the revs to climbing power—about 2,400 rpm. Now he can cut the throttle to climbing power and, at long last, release the safety harness lock which, whilst still securing him in his seat, allows some freedom of movement. He's really batting along now, soaring up to the virgin whiteness of the great banks of cumulus above him. He climbs through them at 10,000 feet. First stage supercharger is now whining like a great dynamo. He's gone on to oxygen, its sweet taste cold in his mouth. They, this lovely creature and he, level off over the cloud, sailing along on top of the world in magnificent solitude. Below him, the coast of Ceylon stretches away to the south towards Batticaloa. Far away to his right the mountains can be seen below the clouds. Adam's Peak, 8,000 feet of mountain in the centre of the island, is far below him. The Pratt and Whitney is purring like a great cat, cantering along, pushing back the miles at 240 knots indicated. What a day to be alive!

He revels in the sheer ecstasy of living. He looks around, underneath, above—nothing. He pushes the stick forwards until the airspeed indicator registers 320 knots. Now back, back, back. He begins to 'grey out' as the forces of 'G' bring on an incipient blackout. The world and the instrument panel become dim and dark. He loses the earth; now it's all sky. The Corsair pulls over into the inverted position, on top of the loop. He eases the stick. Immediately the earth brightens up again as his vision clears and he swoops down, building up a tremendous speed as the earth comes back into view. Now the jungle is fairly rushing up at him. Although he has reduced throttle, the engine is still whining. There is a huge jolt as he flashes through the slipstream of his initial dive (that must have been a good loop!) and blacks out slightly as he pulls out of the dive into level flight again. Now into another dive and the speed builds up massively again. Pull, pull—now he's really blacked out. He feels her go into a steep climb and relaxes pressure on the stick. The blood comes rushing back to his eyes, the dragging weight is lifted from his arms, legs, abdomen. He flicks over the stick and goes into a series of 'upward Charlies'—fast rolls in the climbing attitude—until the power ebbs away and he falls off into a stall turn. Now for a couple of 'chandelles'. A dive, a climb, up and up until she's near the stall. Then rudder and stick to the left and he slides off, falling through the sky at something like 350 miles an hour. He throttles the aircraft again, building up speed. Now up again, on the other side. When it is nearing the stall and the stick is becoming 'sloppy' in his right hand, he pulls the Corsair over and down to the right, dropping out of the sky again. The world is his and he laughs for sheer joy.

Now for home. Where is he? Way, way down at the bottom of a long, grey funnel through the clouds he sees a town. Must be Batticaloa. A gentle dive to the cloud-tops, then he heads north for China Bay. He flies low, skipping along the tops of the cumulus, weaving in and out of the valleys, going through the tops of the high ones. Beneath him, as though through the fast click of a camera shutter, he catches a momentary glimpse of a cruiser or a battleship in China Bay; down, down, 14,000 feet below him. He cuts the throttle, brings back the supercharger lever. Hard right stick and rudder. The great port wing towers over him on his left side and the Corsair falls like a stone, its propeller windmilling. He's diving, in magical silence, near vertically, down the grey, cliff-like wall of a chasm of cumulus, strangely dark out of the sun. With a flash the wide expanse of China Bay is suddenly revealed to him, glinting in the morning sunshine. He sheers off in case anyone becomes trigger-happy. Westwards over the jungle, he jazzes the throttle to clear the engine. Now down to 3,000 feet, he turns eastwards again and comes up to the airfield, looking as though butter wouldn't melt in his mouth.

As I said, Dicky now set about turning us into fighters within the meaning of the act. We practised flying as a Wing, both squadrons together, in the manner of RAF Ramrods which flew over north-western Europe enticing the German fighters to take the sky and give battle. In this we were to be unlucky for, at this stage of the war, the Japanese were already feeling the lack of fuel and aircraft, and in our experience could be drawn into battle only when some cherished prize was at stake. Cork, however, knew what he was doing when he drove us on and on in low-flying exercises. Fighter schools in our days didn't teach ground strafing as we would have to fly in action. There, we had been taught to dive at the target from a considerable height and to open fire when down to about 400 yards. After firing, we had to pull up sharply and disappear from the scene at high speed and low altitude.

There were two fundamental dangers in this method. First, to dive from height was simply begging to be shot down, for we were to find that Japanese short-range flak gunners were good and needed no second invitation. Secondly, a monoplane (and it must be remembered that many of our instructors had learnt their trade on biplanes) has an inherent characteristic at the point of pull-out. After the joystick has been pulled back to raise the elevators and thus recover from the dive, it carries on for x feet in the same plane as the line of the dive itself and only after a second or two does it change its line of flight to that demanded by the new position of the controls. This continued downward trend was known as 'mushing'. If one tried to pull out too near *terra firma*, the 'mush' would put the aircraft and its occupant firmly but untidily into the ground; very often through the target itself.

We were to find that most of the Japanese airfields we attacked were 'single-strip' jobs, carved out of virgin jungle. The enemy knew very well that, in order to attack such a runway successfully, we were obliged to fly down the field longitudinally. A lateral attack at high speed would have flashed us across the field before we had time or room to bring our guns to bear. With this in mind, the enemy positioned his flak weapons and grounded aircraft accordingly. The fields were generally armed very heavily at both ends, with a liberal scattering of weapons down each of the long sides. The best life policy was obtained by flying low and fast—and the faster and lower the better!

Cork had been fortunate enough to take part in some ground-strafing attacks in northern France. With the recollection of these very much in his mind, he led us day after day low-flying at tree-top height the full width of the northern part of the island. Such fun it was, too! Despite the thick undergrowth and the speed at which we were flashing across the tree-tops, there was plenty to see. Wandarus, the friendly slate-grey apes of Ceylon fled from the high branches as we approached. Water buffaloes looked up from the clearings and galloped off into cover. One never-to-be-forgotten morning we surprised a herd of wild elephants crossing the railway line and I fear that the roar of our engines gave them plenty of urge to increase speed.

The Mahaweli river, the largest in Ceylon, flows from the hills south of Candy to the north-east and empties into the southern part of China Bay. The mouth of the estuary consists of acres of tidal mud-flats on which crocodiles in their hundreds basked in the sun all day long. They were brutes, too—the estuarine variety, I was told; apparently much larger than the inland 'mugger' type—and from the air I judged their length to be something in the order of 12–15 feet. Tears may spring to the eyes of animal lovers when I admit that, whenever I passed across the estuary, I took the liberty of shooting two or three. The fact is that I don't like their feeding habits! I also doubt if they would have given *me* an even break had I descended in their midst!

143

We lived ashore on the very edge of the jungle. Basha huts, which were long, single-storey wooden frameworks covered with plaited coconut leaves, were our home. We washed and shaved outside in the dawn sunshine, earnestly watched by groups of inquisitive wandarus. Tree-rats, reminiscent of squirrels, lived in the roofs from which they periodically descended to ransack the chests of drawers in our cabins in order to gnaw away the buttons from our shirts and shorts. Snakes abounded, with cobras and Russell's vipers among the nastier specimens. The insect life had to be seen to be believed. Day was bad enough, but the nocturnal population was fiendish. Mosquitoes bred in their millions and drove us to distraction. Great four-winged beetles, something like two inches long, droned through the darkness of our cabins to thump into our mosquito nets like tennis balls. The only redeeming feature was the firefly. The bright, winking lights in their thousands more than atoned, in their beauty, for all the other crawlers and flyers.

Our entire entertainment ashore was provided by a primitive bar and an even more primitive cinema. The clatter from the insect life and the thunderous downpours of monsoon rain on the roof completely blanked out the sound from the speakers. But the films were so ancient that we knew the scripts anyway!

Life aboard the carrier, out in the bay, was infinitely more genial. For one thing, there were no insect pests. But nowhere could one escape the heat. Nor could she provide food in any better shape than the mess ashore, for there was little you could do with powdered egg, powdered milk, powdered potatoes and corned beef that ran from an opened can in a turgid stream of tepid sump oil conveying a few streaks of red meat.

Rumours of a German blockade runner between the Cocos Islands and the Sunda Strait led to our sailing from Trincomalee on February 22. We flew exercises for two days, then ran into bad weather. Sampson, a Barracuda pilot of 847 Squadron, landed his aircraft very cleverly when his arrestor hook refused to come down. The ship whacked up to full speed and, with such wind as there was (and wind was a rare commodity in the Indian Ocean except in monsoons) produced a wind speed down the deck of 40 knots for his special benefit. We never found the blockade runner—if, indeed, he ever existed—and returned to harbour on March 3.

We sailed on another 'Calcutta sweep' on March 8 hoping, we were told, to draw enemy forces out of Singapore. They chose not to play with us, but the flying was invaluable; and you can't take the Fleet to sea every day just to give the boys a fly-around! On our first full day at sea, 'Tiddles' Brown did a shaky landing and put his port wheel over the side into a gun sponson. He bent the aircraft but he himself was unhurt.

March 10 was a tragic day and no mistake. The party opened up at 1030 when Alan ('Deadly Joe') Vickers did a bad bounce and went headlong into the crash barriers. He was unharmed but the aircraft was a bit of a mess. During the afternoon the Barracudas put in a dummy torpedo attack on the ship. Scott of 810 Squadron, pulling out of his dive to level out for his torpedo run, got into a high-speed stall. He hit the sea with a tremendous impact and disintegrated before our eyes. All three crew were killed instantly.

Some time later I put on a more modest turn. During an exercise I noticed that my hydraulic pressure had fallen to zero. My hook dropped as it should—automatically when pressure failed. I called up the ship requesting an emergency landing and she obligingly turned into wind. I blew down my undercarriage with the emergency CO_2 bottle and managed to get down about ten degrees of flap. I was more than relieved when Johnny dropped me on to the third wire without any trouble.

If that was a bad day, the next was murder. Don Hadman hit the barrier on landing and the rest of us flew around in circles waiting for the flight-deck party to sort things out. I was on next. I crossed the barriers, folded my wings and taxied on to the forward lift. I had just stopped and switched off when there came the deafening scream of tortured metal behind me. Joe Vickers had drifted off to port on his approach. Probably because Joe had lost sight of the batsman, he ignored all signals from Hastings to go round again; and Johnny had to jump for his life into the safety net as Joe hit the port after group of 4.5-inch guns. He then careered up the port side of the deck until he crashed heavily into the great steel stanchion of No 1 barrier, slewing the tail round to rest across the nets, with the nose pointing towards the island.

Because of amateur, albeit willing, interference in clearing up prangs, Captain Cunliffe had ordained that no goofers should approach a crashed aircraft. All rescue work had to be undertaken only by the flight-deck parties. So we stood our ground, Reggie Shaw and I, 200 feet away. Alan Vickers was still in the cockpit, either unconscious or dead—we shall never know. His head lolled to one side and it may be that his neck had been broken by the impact.

So the men who mattered leapt into action. Fire-fighters in their asbestos suits were running out their hoses to drench the engine in foam. A sick bay chief jumped up on to one wing, Doc Alcock, the flight-deck doctor, on the other. George McHardy—against all the rules, but nevertheless most gallantly—climbed on to the cockpit hood on which he sat astride, trying to help the other two to unharness Vickers and lift him out.

So far all was going well. Then, without a spark of warning and with the concussion of seething hot air, the main petrol tank went up in a great explosion. The chief was killed on the spot. Ron Alcock was flung to the deck, horribly burned on head, face and arms. George was blown—a great torch of bright flame—in a wide arc to the sea, 50 feet below. The aircraft was now an inferno, with firefighters covering the engine in foam and flames leaping high from the fuselage. But even these men had to withdraw when the six guns of the Corsair roared into action and sprayed the island with lead and steel. Burning oil and petrol flowed from the aircraft into the ready-use ammunition locker below where three boys, trapped by the aircraft lying across their only exit, were badly burnt. Then came the final catastrophe. The rear end of the Pratt and Whitney power unit was made of magnesium alloy. Now it, too, caught fire. Nothing could extinguish it, nor could anyone now approach because of the intense heat.

Alan Vickers was dead. The chief was dead. George McHardy, picked up by a destroyer and rushed to hospital in Madras, died there from his dreadful burns. Doc Alcock and three gunners below the flight-deck were transferred to hospital with serious and disfiguring burns.

To lose squadron chums, God knows, is bad enough; but to see the faces of their particularly close friends—buddies with whom they had joined up and from whom they had never been parted until this dreadful moment—is something akin to agony. Nothing could be done for the boys who had gone but we tried, as kindly and unobtrusively as we could, to jolly along their friends. Most of them were very young. Some had volunteered straight from school or university and knew little or nothing of life. They hadn't at this stage of the game accumulated much mental stability and were easily shaken.

I have always maintained that carrier life, infinitely happy and enjoyable though it was, did nothing to make it easier for us. As a member of a shore-based squadron, one could at least go off to the nearest town and see a film; or find a few civvies with whom to have a drink and forget 'shop' for a while. One could take out one's wife or girl-friend. But in a carrier we were *there*. There was no escape from it all. Your Corsair was in the hangar, one deck up. The flight-deck, that torrid arena of the grim game of life and death, was only two short ladders beyond that. Life was lived, utterly and completely, within a space of something like 10,000 square yards. Within that area we ate, slept, drank, chatted with our friends, attended church, watched films, took our exercise—and flew, landed or crashed our aircraft. Friendships became, if anything, too close and the hurt was all the more painful for that very reason.

It was a relief to get back to Trincomalee. The goofers had had more than their fill for the time being.

Once back in China Bay, we cast our sorrows aside. We swam or sailed dinghies in the afternoons. Michael Hordern, our FDO and a great friend of the aircrews, was the first man I ever saw swimming with flippers and a snorkel apparatus which, together with a spear-gun, helped him to produce a seemingly endless supply of fish, most of them delectable, for the wardroom table. Some characters sought less attractive denizens of the deep. The coast off Trincomalee abounded in sea slugs, singularly unlovable creatures of the same shape and size as a small loaf of bread, which one usually found by standing on them. They registered their objection to this treatment with a slight, slow squirm which had the startling effect of rocketing the owner of the foot from the water like a Polaris missile. Churchill, a Flight Commander who joined our squadron in the summer of 1944, found unpopularity in several quarters by collecting two or three of these monstrosities and depositing them, like visiting-cards, in the washbasins of ship-mates' cabins. They appeared to possess neither head nor tail, moved at a steady inch per hour and were utterly repulsive in their amorphous grey, decomposed appearance. There is a type of person who can handle such things without a morsel of squeamishness; but Churchill was almost uncanny in his ability to leave them with people whose revulsion knew no bounds and who inevitably had to bribe a braver friend to remove them.

In the evenings we might watch a film in the after lift well, sing around the piano, or merely drink and chat. We were a happy crowd and, certainly in the wardroom, there was no nonsense about ship's officers and squadron officers. (From friends in other carriers, however, we gathered that the absence of any division between the two was not universal, by any means.) Good or bad things in a ship descend from the top; and our Captain and Commander set the style. More than any other senior officers, perhaps, they understood the RNVR temperament. Without their endless wealth of tact, goodwill and infinite good nature, I tremble to think what a holocaust we might have produced. The genius who composed the song 'There's a balls-up on the flight-deck—And the Wavy Navy did it!' was speaking from a wealth of experience. A happy carrier such as ours had to be grateful to a Captain and Commander who, somewhere along the line, had realised that RNVRs were creatures of a type entirely different from anything they had encountered in such numbers so far in their careers and that, as far as they were concerned, rules might conveniently be bent a trifle and discretion stretched a little further than was customary. God knows we tried. But our valiant efforts to conform were directed largely along civvy lines of good manners and behaviour rather than in a determination to master King's Regulations and Admiralty Instructions. In any case, these seemed to us so voluminous and detailed that we conveniently decided that they could not possibly be assimilated in just *one* war! The undoubted fact that it worked was entirely due to these two gentlemen.

Towards the end of March we were at sea again, trailing our coat in the Indian Ocean. Some strikes were in the offing but without *Victorious*, whose arrival in China Bay we expected very shortly, we couldn't tackle the job alone. The great *Saratoga*, the last big carrier of the US Navy's old guard, was coming round from Esperitu Santos in New Britain to join us for a time; and we were out to rendezvous with her.

She made an impressive sight as she and her three attendant destroyers climbed out of the southern horizon to meet us. They had run into a typhoon whilst crossing the Great Australian Bight and had taken some punishment, but *Saratoga's* menace and power were there for all to see. On the day following our rendezvous she proceeded to show her teeth. Her complete air group—Air Group 12, said to be one of the most efficient striking forces in their navy—disappeared over the horizon. An hour later they returned to deliver a devastating simulated attack on their own vessels. Dive-bombers (Douglas Dauntlesses), fighters (Grumman Hellcats) and torpedo-bombers (Grumman Avengers), all at the very peak of efficiency, gave a display which took our breath away.

We saw quite a lot of each other in Trincomalee. Some of them had been instructors during my time at Miami and it was good to see old friends. One such was Commander Joe Clifton, the Air Group Commander. 'Jumping Joe' was one of the great characters in my life—and in many others. He was an average-height, thick-set, tough-looking guy, as hard as they come, who had played football for the US Navy—and in America that speaks volumes. He had taught me air-gunnery at Miami. He talked loudly and interminably with only short pauses to allow the intake of breath and smoke from a large cigar, without which he was never to be seen. He was no respecter of persons and it would be a gross understatement to say that he didn't suffer fools gladly.

I was driving our big Ariel bike from the airfield back to the mess at China Bay one morning when I met Joe with three or four of his boys indulging in a strange exercise for Americans—walking. I stopped to pass the time of day.

'Where in hell d'you learn to ride that goddam thing, Hans? Only cops ride them back in the States!'

We talked. All the time Joe was looking over the machine.

'D'you know, Hans? I ain't never ridden one of them. How's about checking me out?'

I dismounted and went through the cockpit drill. The 500 cc bike was not lacking in urge and I emphasised that the clutch called for a dainty hand on the controls; something for which Joe was not particularly noted, on the ground or in the air. He settled himself into the saddle and positioned his cigar firmly and squarely in his mouth. He set his face in that characteristic look of determination and was ready to go.

'Now, Joe! Easy on that clutch!'

Up went the revs, bang went the clutch. The bike took off as though rocket-assisted and, with Joe hanging on for grim death, shot through the open doorway of a basha hut to disappear through the rear wall, leaving a well-defined aperture—'Man on motorbike passed through here.' We ran to the back of the hut. The bike, with engine stalled, lay steaming gently in the noonday heat. Joe, flat on his back, was laughing gently through a dark brown, sticky mush which had been a cigar.

'God*dam*, boy! That sure is one hell of a machine! I reckon those cops back home are no fools! Sure as hell would like to get the hang of it!'

For two or three weeks we flew and sailed together, attacking the Fleet and making a series of dummy operations against Ceylon itself, which in turn retaliated by testing our own defences with purposeful attacks by RAF Beauforts and Beaufighters. By then we were ready.

One more catastrophe had to be endured; and again *Illustrious* was struck a hard blow.

As we approached Ceylon after some days exercising, we were ranged for a dawn take-off, with Dicky Cork heading the line. The Indian Ocean in April is flat calm and at dawn there is virtually no wind. For almost half an hour the Captain cast around trying to find such wind as there was and eventually settled on to a course. Away went Cork, but the wind was so negligible and his take-off—including a breathtaking 'sink' over the bows—so hazardous that the rest of the flying programme was cancelled. Dicky was given a course to steer for China Bay and the fleet turned to follow him to the coast.

As we came through the boom and sighted the signal station we were greeted with quickfire flashes, telling us that the runway was out of use because of a bad crash. Though I believe I was the first to put two and two together, I claim no pride. Our arrival in port only confirmed what I had surmised already as an appalling tragedy.

Cork arrived over the airfield—then controlled by the RAF—and prepared to land in the half-light of dawn. The controller gave him a red on his Aldis, since he had just given permission to a young pilot, Anderson (coming out to do deck-landing trials aboard our ship), to taxi down the runway for take-off. Cork accordingly tucked up his undercarriage and did another circuit. He now made another approach. For reasons which we shall never know, he ignored another red on the Aldis *and* a red Very light. He pressed on with his approach and landed on top of Anderson, who by this time had reached the middle of the runway.

No wonder the shore station's signal had been lacking in detailed information, for both men were burnt beyond recognition. The next morning we took what was left of them to the little cemetery in Trincomalee. We had never met Anderson. Cork was one of us and would be sorely missed.

I was a long time getting over that one. Silently, I swore like a trooper to think that someone like Dicky, who had already gone through hell and high water, should throw his life away so contemptuously. He deserved a better fate.

Sad, yes. But they would both have been proud and happy to see the full *Saratoga* air group lined up with our own as a guard of honour as we slow-marched them to their final landing.

During the first month or two of our long stint based on Trincomalee, it became necessary to change our Corsairs to a later mark. The aircraft were brought in crates from the States to Cochin, on the south-west coast of India, thence taken by road some miles inland to Coimbatore, where there was a Royal Naval Air Repair Yard. Here they were reassembled and test-flown before being issued to the carrier squadrons. We flew our old machines up to Coimbatore and brought the replacements back to China Bay.

And now, at long last, with a trail of destroyed and broken Corsairs and Barracudas and a lamentable loss of young men behind us, we set off to war. The objective was Sabang, on a small island off the northerly tip of Sumatra. The harbour was used by shipping servicing the Japanese armies in Burma and this, together with a large airfield at the back of the town, was a target worthy of our attention.

We sailed on April 16, in company with *Saratoga, Renown, Valiant* and *Richelieu*; and the cruisers *London, Newcastle, Gambia, Nigeria* and the Dutchman *Tromp*, with escorting destroyers. These, numbering ten in all, including three Americans and the Dutchman *Tjerk Hiddes*, joined us at sea, together with the cruiser *Ceylon*. At 0650 on the 19th we flew off, our component being 17 Barracudas and 13 Corsairs.

My first sight of enemy territory was of a luscious green island, basking in the early morning sunshine. It was all so very beautiful that when red flashes burst from the deep, verdant green, I felt considerably put out. Good God! It's enemy fire! Why I was surprised I can't imagine. I can only suppose that I was appalled that some vandal should set fire to Paradise. We dived down ahead of the Barracudas, firing enthusiastically at warehouses and quays and suddenly found ourselves at the far end of the harbour, unscathed. We were still green and hadn't yet learned about targets of opportunity. So we milled around like a lot of schoolgirls and left it to the Barracudas, who made a splendid attack on the harbour and oil installations. The Corsair boys returned to China Bay with a feeling of anticlimax. We had been to the enemy and had found no opportunity to cover ourselves with glory. But we would learn.

Before we sailed from Ceylon on our next operation together, *Saratoga* and ourselves paid a short visit to Colombo, fetching up there at the end of another exercise. *Saratoga* went to a lot of trouble to stage the party to end all parties and invited our C-in-C, Admiral Sir James Somerville, and other Fleet officers, and our own air group, partly to repay our hospitality in entertaining them aboard *Illustrious* in China Bay. (This in itself had proved to be an alcoholic feast of Olympian proportions!)

Saratoga threw her party ashore at the Prince's Club and Joe Clifton, as her Air Group Commander, was in full charge. They took over the club completely for the night and invited every eligible woman in sight. Great were the goings-on. Since American warships are officially—and surprisingly effectively—dry, their boys really go to work on the liquor when the flood-gates are opened. And this night was no exception. Their ship's band provided a dance orchestra of 14 or 15 players, all of a highly professional standard.

Shortly after the musicians had enjoyed a brief rest, I was sitting in a nearby lounge chatting to some American friends. There was suddenly a bull-like bellow for 'Hans! Where the hell is Hans, for Chrissake?' It was Joe. Not since the late lamented death of Stentor has anyone but Joe achieved such vocal power. He hove in sight.

'Hey, Hans! For God's sake move your ass and get on that goddam piano, will you? That lousy goddam pianist! The sonofabitch has passed out! Be a pal, willya, and pitch in with the other guys!'

'It doesn't surprise me. He was as pissed as a newt the last time I saw him.'

'Wassat? What did you say?'

I repeated it.

'What the hell's a newt, for Chrissake?' Joe's interests were a bit limited and obviously didn't include the study of fauna. I told him.

'Is that right? And just how the hell do newts get—what did you say?—pissed?'

I had to confess that I was beaten on that one.

'Hey! Is that a Limey expression? Sounds good. Must remember that one. Anyway, fuck the newts, Hans. Get on that goddam piano, there's a good guy. That sonofabitch is finished for the night, that's for sure.'

I went over to the grand piano and sat down. The nearest musician was the lead saxophonist. He was a New Yorker, slim and dark—probably of Italian origin. He was a man of few words. He half-turned towards me and said from the corner of his mouth:

'Sweet Sue, in G. OK, One-two.'

It was a long time since I had enjoyed playing so much. These boys were—as I found later—all professional musicians, drafted into uniform for the duration. They played the whole night without a note of music in front of them and never put a foot—or a finger—wrong. It came as an exciting challenge to me when I found that they automatically assumed that I was in the same category. With only a couple of bars' notice, the leader would remove the reed of his instrument from his mouth, half-turn to me again and laconically call upon me to modulate to F and play a piano 'break' for half a chorus. For an hour and a half I revelled in the company of true musicians and learned more than any teacher could have imparted in a year.

On May 3 we sailed again, for a final exercise before another operation. Shortly after leaving harbour, two of our Barracudas collided in mid-air and Walmsley and his crew of two were killed when their aircraft went into a spin. Buckland managed to ditch safely outside the harbour from where he and his crew were rescued by the American destroyer *Dunlap*. We carried out a big fighter exercise in the afternoon, marred only by two heavy deck prangs by Eric Rogers and Tony Graham-Cann, both fortunately unhurt.

Whatever was in the wind, it called for Avengers, good torpedo-bombers built by Grumman of Long Island. So our Barracudas were flown ashore and we took on Avenger Squadrons 845 and 832. Just before the change-over was effected, Admiral Mountbatten visited us in harbour and combined a social call on the Captain with an official visit in his capacity as Supreme Commander of the forces in South-East Asia. He was brought to the flight-deck by the after aircraft lift and was immediately introduced to all the heads of departments.

'Bull' Cullen, Commanding Officer of one of our Barracuda squadrons, was standing on my right. He shook hands with the great man.

'So you fly Barracudas, Cullen? And what do you think of them?'

'Very good aircraft, sir,' said Cullen, standing rigidly to attention and staring fixedly in the direction of Rangoon.

'*Really?*' said the Admiral. 'I've had other comments. Have you flown better aircraft?'

'Er, yes, sir. I think I have.'

'*Much* better aircraft? I'll tell you why I want to know. I have just left your opposite number down the line there and he tells me they're bloody awful.' A pause. 'Do you *really* like them?'

'Er, not exactly, sir. We *could* have better.' Poor Cullen wasn't enjoying this a bit.

'That's more like it, Cullen.' There was another short pause. 'In fact, I suspect you dislike them just as much as he does.' Cullen was listening intently. Then the Admiral spoke again, very softly and infinitely kindly. I suppose I was the only outsider to hear. 'Listen, old chap. What I am here for is to have you tell me precisely what you think. Never try to tell me what you think I might like to hear. There's a good chap—and the best of luck.'

You're wasting your time trying to flannel a man of Mountbatten's calibre.

During the same day he visited *Saratoga*. In the early evening I went across to her for a meal with old friends. Later, some of us decided to return to *Illustrious* for a drink. 'Baby' Winterrowd turned down the invitation.

'Hell, no!' he said. 'I got more to do than go drinking. I gotta get a letter off to my Mum. It isn't every day I shake hands with a real live English lord!'

Whenever the Fleet lay in China Bay between operations at sea, we landed some or all of our Corsairs on Trincomalee airfield to continue flying practice. This constituted in reality an endless fighter refresher course in which we practised low flying over both jungle and sea, dog-fighting with gun cameras (the films from which were later screened and the results assessed) and, with the co-operation of nearby RAF Spitfire squadrons, ground-strafing runs over their airfields.

After the Sabang operation, Joe Clifton from *Saratoga* and I exchanged aircraft for a local flight. It was my first experience of the Grumman Hellcat and, despite my fanaticism for the Corsair, I was certainly enamoured of it. Its cockpit was similarly roomy and efficiently laid out. Its performance, too, was much the same but in landing particularly I found it a lot safer and easier to handle largely, I think, because of its superior visibility and better stall characteristics.

We sailed with our full fleet and *Saratoga* and her destroyers. On May 15 we edged our way slowly into Exmouth Gulf, on the northwestern corner of Australia. A more desolate place cannot be imagined. This great bay, surrounded only by sand, scrub and pitifully stunted trees, shimmered in a suffocating heat. The air was lifeless—as, indeed, was everything else. The only signs of activity were aboard the oil-tankers, preparing to refuel us. We sailed again the same evening, heading north and going fast. We were aiming for Java.

At 0705 next morning we took off and, thanks to assiduous practice over the past few weeks, we joined up in quick time—from *Saratoga*, 24 Hellcats, 12 Avengers and 18 Dauntlesses; from *Illustrious*, 16 Avengers and 16 Corsairs. We had two accidents. One of the Avengers literally fell over the round-down into the sea and another ditched soon afterwards through total loss of power. All six crewmen were saved.

This time we knew what we were about. We flew 70 miles to the coast and quickly crossed the island to attack Sourabaya on the north coast. Our targets were the Wonokromo oil refinery and the Bratt engineering works, both to the south of the city; and the big harbour. All went well. I had two flights to escort our Avengers and *Saratoga*'s Dauntless dive-bombers attacking both the southern targets and we successfully saturated the anti-aircraft defences without suffering any losses. Hathorn, the Dauntless squadron CO, made a classic attack on the oil refinery which severely damaged the three retorts. Our new Avenger bombers attacked the engineering works with bombs specially long-fused for low-level work, which they delivered with letter-box precision. One or two aircraft which sought to interfere—though not in our part of the sky—were readily shot down. Our only casualty was one of *Saratoga*'s Avengers. Her squadron was busily engaged in torpedoing ships in the harbour when Rowbottom, their CO, was badly hit. With commendable airmanship he managed to coax his dying Avenger out into the bay, where he finally ditched. Fortunately he and his crewmen, although captured, survived the war. The hearts of my own flight fluttered briefly but excitingly when, in the middle of shooting-up a coaster heading up the bay towards Sourabaya, we found ourselves surrounded by crossfire from a flight of Hellcats, hellbent on doing the same thing. The moment passed.

On the way home I took up my position as stern cover. My first realisation that the American strike leader was leading us through the wrong pass in the mountains came when I saw a flight of Hellcats diving below us, obviously heading at a rate of knots for the surface of Java. There, far beneath us, was a great airfield with a welcoming spread of parked aircraft. I thought quickly. All the fighters had used a lot of ammunition; and four aircraft wouldn't be carrying sufficient to deal with the great array of tempting targets below us. If I waited for permission to attack the element of surprise would be gone. I prayed hard—and took my flight down in a great sweeping dive to the airfield. This was Malang, an important Japanese Army Air Corps base—and we had them on toast.

I was breaking the rules. My job was to provide stern escort for the bomber force and now I was gallivanting on a private jolly (for which I was later censured—and rightly so—by Captain Cunliffe). Nevertheless, here I was; and for the first time I realised the power and majesty of the Corsair. At over 300 knots, with my three boys well spaced out in line abreast, my aircraft slid into the airfield.

Closing quickly into firing range, my first impression was one of bodies rushing like ants all over the field. Some were heading for AA emplacements, others dashing for the hangars, presumably to taxi out aircraft from the fires which the Hellcats had already started. As I flattened out at about 30 feet, heading for a row of parked fighters, my first burst blew to hell a machine into which a pilot was climbing. Tracer ricochets were flying in all directions in front of me and my six guns were thudding away with a healthy, dull thump, a bass *Te Deum* to the painstaking work put in by my armourer. I flashed across the airfield boundary, went into a screaming low turn, pulling streamers from my wingtips. Then I was firing again, the .5–inch shells banging into a group of three two-engined aircraft. There seemed to be no gunfire from the field. Fires were raging all over—hangars, aircraft, living quarters. We made another run at a small group of fighters—and then there was nothing left to hit. We climbed away, joining into formation again, grinning hugely at one another through the Perspex of our cockpit hoods.

Johnny Baker had a yearning to blow up a railway locomotive—which I sincerely hope he has long since abandoned—and I agreed to loiter over Malang town while he and his wingman went down to the station, probably to consult the timetables to see what was due to arrive. Whilst Brynildsen and I circled lazily over the town at about 8,000 feet, I became intrigued by a large black building in the town centre. What on earth was it? One sure way to find out. Telling Neil to stay put and to cover me, I dropped my port wing and fell quickly to around 2,000 feet; then headed down, straight for the mystery building, and delivered a two-second burst through the roof. The result couldn't have been more dramatic. Doors on all sides burst open to disgorge hordes of people into the streets, milling back and forth like a disturbed nest of ants. Then I got it. I had frightened the living daylights out of a cinema show—or a cockfight, to which I believe the Javanese are more than partial. For a moment I felt myself to be the biggest heel of all time. Then I thought again and decided they should have more to think about at ten in the morning!

On the following day, sailing back to refuel at Exmouth Gulf, we said farewell to *Saratoga*. We had enjoyed their refreshing company, both ashore and afloat. We had admired their efficiency and single-mindedness. We had made new friendships and had cemented old ones. It was a sad moment as she steamed slowly past, acknowledging our salute, our full-blooded cheers and our farewell to good and brave friends. Then she and her destroyers slid into the murk of the gathering darkness to the south. Godspeed!

10

'On the road to China Bay, Where the flying Corsairs play'

Apart from continuous flying practice from the airfield and the occasional one-, two- and three-day exercises at sea, we idled away a month at Trincomalee. Despite the freedom from operational anxieties, however, we just couldn't escape from the ever-present menace of death. On the last day of May, Brian Guy of 1830 Squadron, taking part in an exercise out at sea, flew into an electrical storm and failed to reappear. Although arduous searches were carried out at sea and along the coastal strip, nothing was found. Ten days later during an exercise at sea a Barracuda of 810 Squadron hit the sea in high-speed stall and all three crewmen were killed.

Since March we had been getting acquainted with a new flight-deck doctor, Robert Ellison, who had replaced the unlucky Alcock. Bob was, I believe, one of the first RNVRs to undergo a course in aviation medicine and was, therefore, the ideal chap to look after us. His main purpose aboard the ship was to watch aircrews for signs of crack or strain; and as a result he found himself spending most, if not all, of his time with us. He was a good listener and never appeared to weary of accepting for further consideration all our moans, worries and frustrations. As time went on, we needed more and more someone of his type on whom we could unload our fears.

That same month, too, our CO, who had been operational since the commencement of the war, departed quite suddenly for the UK and within an hour, after a three-minute conversation with Captain Cunliffe, I found myself in charge of the squadron. Promotion, after wending its way through the usual channels, followed a few weeks later.

Now came another operation which we would carry out alone. The family, of course, came along with us—*Renown, Richelieu, Ceylon, Nigeria, Gambia, Phoebe* and seven destroyers. It can't have been much fun for them, although I reckon it was preferable to swinging round a buoy in China Bay. Our objective this time was the harbour and airfield of Port Blair in the Andaman Islands, that pendant of small islands which appears to be suspended from Calcutta, down through the Indian Ocean.

We made our landfall soon after dawn on June 19; and the course given to us was a good one, for we hit the main island of the group right on the nose. As we approached the coast I gave the order to purge the wing-tanks. At this time, each wing of the Corsair contained a small built-in petrol tank, both of which we endeavoured to exhaust before going into action. These, unlike the main tank, were not self-sealing and were extremely vulnerable to gunfire; especially so when they were partially or fully exhausted, because of the highly explosive vapour still captured in them. The Corsair was fitted with bottles of CO_2, opened by a valve in the cockpit, with which to purge them and render them reasonably harmless.

When I gave the order Gordon Aitken, a lovable character and a great pilot but one given to engaging moments when his head became firmly tucked into the nearest bank of cumulus, promptly opened the wrong bottle and blew down his undercarriage. (Once extended by this method, the undercarriage could not be retracted again without adjustments by the maintenance crew.) This was great! I was, unfortunately, in no position to kick his backside and had to restrict myself to ordering him to return to the ship. He would have looked a proper Charlie flying around at very limited speed with all that drag on him. Worse, he would have been a sitting duck.

With a flight led by Percy Cole, we gave the airfield a going-over and destroyed seven or eight fighters which the Japanese had most thoughtfully lined up for us at the end of the runway. The fury of the short-range flak showed how annoyed they were and there was no end to the host of red balls that rose lazily in arcs and flashed past our faces as they just missed astern. Johnny Baker chased a mechanic across the airfield and put him out of the war. The boys shot up hangars, huts, living quarters, petrol bowsers and other odds and ends. The only serious trouble we encountered was an imposing row of machine-guns lined across the bottom of the runway strip. The Jap boys manning them were the bravest of the brave for they steadfastly stuck to their guns in the face of our terrible fire, refusing to the end to put down their heads.

By this time the bombers had arrived so we sheered off, Cole to the south, myself to the north. On Mount Harriet we found the radar station. With the last of our incendiary ammunition we burned to the ground the station buildings and then, in a wave of completely unjustified optimism, tried our luck with armour-piercing shells on the masts themselves. A very brave Japanese gunner, squatting on a small platform set among the girders halfway up one of the masts, had a go at me as I passed at his level. I yelled to Reg Shaw, half a mile astern of me, to get the bastard. He duly obliged. Our .5-inch bullets packed a considerable wallop and this gallant fellow hurtled from his platform to the ground as though catapulted.

Two of us were hit by light flak. Johnny Baker had a 40 mm shell-hole bored cleanly and clinically through a blade of his propeller, making his engine run very roughly. I collected a shell—probably 20 mm—from below and ahead which passed neatly through the propeller without touching it. It sheered off the vanes from the top centre cylinder of the engine and finally burst through the engine cowling, leaving something like a head of aluminium cos lettuce sticking out on top.

When there was nothing left to go for, we rendezvoused out at sea, east of Port Blair, over one of our submarines. This 'boat' was one of two temporarily withdrawn from their patrol areas in the eastern Indian Ocean to act as air/sea rescue vessels for the operation. We found her four or five miles out, cruising in lazy circles, with some of the crew relaxing on the casing and one or two officers waving quite merrily to us from the conning tower.

'Well! I'll be damned!' I said to myself. 'Talk about cool sods!'

We dipped our wings in salute and set course for the fleet.

Reggie Shaw provided the real excitement of the day when he found to his horror that the undercarriage would descend only halfway—and there it stuck. This is a bloody awful predicament. One cannot ditch with safety, for the undercarriage would snap the aircraft on to its back, with possibly fatal results. Nor can one deck-land, an effort which would not only tear the deck installations to rags and tatters but would probably pitch the aircraft over the side into the bargain. The only option is to bale out. So we told him, by the ship's radio, to go ahead of the destroyer screen and get on with it. We suggested that he should open his hood, invert and release his safety harness.

He did. Nothing happened. He inverted again. Again no body emerged.

'What the hell are you doing, Reg?'

'I can't get out!'

'Don't be so bloody stupid! Climb out then, you stiff!'

The ruderies produced results at least. He clambered out on to the wing and, after some hesitation, jumped. He fell, fell, fell . . . No sign of a parachute. Standing on the flight-deck, hands shading our eyes, we were beside ourselves with horror and frustration. Then we began to shout;

'*Pull* it, Reg! For God's sake, *pull* the bloody thing!'

The great white flower finally blossomed and he floated the last 200 feet gracefully into the ocean. God! He had certainly cut it fine!

Later, safely back from the destroyer which had picked him up, he told us that the anaesthesia of floating, with warm air flowing over his body like a refreshing shower, had robbed him of the vital urge to pull the ripcord. It had brought him close to death.

The rest of us returned in more normal fashion, safely and without prangs. Our boss, Ian Sarel, Commander (Flying), never failed to greet our return as a friend. Ian, of course, was a pilot and had taken part in one of the great and earliest actions of the war, when Skua dive-bombers had flown from the Orkneys to sink the German battle-cruiser *Königsberg* in Bergen harbour. For this he had been awarded the Distinguished Service Cross.

Watching deck-landing from 'goofers' could be more nervously exhausting than carrying out the landing itself. To the onlooker, a Barracuda's landing looked hazardous enough. Yet it could approach from dead astern in a steady, descending drone to the deck. But every Corsair looked a certain crash. The beast's long nose, which gave the pilot extremely poor visibility in the 'nose-up' landing attitude, shut out completely any idea of approaching from dead astern. In order to keep both deck and batsman in view, the pilot had to approach the round-down in a great, sweeping, descending curve from the ship's port quarter. In many instances he was still turning as he crossed the round-down. The batsman would then straighten him up, simultaneously giving the mandatory signal to cut the throttle. The aircraft would then sink into the wires.

As I have said, to watch this from goofer's gallery was nothing less than horrendous. It calls for little imagination to realise why Commander Sarel's hair turned grey during the commission, for he had to watch every landing. Yet he was a quiet, serene man who was never known to flap. He was tall, gentlemanly, with a slim, boyish figure, a ready smile and an endearing penchant for standing at the end of the wardroom piano with a drink in his hand and a song always on the tip of his tongue. He was a fine officer and a grand shipmate.

There is little doubt that the operating of aircraft from the deck of a carrier is a highly professional business which involves not only the carriers and their charges but also every ship in the Fleet. For both flying-off and landing-on, the carriers must sail into the wind in order to increase the relative wind speed over the deck and, of course, to enable the aircraft to land as near into the eye of the wind as possible. It will, therefore, be appreciated that if the course to be made good by the Fleet is, for example, due west—270 degrees—and the wind at the time is blowing from due east—090 degrees—it is necessary for the Fleet to make a turn of 180 degrees and to pursue a course of 090 degrees until all aircraft have taken off or landed. Why must all ships in the Fleet turn? In enemy waters where submarine attack is possible, the destroyer screen is there to cover the major ships—battleships, crusiers and carriers—against such an attack. If the carriers were detached, unescorted, to operate their aircraft, they would be highly vulnerable for anything up to 30-40 minutes. In dangerous areas, therefore, it is essential that the destroyer screen remains intact.

Every minute sailed on the course for operating aircraft, therefore, is delaying the Fleet's progress; and to reduce that time wasted it is essential that the squadrons' drill in the operations of landing or taking-off shall be as expert and efficient as is humanly possible.

The main requisites so far as taking-off is concerned are; efficient 'spotting' of the aircraft on the deck, so as to maintain a steady flow of machines from their 'spotted' positions to the take-off point; and a fairly exciting turn to starboard by each aircraft as soon as possible after leaving the deck so as to take its slipstream away from the line of the deck and clear of the path of the following aircraft. The great art in landing lies in the interval of time and distance taken by aircraft on their landing pattern around the ship. If the interval taken is too great, time is wasted since valuable seconds are being thrown away while the batsman awaits the oncoming of the next aircraft. If the interval is too short, the batsman may well have to 'wave off' an oncoming aircraft because the preceding one has not yet cleared the barriers. Valuable time elapses until such time as the next aircraft makes his final approach.

Slick work, too, is demanded of the flight-deck parties. As soon as an aircraft hooks a wire, members of those parties must rush from the nets to disengage the wire, to allow the aircraft to taxi forward. The wire operator must quickly rewind the wire in readiness for the next landing; and the barrier operators must lower both barriers as soon as an aircraft is hooked and then re-erect them immediately the landed aircraft has taxied across them to the forward end of the deck.

With every man concerned doing his job efficiently and with squadrons at peak performance, aircraft in our ship could take off at intervals of 12 seconds and land at the incredible rate of one aircraft every 22 seconds.

The official form on which to report an accident was the A25. Since most Naval pilots have completed at least one of these during their service, it is hardly surprising that the form figured largely in song and story. The chorus of the A25 song ran:

> *Cracking* show! I'm alive!
> But I've still got to render my A25!

The verses were legion and varied from faintly respectable to downright obscene; but they were all uproariously funny. Since deck-landing alone accounted for so many reports on this form, the song naturally returned again and again to incidents on the flight-deck. For instance:

As I float up the deck and I see Wings' frown,
I can tell by his look that my hook isn't down.
A dirty great barrier looms up in front—
Then I hear Wings shout—'Switch off that engine, you . . .!

And again:

When the batsman gives 'Lower' I always go higher;
I drift off to starboard and prang my Seafire.
The chaps up in goofers all think I am green,
But I get my commission from Supermarine!

The beginning of July brought us a new 'owner'—a change we viewed with a certain amount of disquiet, as Captain Cunliffe was the type of leader one hopes to retain for ever. On July 3 we dined him formally in the mess—a very special occasion which Commander Wallis superintended with the ease and efficiency which attended everything he did. The new captain, Charles Edward Lambe, arrived on July 6. As he ascended the gangway ladder, the cruiser *Nigeria*, moored half a mile away, flashed a signal—'Where's your piano?'. It seemed that in peacetime days our new Captain, a musician of some ability, had carried a piano around with him! We were soon to learn that musicianship was only one of his many attributes.

Two days later we went to sea, largely to show our paces to our new Captain. The air group rose to the occasion. We had a splendid day of exercises—no prangs, no 'hearts-in-mouth' and every landing a copybook job.

The following day was Sunday and, after Divisions, the officers pulled a cutter ashore bearing Captain Cunliffe on the first stage of his journey home. It was a moment in history. We had intended to honour him with a flypast *en masse*, but my diary tells me that RAF Command in the island refused us permission. It doesn't tell me why they jibbed!

It was said that Captain Lambe was an anxious as the rest of us to get to sea again. He was probably already suffering from the lassitude induced by the humidity of Trincomalee and was sighing for the sea breezes which, although they varied only between warm and hot, at least gave some relief.

The opportunity came on July 22 when we sailed again for Sabang, on the famous 'top left-hand corner' of Sumatra. To feel the great ship's movement underfoot again; to ride with her majestic heel to starboard as the wheel went over as she passed the boom; and to stand on the quarter-deck watching the awesome wall of water mount higher and ever higher as she worked up to 20 knots—there was a wonderful exhilaration to all this, impossible to describe to those who have never gone down to the sea in ships. She had life and we were lucky to be part of it.

This time it was to be Sabang with a difference, for the big guns were to have their say by bombarding the port from some 12 miles out. As *Victorious* had joined us two days earlier, our air power would now be twice as effective. We were all Corsairs; the Barracudas had no part to play in this operation and had been put ashore.

For the bombardment, fighters had been laid on to undertake the spotting for the battleships. It would be their duty to circle the target area and to report by R/T on the accuracy of the fall of shot. Two Corsairs were allocated to each battleship; and to make the job easier the big gunners would use coloured shell bursts—*Queen Elizabeth*, for instance, would fire shells with blue bursts, *Valiant* white and so on. All this had been well and truly rehearsed.

Three days later, at 0535, our flight was first away from the ship, leading a strafing force from both carriers to keep Sabang airfield quiet. We made a good landfall and were over the airfield at 0600 precisely; a bit too early, as it happened, for it was almost impossible to see what was on the ground. Within minutes, however, the sun came rocketing out of the eastern horizon and we were able to go to work. There were two aircraft standing out in the open, plainly visible; and another two in revetments. All four were destroyed. Hangars were set on fire and we used incendiaries on the barrack blocks. Daybreak is an unpardonable hour to attack *anybody*. A man is never at his best when struggling into a pair of trousers, particularly when the process is somewhat hindered by bursts of incendiary fire zipping through the hut. Certainly the Japs who, rushed out of those barracks, some of them clutching platefuls of whatever the Japanese soldiery ate for breakfast, must have disliked it intensely. A lot of them, breakfast or no, died that morning.

Then we climbed up to 10,000 feet to get our second wind. The spotters had arrived to take up their positions for the bombardment and we could now only await the arrival of the big ships. In the meantime we were scanning the harbour and set off quite a panic when I reported to the Fleet the presence of a submarine moored alongside one of the quays. They gulped a couple of times and asked me to make sure, so we went down to 2,000 feet and had a good look. With a very red face I had to admit that I was wrong. What it turned out to be was a small coaster with a tiny superstructure amidships; and the Fleet was so relieved that they forgot to give me a blast for poor ship recognition. Then the first of the shells came droning in and we needed no reminder to get the hell out of it.

Fifteen-inch shells are the very devil for demolition work. The big warehouses along the sides of the quays were systematically pounded to rubble and I remember quite vividly seeing one actual burst. A tremor blurred the quayside; then a warehouse literally took off and rose towards us in one piece. At some height which it was impossible to judge the building then disintegrated and fell to the ground in a monstrous cloud of dust and smoke.

The flak gunners were wide awake by now and were becoming more menacing and much too accurate. After a minute or two's search I found at least one battery which was giving the spotters a few headaches. Three guns were dug in on the crest of a hill on the southern end of the airfield and we did a quick flash over the position to see how the land lay. Back at 8,000 feet I summoned another flight and told them to attack low and fast from the southern side. I allowed a few seconds for the low-flying flight to get in their burst of fire, in the hope of unsettling the enemy by strafing him from an unexpected quarter; and then we were roaring downhill, frontally attacking the position. Once you are committed, nothing seems to matter. We saw the great muzzle flash as one of the guns was fired. I remember seeing the upturned faces of the gunners as they looked for a hit. Where the hell the shell ended up I don't know. We were past the point of no return and all that seemed to matter was that we should destroy them. And then we were within range. The Corsair shuddered as the six guns hammered away with their deep thud. Chunks flew off the gun mountings and bodies were hurled to the back of the gun emplacements. Then we were flattening out, our wingtips throwing off great streamers of vapour as we flashed over the gun position at 30 or 40 feet and out to sea.

We had carried out our mission but as the big ships were still busy it seemed a pity to go back. I looked around for something else to hit and suddenly remembered a fat merchantman of two to three thousand tons apparently anchored in the middle of the harbour. It seemed to have escaped damage from the bombardment. We reformed quickly and dived down again in line astern, firing with armour-piercing bullets at the ship's water-line. We had long been assured that a close pattern of .5-inch ammunition could tear up the deck of a destroyer, so a cargo ship's hull should be vulnerable enough. Our attack must have perforated her, at least, for she lost no time in getting under way and heading for a quay—to avoid foundering, I hoped.

And then it was time to go. The bombardment had lasted 20 minutes. Even the destroyers had enjoyed a field day, for some of them had come up to the harbour entrance to discharge their torpedoes at the wharves and jetties.

This time the Japs were well and truly nettled. We had been back on board only a short time before they showed themselves in the vicinity of the Fleet and our standing patrols became busily engaged. Keith Munnoch's flight shot down a Sally and Bud Sutton, 1830's Senior Pilot, collected a Zeke. We had no luck. Two minutes after we had landed-on after an afternoon patrol more enemy aircraft appeared and attacked the Fleet. They paid dearly for their temerity. Both squadrons of the ship and a flight from *Victorious* ran up scores, with three Zekes destroyed and two more damaged.

Les Retallick of 1830 Squadron was our only casualty. From a height of 10,000 feet he was conscientiously photographing the target area with his large vertical camera when he took a burst of heavy flak. There was an explosion in the centre of the fuselage which set the aircraft on fire and rattled up the protective sheet of armour-plating behind his seat with such force as to pepper his shoulders with fragments. He lost no time in making a classic bale-out; this immediately over the airfield, which gave him considerable food for thought. Such wind as there was, however, very decently carried him out to sea. He survived two hours in the water during which he was most unsportingly potted at by Japanese shore batteries, before being safely picked up by a whaler from *Nigeria,* one of whose officers had carefully pinpointed the position of Les' entry into the Indian Ocean and had set afoot plans to rescue him as soon as the ship had finished plastering Sabang with her 6-inch guns.

Les duly rejoined us on our return to China Bay, where Willie Macgregor, our PMO, got in some practice in extracting the steel splinters from his back. As I said to him later, hardly the sort of thing that a South London schoolmaster should have to endure on a Tuesday morning.

Thanks to a meeting aboard our ship with an ebullient character called Farnfield, an RN Lieutenant-Commander, I was invited to spend a couple of days at sea in his destroyer *Quality.* It was a refreshing change from 'big-ship' life. In company with two other destroyers we practised a number of evolutions including a high-speed run which thrilled me beyond belief. Destroyers are all engines and weapons; and her fantastic acceleration as she quickly worked up to about 35 knots, the vibration beneath one's feet from the mighty turbines under the 'iron deck' and the mountainous cliff of water which built up astern as she lifted her bows, dug in her stern and slid across the tranquil sea left me speechless. Farnfield, clad in cap, white shorts and gym-shoes, slapped his expansive tummy with glee as he revelled in my astonishment at his darling's paces. He was a destroyer man through and through.

On the second afternoon the three of us 'hunted' one of our own submarines who delayed her departure on patrol sufficiently long to participate in our exercises for a couple of hours. She submerged as she left China Bay in the morning and after lunch we set about finding her. Eventually *Quality* and another destroyer got cross bearings on her and, in accordance with arrangements made earlier, Farnfield ordered a hand-grenade to be dropped over the mark. We stood by, awaiting the appearance of a small marker buoy which the submarine should send up on being detected.

Nothing happened. Farnfield again took the destroyer over the mark and dropped another grenade. This one, too, produced no response.

'He's got his bloody head down!' Turning to his First Lieutenant he said: 'Let's rouse the lazy bugger! Give him a depth charge on a deep setting!'

We went round into a great circle, building up to a breath-taking speed. As we did so, a depth-charge was being prepared on the launching rails down aft. As we crossed the mark again, down went the charge. In a few seconds the muffled detonation came to our ears, the surface of the water astern of us shivered, then erupted into a great explosive cascade of water. Once more we stood by.

In about three minutes the submarine's nose slowly emerged. She surfaced fully and her signalling lamp went into action—a damned sight too fast for me to read.

'What does he say?'

' "Thank you for awakening me. I was enjoying my Sunday afternoon." '

There were times when we considered that the heat was a greater worry to us than the thought of battling with the enemy. It seemed to be something to which we couldn't adjust ourselves. British ships of that generation weren't designed for those latitudes and, in the absence of any form of air-conditioning, even the shortest possible time spent in an enclosed space could be purgatory. Our life in Ceylon and the Indian Ocean was certainly subjected to the onslaughts of this oppressive heat. It affected tempers and efficiency and a great deal of understanding was necessary to maintain morale; certainly a great deal of imagination, which King's Regulations and Admiralty Instructions didn't cater for.

What with cricket and football matches, deck hockey leagues, darts matches on the mess-decks, lectures, discussion groups and gramophone recitals, we managed to keep the boys happy enough and our Adjutant, Steve Starkey, was indefatigable in his efforts to keep their minds and bodies in good trim. In those latitudes morale is everything; and all his efforts had that as their goal.

Entertainment of a more exciting nature was always being provided in some form or other. I was in the hangar about 1600 one afternoon when a messenger summoned me to see the Commander in the wardroom.

'You have a young man called Demaine in your squadron, Hans. What is he?'

'Electrician, sir. A good boy.'

'Yes—I'm sure. He wants my permission to dive from the Admiral's bridge.' He grinned at my expression. And well he might! Good God! What height was that? Hell! it was 80 to 90 feet! But the Commander was carrying on. 'He's *your* man. Provided you have no objections, it has my blessing.' He paused for a moment. 'He obviously has every confidence in his own ability; and I don't like battening down on a good man.'

I went up to the flight-deck. A fair 'gate' had gathered from which rose a hum of anticipation and excitement. I ran up the ladders to the Admiral's bridge. Demaine was standing on the outer rim of the deck, only his hands on the upper rail preventing him from falling into China Bay. There was a sea of upturned faces beneath him, their owners clinging to every possible projection from the starboard side of the deck and ship. Demaine grinned at me as I walked over to him.

'Tired of the food, Demaine? Or are you having electrical trouble?'

'The lads want me to have a go, sir. I can do it all right, if you say it's OK.'

'Off you go, then.'

He braced himself for a couple of seconds, then he was off. He sprang out away from the ship in a great arc, his body arching as he fell away from me at an incredible speed. He straightened out to a knife-blade an instant before he hit the sea, his clenched fists battering a hole into the water. There was only a 'plop'—no splash—as he sliced into the water. Magnificent.

A burst of cheering greeted him as he surfaced. It came from other ships nearby, too, in addition to our own. He crawled quickly to the starboard brow and met me at the door from the flight-deck to the island.

'The lads want an encore, sir!' he gasped, his great chest heaving from his exertions.

'I'll bet they do! Jack, you were great! I didn't know we had a star on the strength! But no more, old son. And don't take any notice of *them*; believe it or not, the same crowd watch deck-landings and you can take it from me that a fair percentage of 'em are hoping you'll break your bloody neck. Be happy with one—you're too good a lad to risk your life again.'

One of the benefits emanating from a happy ship or squadron was the remarkable absence of trouble among officers and ratings alike. Naturally there were occasions when their halos tilted a little, but only one serious incident comes back to me.

Since the squadron's days at Stretton, almost a year earlier, we had been bedevilled by petty thieving in the ratings' quarters; and some of it was quite serious. Petty Officer Turner and I had spent a lot of time and effort trying to apprehend the culprit, but without success.

Most crimes rear their ugly heads at some time or other in the Navy, as in any other organisation where men in large numbers are gathered together. The great majority of them are dealt with in a calm, gentlemanly manner with neither rancour nor hard feelings. Drunkenness, setting fire to bunks or hammocks whilst in a drunken stupor, absence without leave, striking a superior officer—all these are taken in the Navy's stride.

But theft is something the Navy finds impossible to forgive. There is no privacy in a ship. No lockable drawers or cupboards. No private safes. If one cannot trust one's messmates, life is not worth living and the stability of the system falters.

Eventually this lad was caught. Another rating, living ashore at Trincomalee and suffering from a mild attack of sunstroke, was confined to his bed. Resting in his bunk behind his mosquito net one afternoon, he saw the culprit systematically rifling through his messmates' gear. He leapt from his bed and grappled with the thief, who pitched out of an open window a wrist-watch he had just 'found'.

Later, I was asked by the Commander to read the Warrant which would commit the rating to detention. The fatal document in hand, I went up to the hangar deck. There, on the lift, was the squadron drawn up in a hollow square, officers lined up facing the ratings. I took my place in front of them and read out the sentence. I was halfway through when the prisoner started to sob as the solemnity of the occasion overwhelmed him. With an unbelievable effort I managed to keep my voice steady. Some of the ratings began to shuffle with embarrassment, to be stopped in their tracks by a rasping censure from Turner.

The Marines marched him away to his weeks of hell upon earth. I felt as though I were about to serve his sentence for him.

When in harbour we had, of course, the cinema. On board, our Odeon was situated in the well of the after aircraft lift, the screen suspended on its forward bulkhead with the projector shining from the after bulkhead. If we were lucky enough to be in harbour on a Sunday, this was 'Officers' Night at the Movies'. Naturally enough, the quality of the films, both in content and physical condition, varied. What *never* varied was the quality of the wisecracks from the audiences. Film stars of the time would quickly have acquired inferiority complexes had they known that, despite their best endeavours, every film became a farce.

Any ratings who had missed a film during the week would catch it on Sunday when, since the officers occupied the 'stalls' on the lowered lift itself, they would sit on the flight-deck, legs dangling into the lift well, looking down from the 'gods'.

Their ribald comments on *any* film were worth a king's ransom; and were even more hilariously lurid whenever tragedy or high drama appeared on the screen. Detectives were loudly informed of the doings of their suspects, five minutes ahead of schedule. Love-sick swains vowing undying love were vociferously advised 'Yer want to leave that bit alone, mate! She's bin in the stokers' mess all weekend! 'Ad it from 'ere to there, she 'as!' Movietone newsreels probably took the biggest beating of all. Their commentators—no doubt in a laudable endeavour to boost civilian morale during those depressing middle years of the war—were inclined to turn every slight advantage gained in the field into a major victory; and every reverse into a temporary and trivial setback. There was much talk of 'our brave lads, with their tails well up'. This was enough to send our matelots into paroxysms of Rabelaisian ecstasy from which the much-maligned 'Pongoes' emerged none too well.

When 1,800 of you are obliged to live together in a big iron box, you *have* to try, don't you?

Perhaps more so in harbour than at sea, the wardroom could burst into song at the drop of a hat. Sometimes after supper, around 2100, there would be a suggestion that the piano should be brought across. Man-handling quickly moved it from the dining-mess across the passage into the wardroom and in a matter of seconds the sing-song was under way.

Most of our songs were sung with everybody word-perfect as they roared out the full-blooded choruses; and there was no shortage of soloists, each of whom had a verse or two of his own pet ditty to contribute. We were lucky to have as shipmates the well-known actors Michael Hordern, Robert Eddison and Douglas Storm. One of our company for six months or so was the BBC producer Malcolm Baker-Smith, who was collecting material for a projected film on the subject of life aboard carriers. These indispensable shipmates not only joined in the singing with professional gusto but were, from their calling, clever enough to write new and topical material for us to sing. More than that, they would stage one-act plays at short notice, write pantomimes and contribute in every way to the wonderful spirit that abounded in the wardroom.

Standing around a piano, singing songs, drinking, with perspiration streaming down one's face and dripping from the chin, might well fail to appeal to modern young men as a relaxation. To us it was a life-saver. To be with good and true friends, indulging in harmless, uproarious fun, was something which enabled us to relax completely from the nervous tension of our jobs, to survive the absence of our nearest and dearest and to recover from the shock and grief caused by the loss of our comrades-in-arms.

As a change from pounding out accompaniments to nautical ditties, fun though they may be, it was refreshing to be called upon to play more serious music. We had a fair sprinkling of messmates who found peace and tranquillity in sitting round the piano in the quiet of the dining-mess when Bob Finlay or I played snatches of Beethoven or Dvorak, Schubert or Tchaikovsky. Steve Starkey gave talks on musical appreciation to our squadron ratings and would ask Bob or myself to play bits and pieces to illustrate them. When darkness fell soon after 6 pm the evenings were long; and our faithful Chappell upright was nothing short of a godsend.

A promise of relief from the dubious joys of life in Ceylon flickered when a rumour spread that the ship's boilers were in need of major refit—and that it would be necessary to go to South Africa for the job to be carried out. Strangely enough, the fighter boys didn't exactly roll around the deck in ecstasy. In fact, Mike Tritton suggested to the Captain that we might be temporarily seconded to the RAF on the Burma front if the ship was to be off station for any length of time. We felt that concentrated operations up in the north would give us invaluable experience. Eventually the answer had to be 'No'. The problems of transporting squadrons and stores and of maintaining steady supplies of spares for our aircraft when we got there would be insuperable. We had to settle for South Africa. Perhaps, after all, a change from the sweaty, primitive charms of Trincomalee would do us no harm at all!

11

Interlude in South Africa

We sailed for South Africa on July 30, leaving behind us at China Bay Jimmy Clark, Matt Barbour, Ken Seebeck and Neil Brynildsen, all of whom were returning to New Zealand for leave. I myself was looking forward to a few weeks in a more temperate climate. Prickly heat was knocking hell out of me and it seemed that my tummy was occupied for most of its time in doing slow rolls.

Eventually, after brief calls at Addu Atoll and Diego Suarez, we arrived in Durban on August 9. We tied up alongside, refuelled and were away again by 1600. We were obviously in a hurry!

The weather now showed us what the Roaring Forties could do. Never had I seen such great seas or such an awesome swell. Despite the height of the flight-deck above water level, we were taking it green and some of the aircraft parked on deck suffered heavy punishment. Great fun, though! Two days later, off Cape Agulhas, the entire air group took off and flew to the naval air station at Wingfield, a few miles out of Cape Town. We were too large a force to be accommodated at Durban, so here we were for the next two to three months. Having disembarked our ratings, unloaded our spares and personal gear and made her farewells, *Illustrious* returned forthwith to Durban to get on with her boiler refit.

The first thing was leave. Within three days of our arrival, thanks to the magnificent and entirely unselfish work put in by the South African Women's Voluntary Service, all our ratings had been despatched on a fortnight's holiday, with all travelling expenses, accommodation and maintenance free; and aircrews on a longer leave of three weeks. South Africa welcomed us with open arms and her hospitality, already world-famous, knew no bounds. Fanny Forde, our Barracuda wing leader, had been there at some time earlier in the war and had an open invitation to stay with a family in Johannesburg. What was more, the invitation included a friend. He asked me to join him in spending our leave there and a telephone call fixed it up.

We spent 36 hours on the famous Blue Train, rising out of the Cape to the Great Karroo and steaming, hour after hour, across the wide, boundless veldt. During that wonderful train journey I saw for the first time wild ostriches speeding across the flat, featureless landscape with their amazingly fast trot.

At 8.30 in the morning of the third day we pulled into the main railway station of the City of Gold. For three happy weeks we lived the life of princes at the home of Eric and Kay Gallo, whose lovely house out at Sandhurst was laid wide open for our enjoyment. They were the finest of hosts. Never for one moment did they try to organise us, but whatever we wished was simply provided without a second thought. We had a wonderful time.

There were plenty of the lads spending their leave in Jo'burg. We ran into them in bars, in restaurants and in night spots. One afternoon I ran into Gus, quietly sinking a few beers.

'That was a lovely girl I saw you with last night at the Star Dust. Where on earth did you gather up sufficient influence to meet *her?*'

'Isn't she a pippin, Hans? Talk about a lovely face! Did you ever see anything like it? And what about that pair of tits? Legs too—haven't seen anything like it for years!' He paused to put away the bottom half of his glass of beer. 'Trouble is, she's such an old bag!'

I ran into Mick Ritchie in a night-club where we had gone with Eric and Kay. Mick was red-faced from the pressure being applied to his abdomen and chest by the arms of a beautiful Wren who wasn't the least bit ashamed to be seen making powerful advances to a great seduction. When the moment offered itself, I told Mick that I feared for his safety.

'But, by God! Mick, she's a lovely girl!'

'Yes. As a matter of fact, I met her at a private party an evening or two ago. She was with a big Pongo Captain then. Now I find her here with a couple of girls. I thought I'd better find out the score before going into action, so I asked her where the Field-Marshal was. "Oh! *Him*!" says she. "He's gone back to his unit. You know how it is—the King is dead—Long live the King!"'

Three weeks of hectic living passed all too quickly. It was a sad moment for me when I leaned out of the carriage window of the famous Blue Train to wave 'good-bye'. We had enjoyed a never-to-be-forgotten holiday whose happy memories took a long, long time to fade.

Life on the air station at Wingfield was luxurious after the confines of the ship and the primitive life ashore at China Bay. The sight of fresh fruit and vegetables; jugs of milk at every meal; unlimited butter; bread with not a trace of a weevil—all these appeared in endless profusion. South Africa, it seemed, was a bottomless cornucopia. And there was news. Terence Shaw, our Operations Commander, had left the ship, to the sorrow of every officer in the mess. He had been replaced by John Smallwood, who had decided to come to Wingfield to make our acquaintance rather than await our return to the ship. There was excitement for the squadrons, too. Our pilot complements were now to be increased to 20, with 18 aircraft; and as a result of the disbanding of 1838 Squadron, eight new boys now joined us: John ('Wong') Lee, a tall, good-looking lad from London; Ron Ayrton, a young man from Essex; Jimmy James, tall and cheerful, who enhanced the squadron considerably by virtue of his straight stripes; Jerry Morgan, a Canadian from Montreal; and four New Zealanders—Evan Baxter, Ben Heffer, Jack Parli and Adrian ('Winnie') Churchill.

Jack Parli and Winnie Churchill were highly experienced pilots and tough, hard-boiled characters. They were an asset to any fighting unit and were old enough and sufficiently stable to be good leaders. I had no hesitation in making them Flight Commanders. In view of the increased size of the squadron, I now decided that we could stand two senior pilots and I accordingly appointed Jack Parli to work alongside Keith Munnoch. I couldn't have done better.

Life, however, wasn't all beer and skittles. Minor troubles had to be attended to. When the ship was nearing South Africa, commanding officers of all squadrons had been given two memoranda to be read out, loud and clear, to their assembled units. The first one related to our general behaviour whilst in the Union. Apartheid was pretty hot stuff at that time and, to put it in a nutshell, we were warned that association with the black population would bring down coals of fire on our heads from the white community.

I have already told how excellent were the arrangements made by the WVS for leave to be given to our people. Three of my ratings went on two weeks' holiday to a private hotel in Cape Province, owned and managed by a widow of English origin. On their second night at the hotel, this dear lady heard unusual sounds in the early hours and, to her unspeakable horror, found my young men in bed with three young negresses of the hotel staff. She promptly handed them their return rail vouchers and sent them packing on the following morning.

The Captain punished them by denying them shore leave for the rest of their stay at Wingfield. A few days later they were in deeper trouble when it was found that their escapade had left them with a legacy of gonorrhoea. They paid dearly for their defiance in the face of express orders.

The other Admiralty Fleet Order promulgated at the same time concerned aircraft. The two main landing wheels of the Corsair were made of aluminium alloy and carried large tyres inflated to a pressure of 120 lb per square inch. To inflate these, our ratings used compressed air bottles of a pressure of 1,300 psi; not the sort of thing for children to play with. One rating—I think in _Victorious_—in recent weeks had inflated a tyre and had elected to guess its pressure rather than go to the trouble of fetching a pressure gauge. In fact, he had inflated the tyre to such a pressure that the wheel had broken in two under the strain. Half of it flew straight for his abdomen, cutting him neatly into two portions. Not surprisingly, he was very dead before he knew what had hit him. So the gipsy's warning went out—*don't blow up tyres without having a pressure gauge in hand.*

Some days after our return from leave, I was poking my nose around our hangar and the concrete apron surrounding it, where mechanics were servicing aircraft in the brilliant sunshine. As I ambled up to one of the aircraft, I saw a rigger on the point of wheeling away a light trolley carrying an air bottle. As he left the Corsair he kicked the tyre perfunctorily with the toe of his large Navy boot. He looked up and wished me 'Good-morning'.

'Good-morning to you,' I replied. I nodded down at the wheel. 'Tyre all right?'

'Yes, sir. OK now.'

'What's the pressure?'

'OK, sir.'

'I asked what the pressure was. What is it?'

He looked distinctly uncomfortable.

'120, sir.'

'Will you put the gauge on and check it for me, please?'

Now he looked *very* sorry for himself.

'You have a gauge, haven't you?'

'No, sir.'

'Then you must have very sensitive toes. Go to the store and get one, quick.'

In two minutes he was back, having signed for a gauge from stores. He handed it to me and I tested the tyre. I gave it back to him.

'*You* try it . . . What does it say?'

'200, sir.'

'That's what I made it. Tell your Petty Officer to bring you to my office in five minutes.'

I summoned RPO Turner to the office, too, and in five minutes the three of them were there. I reminded them of the AFO and of the day when I had read it out. Had they all been there? Yes. I looked at the rigger.

'Apart from the possibility of killing yourself, you obviously don't give a damn for Sub-Lieutenant Shaw's life. If that tyre had burst on landing and Mr Shaw had been killed, you would have murdered him just as surely as though you had put a bayonet through him. And we wouldn't have heard one bloody cheep out of *you*.' I thought for a moment. I would have preferred to put the whole thing in the hands of

Commander Wallis, but he was in the ship, far away in Durban. I looked at Turner, then back to the culprit.

'I don't know how long we shall be here, but you have seen the last of Cape Town. Your PO will watch you like a hawk from this moment. Any more slackness or sheer bloody laziness like this and you will face Captain Lambe the minute we get aboard the ship again. Now go.'

To be fair, it must be said that the great majority of the maintenance ratings did a fine, honest job, usually under very trying circumstances. The fact that so many of us survived is a great tribute to their skill and devotion to their jobs.

Not long after the new intake of pilots had joined us, I was looking through my office window when I saw Jerry Morgan leading out a flight for take-off.

Jerry, a Lieutenant RCNVR, was a short, slim lad who had already created an impression of being somewhat on the cocky side. He had been heard to say that he could 'fly the crates they come in'—a typical fighter-boy's line-shooting comment, to be sure; but, taken in conjunction with his short stature, we had put two and two together. So I was interested to see how he shaped as a pilot.

As Flight Commander he took off first; and in a manner too nearly suicidal for comfort. He held down the nose long after gaining flying speed, raised the undercarriage and took off in a screaming turn to port with the wingtip no more than a foot or two from the grass until he reached the perimeter when he pulled up, still in a sharp turn.

It should, perhaps, be explained that piston-engined aircraft of those far-off days had a nasty, if rare, habit of cutting-out on take-off, a crucial time in any flight. (To be honest, I never heard of this happening to a Corsair.) This could happen if the engine had not been thoroughly warmed up before take-off; if water or moisture had got at the petrol; or if there was a sudden failure of the ignition system. There could be many reasons. Graveyards near airfields contain the bones of many a pilot whose engine has died on take-off, for generally this means death. Many pilots have attempted to glide back to the airfield but few, if any, have ever made it. The one hope of survival is to hold a straight course and ease her into the ground. If you're heading for a racecourse, a golf course, a lake—or even a stretch of motorway—you'll live. On the other hand, if the nose is pointing inevitably at the Albert Hall, the centre of Wakefield or Winchester Cathedral, you're a dead duck. This is why a pupil under training is taught to climb straight out of a field and turn only when he has sufficient height to give him room to manoeuvre should the worst happen.

Morgan's take-off was contrary to all the laws of survival. I told him so in no uncertain terms when he landed. There was no particular

174

CARRIER PILOT

objection to suicide, I said, but to put at risk the lives of innocent people working in the admin buildings which he had only just scraped over on his take-off was unforgivable. So—'don't bloody well do it again!'

True to form, he chose to ignore the warning; and two days later he imitated his first effort, possibly even more spectacularly. Who he was trying to impress I don't know; his squadron chums, the Wrennery or himself.

I ran to my aircraft and called him up on the R/T. When I ordered him peremptorily to land, he started to argue. Cutting him short, I told him that if he uttered one more word I would come up and 'bloody well shoot him down'. (Shades of Eric Monk!)

Ten minutes later he landed. I grabbed him by the arm and dragged him into the office. Full of protests and indignation, he pushed his Lieutenant's stripes at me. This I ignored and grounded him for a fortnight. This hurt him, for he loved flying as much as the rest of us. When he chose to remonstrate, I added insult to injury by committing him to be duty boy for the same period. This certainly went in deeply, for he was very conscious of his rank.

He stormed out, hating my guts. As he closed the door I muttered to myself—'Now *that* should stop you, my boy!'

But it didn't.

One night during the week following our return from leave, eight of us emerged from a film in Cape Town about 10.30 pm, ready for something to eat. We were a voracious lot and ready to tackle any of the marvellous food which South Africa put before us. I spoke to a policeman on his beat and he suggested a night-club, just round the corner.

It was a comfortable spot. Nothing pretentious, but chummy and inviting. A few couples were dancing to a seven-piece band under subdued lighting. The waiter suggested ham sandwiches and beer which appealed to all present.

Later, when presented with the bill, my hair stood on end. Food and drink were cheap in the Union but, even allowing for the usual 'stick-on' encountered in any night-club, this was ridiculous. I handed it silently to Jack Parli who was sitting beside me.

Jack was a large young man, of average height but thick-set and all muscle. He had shoulders like Joe Louis. He whistled under his raised eyebrows.

'Christ, boss! You're surely not paying *that*?'

I assured him that I had no intention of doing so. I would see the manager. Jack asked if he could accompany me.

The manager was a large, unhealthy-looking mountain of flabby flesh who didn't impress us at all. He bore the look of a man who spent all his life indoors and who slept at the wrong end of the day. I showed him the bill and told him what we had consumed. Without any aggression, I assured him that I had no intention of paying it in its present state.

He shrugged his shoulders.

'You pay it or I call the cops.'

So I tried gentle blackmail. There was over 100 of us out at Wingfield, many of whom would be finding girl-friends and would need somewhere for food and drink. If he were reasonable and played ball with us, he would make a bomb. But he didn't see it my way. Pay or else.

Jack spoke up.

'Mind if I say a word, boss?' I told him to go ahead. 'It's like this. What the boss really means, though you don't see it, is this: alter the bill now or call in the decorators first thing in the morning.'

The bill was halved before our very eyes. Marvellous! I hadn't realised what great psychologists New Zealanders were!

The manager never regretted it. He made his fortune out of us.

The Union of South Africa had contributed magnificently to the funds of the Navy League and was still doing so at the time of our visit. The Captain suggested that we might put on an Air Day for the inhabitants of Cape Town and that an admission charge would raise quite a stack as donations to the League's funds.

Fanny, Michael and I got down to it. The bombers put on a show over the airfield, the fighters carried out some aerobatics, singly and in formation; our aircraft were on view and officers and ratings were on hand to explain things and to answer questions. Finally, we rounded off the afternoon with a simulated strike on the airfield. We arranged that the Barracudas' attack would be prefaced by a ground strafe by 16 Corsairs. Churchill, Cole, Sutton and I would lead four flights of four in quick succession across the field.

My one worry was Churchill, for Winnie was a mad sod.

'Winnie: one run—then get the hell out of it. I'll be only seconds behind you and I don't want you cluttering up the field. Get in and get out—as far as Cape Town if you like.'

All went famously. We were in the right place at the right time and Bud Sutton was just clearing the field as we swept in from the north at about 300 knots. We were low, too—down to ten to 15 feet.

At the far end, beyond the airfield's perimeter track, was a sports area with rugby goalposts. Beyond that a road; and across that, appropriately enough, a cemetery. I was just about to lift over the goalposts when four Corsairs appeared over the cemetery well spread out, low and fast and coming straight at us. Churchill. How on earth we missed each other I shall never know. At a collision speed of 600 knots you have no time to think, worry or dodge. Certainly you have no time to hope.

The audience loved it. They thought it marvellous—'and so well-timed!'

'You crazy bastard!' I said to Winnie, when I had torn him off a strip. 'You'll do that once too often!'

Neither of us knew how prophetic that was.

The ship sent down to us a couple of Franks' flying suits. They were the most amazing contraptions both in appearance and construction, but there was no doubt that their concept was brilliant. When a fast-flying aircraft is pulled sharply out of a dive or, if flying in the horizontal plane, pulled into a steep turn, both it and its pilot are subjected to increasing forces of gravity. When the sharp turn or drastic pull-out comes, the tendency is for the blood in the human body to rush downwards because of sheer centrifugal force—in other words, towards the outside of the turn. Blood from the head and upper parts of the body rushes to the legs and lower parts. Furthermore, the weight of the body increases in direct proportion to the number of G forces imposed.

A pilot's first intimation of the oncoming force of G is a greying-out of vision and hearing ability. An increased application of G produces black-out. Vision goes completely, the sense of hearing is reduced still further and the weight of arms, legs and thighs becomes uncannily and incredibly increased. It becomes impossible to lift one's hands from throttle lever or joystick, or one's feet from the rudder pedals. Yet one can still fly and is reasonably conscious.

The next stage is complete unconsciousness. Probably Nature takes over then, to provide its own remedy by relaxing the pilot's tensions and thereby allowing the aircraft to emerge, even though slightly, to a less acute turning arc.

This Franks flying suit was designed to postpone the moment of black-out which hits every pilot subjected to six or six and a half times the force of G. The effective force varies according to the individual, but generally between those two points.

The suit encased the abdomen and legs into an almost unbearably tight pair of trousers which, of double-thickness gabardine, held an enclosed bladder containing two gallons of water. As the force of G caused the blood to try to rush to the thighs and legs, this great amount of water rushed downwards before the blood could get around to it and held the blood vessels of the lower part of the body to their normal dimensions. It exerted sufficient pressure to prevent their dilation, thereby ensuring that the blood remained in the upper part of the body.

177

I rigged myself out in this complicated outfit one morning, under the eye of Commander (Operations) at whose orders I was to carry out these tests. My Corsair had been specially equipped with an accelerometer which would show me precisely what forces of gravity I would be imposing. I flew well out into Table Bay and carried out some pretty hair-raising dives and high-speed turns at over 300 knots. Our resident Chance Vought engineer had expressed an opinion that a force of 9G would cause the Corsair's wings and fuselage to part company; a viewpoint which, naturally, deterred me from trying to pull to 10G! However, there was no point in half-doing the job; and I found that I could go to 8G without the slightest suggestion of even a 'grey-out'.

At 8G the effect was comical—if one is capable of seeing the funny side. The cheeks of my face were drawn downwards to give a grotesque appearance which I didn't recognise as the thing I was accustomed to scraping daily with a razor. My ears were elongated to something approaching a spaniel's. I had at that time a small partial upper denture. This was forced down on to my tongue with such power that it was impossible for me to budge it. The whole of my body was plunged down into the seat with a devastating force and my arms and legs—now eight times their normal weight—were utterly immovable. But I didn't black out!

When we eventually rejoined the carrier, more experiments were carried out by all of us. The suit, however, despite the fact that it achieved its purpose, was never put into general use for we felt that, where deck-landing was concerned, it was more of a hindrance than a help. In spite of sophisticated instrumentation, a pilot still derived enormous help and comfort from the seat of his pants. The sensations transmitted from the aircraft through his rear end told him a lot before his instruments could. That confounded bladder, which caused the pilot to sit on a small lake instead of the hard base to which he was accustomed, was his undoing; the seat of his pants was no longer there to help him.

I have given some account of the blotting of copybooks here and there. It was towards the end of our sojourn at the Cape that I blotted my own.

It appears that one Mynheer van Reebeck founded a victualling station at Cape Town for the Du h East India Company as far back as 1652 and South Africa has treated the date of his arrival in that wonderful Bay as a public holiday ever since. So, on the 292nd anniversary I gave a day's leave to three parts of the squadron. With nothing else in the world to do and if only to give myself an appetite for lunch, I agreed with PO Vincent to test-fly my machine on which he had just replaced the propeller oil seal.

It was a day made for flying. Cape Province basked in the morning sunshine and all was well with the world—and with me. As I headed for home I found myself passing over Retreat, the rural area where Nick Loew lived. He was a wealthy Boer who owned a beautiful estate, handed down through his family from the early 18th century, where he grew vines, made wine and bred hunters. Fanny Forde and I had spent a weekend there with him a week or two back, when he had complained that he had seen nothing of these wonderful aircraft we had at Wingfield. This seemed to be as good a time as any to rectify that omission. I had no difficulty in finding his house; and there, standing by the side of the swimming pool, was Nick himself, waving madly.

Still full of zest and the joy of living, I treated him to his own private low-flying display, rounding off with a sequence of aerobatics. My exuberance was short-lived. When I landed, our new Commander (Operations), John Smallwood, awaited me, with puffs of steam rising from his collar. I tried a bit of straight-faced flannelling, but John was too clever for that and in no time at all I was standing before Captain Farquhar (whom I had known earlier in the war at St Merryn—regrettably only slightly, for he was an affable and most gentlemanly soul).

It must be said that we were having trouble getting used to John Smallwood's ways. Obviously as a new broom he felt constrained to sweep clean. His manipulation of the broom seemed a little energetic after Terence Shaw's gentle approach to life. What was more, mutual understanding hadn't been particularly encouraged when, after an interesting lunchtime session, Johnny Hastings—possibly with a view to participating in the next Olympic Games—had seen fit to throw a plank at him, to the accompaniment of rousing cheers. The fact that he missed was neither here nor there.

Still, I couldn't blame John for carpeting me. He had no alternative, for he was taking his instructions from no less than the Chief of Staff of C-in-C South Atlantic, to whom my low-flying jolly had been reported by General I. P. de Villiers, GOC all forces in the Union of South Africa. The complaint was that whilst I had been busy flying through Nick Loew's back garden, I had been giving similar treatment to the General's. This was no doubt true, although it must be said that, if the General's house was where Johnny Smallwood said it was, I had at least been very careful not to hit it. The heat was on. It was to be a court martial and nothing less.

The Captain, therefore, was obliged to confine me to the station, but he generously staved off John's demand that my wine-bill should also be stopped.

The days wore on. Rumour had it that the court martial had already been named and that the hearing was only a matter of days away. Smallwood said that I should lose no time in finding myself a 'prisoner's friend'. I could see myself behind bars already and didn't enjoy the sensation. However, I had to get on with it. The best person I could think of was Ian Sarel, whom I felt sure could be relied upon to say nice things about me. I rang him up in Durban. He called me a lot of extremely rude names, but asked me to let him know as soon as I had further information. He would hold himself in readiness to come. I felt depressed and very angry with myself. On the other hand, I hadn't killed anyone, nor had I damaged any property. I tried to believe that nothing too drastic could happen to me.

On the following evening I was sitting alone at the wardroom bar. All the lads had long since flown to the bright lights of Cape Town. I was taking it very gently, sipping like an old lady, when the Captain came in. He gave me a cheery 'Good-evening, Hanson!', insisted on refilling my glass and took a neighbouring bar-stool.

'A bad business this, Hanson—very bad. And I don't like the way things are going. What does Captain Lambe think about it?'

'When he hears about it, sir, he'll be madder than hell—and I won't blame him for that.'

Captain Farquhar put down his drink and stared at me.

'Do you mean you haven't told him?'

'No, I haven't. I don't know the drill for this sort of thing and thought that you or Smallwood would have reported it to *Illustrious*'.

'Heavens above! And I had been thinking all along that you would have been in touch with them! I must get on to this right away. We haven't a moment to lose!'

He knocked back his drink and ran. It must have been the best part of an hour before he returned. He was smiling—a good sign, I thought.

'I think there's an even chance we might just scrape you out of this. I managed to get a telex through to your Captain and here's his reply. I can't show all of it to you'—he folded the paper and handed it to me—'but you may read the last two lines.' What it said was—'Above all, tell Hans not to worry. Everything will be all right.'

I was overjoyed. We had had no time at all as yet to get to know our new Captain, but there were indications that he could turn out to be as fine a man as his predecessor. At any rate, he wasn't going to have me thrown to the wolves.

'I'll see you tomorrow.' The Captain was off.

We drove down to Cape Town at 1100 on the following day. On the way, the Captain put me wise.

'It's all right. It's as good as over. Captain Lambe suggested the course of action. There was no point in trying to tell Staff to run away and forget it. They are hell-bent on giving you the works. It seems that the South African boys have been doing quite a lot of nuisance low-flying recently and a decision had been taken that the next case would be made into a stormer. You happen to be that case. Instead, he told me to see the General. I came down early and had a long chat with him. As I—and Captain Lambe—thought, the crux of the whole thing is that the General doesn't realise fully what a Naval court martial can do to you: you could lose your squadron and your half-stripe; and you could be returned to UK, more or less in disgrace, to spend the rest of the war stooging. A complete waste of a man who can do better things. When I told him this he was appalled. All he wanted was that your backside should be kicked and it looks as though this is what you will escape with. He has, in any case, assured me that he will not give evidence at the court martial.'

We reached GHQ. Admiral Burnett, a seadog with a large red face who could have eaten me as a second course, made very short work of me. There wasn't a lot left of me as I made my way out. My hand was on the door knob when he said:

'Just one thing, Hanson.' He was speaking more quietly now and there was the suspicion of a grin on that large, red face. 'Next time you go low-flying, please be a good chap and take the trouble to find out who lives next door. Save us all a lot of trouble!'

They're all just big, bouncing boys at heart! I then thanked the Captain for all he had done for me.

'You're not finished yet. You owe the General an apology. After all, he's the one to whom you really owe your escape.'

So we went along to the General. I went in alone. General de Villiers was a great man. He was of the same vintage as Smuts and had served with him in the Boer War, leading his own commando against the British. He was a great gentleman as well as a great soldier.

'Come and sit down, my boy! Would you like a drink, eh?'

'Thank you sir; but it's a bit early.'

'Really! I understood you Navy chaps drank at any time!'

Then we talked about it.

I tried to tell him that low-flying was our job and our life. But I didn't pursue it. It was evident that he thought all flying machines were unsure things. I was more than a little touched because, despite the fact that my misdemeanour had caused him no little concern, he had been more worried about my own personal safety than anything else. He was marvellous and we parted the best of friends.

When I emerged at length, I took a deep breath and told the Captain I felt a new man. He just grinned and drove me back to the station.

I celebrated my acquittal by going to a film in Cape Town with five or six friends. Later we dropped into our regular night-club for a sandwich and a beer. We hadn't been there long before the club hostess, Sophie, drifted across to greet us. She was a cheery soul and readily sat down to accept a drink. After two or three more, she declared herself to be in the mood; and surveyed the faces around the table with a look of confident expectancy.

Now Sophie was about 35 and a fine mountain of a woman, of enormous proportions. I would have said that Sophie was on a loser from the start. She wasn't just fat. The blubber hung from her in folds and was scarcely restrained by a black evening gown which bulged ominously and terrifyingly from neck to ankle. There was a silence of utter disbelief, broken only when one of our young doctors spoke up:

'What you need, Sophie, in that condition is a good doctor to give you the once-over. Where's the examination room?'

Sophie stood up without a word and they disappeared. She had a flat on the top floor.

Doc reappeared some time later. He resumed his seat and started in on another half-pint of beer.

'Remarkable woman, Sophie,' he said. 'Wonderfully manoeuvrable for someone of her displacement. Handles really quite well at all revs.'

We were lost in admiration.

Thanks to some excellent organisation by Steve Starkey, we threw a party for the squadron at the Kelvin Grove. It was a night for the ratings to sit back and enjoy themselves, with the officers taking care of the chores. They had managed to muster an incredible number of females and the amount of food and drink consumed was staggering. Everybody had a thoroughly good evening.

Later, not unexpectedly, some of the kids took decisive steps to develop acquaintances they had made during the party. Evan Baxter, one of our new pilots, seemed to have proved himself a worthy successor to Ken Boddington and Dicky Cork in the field of womanising and had a track record which left Casanova very much in the amateur class, with L-plates back and front and egg on his face. He had found himself a pretty little number at the party and had danced with her for the entire evening. With true hospitality, he was invited to spend the night with her. He needed no second invitation. In order to be back aboard the ship (now returned to us from Durban) he asked the girl to set an alarm for 0700. They beat the alarm to the draw and pressed the button before all hell was let loose. Evan kissed his girl-friend—'See you tonight at seven'—and made for the bedroom door. His hand was on the handle.

'Don't make a noise going through there. You have to cross Mother's room to get out. She wouldn't mind at all, but it's too early to awaken her.'

Bax was made of stern stuff and his experience was infinite, despite his tender years and cherubic face. His various campaigns had been fraught with similar difficulties. He went into his drill. Off came his shoes, the laces were tied together and the whole affair slung round his neck. He was off.

By the faint morning light filtering through the curtains he could see the exit door on the far side of Mama's room. When he reached it, he hesitated: 'Must just have a look at Ma before I go.' Her fair hair was strewn seductively over the pillow. Beside it, a gentle wheeze issuing from its open mouth, reclined the happy face of one of his Kiwi chums. Evan was at his side like a shot.

'Come on, you snoring bastard! Thirty-five minutes is all that's left between you and the rattle! Get a jerk on!'

Father, it seemed, had been captured at Tobruk and was now languishing in some lousy Italian POW camp. Mother just had to have her creature comforts.

As Neil Brynildsen would have said: 'War can be cruel 'ard!'

As I said, *Illustrious* had now come back for us. She was ploughing through heavy seas around the Cape when, at 0800 on October 13, we took off from Wingfield to have our first look at her for two months. The weather was glorious, with an azure sky and not a cloud to be seen, although the 'white horses' out on the open sea gave us a pretty good idea of what the Roaring Forties were up to again! We renewed acquaintance with our shipmates by flying the air group in a spectacular tight formation over the ship. Our 36 fighters were in six columns of six, flying in line astern. They looked marvellous and their accurate drill was a pleasure to see. As we crossed the ship from stern to bow I was lucky enough to spot a greyish-white plume falling in a windswept arc from Bud Sutton's aircraft, leading one of the columns.

'Bud! You're losing all your oil! Get down quick!'

More luck was to come—and efficiency. The ship was heading into the teeth of a half-gale. She must have heard my urgent R/T call, for I saw a batsman running down to his position on the flight-deck. Bud, too, behaved with admirable promptitude. He didn't question my call but fell out of formation like a stone, at the same time confirming to the ship that he was coming in for an emergency landing. He made the deck safely and was taxiing forward when his engine packed in completely. The main oil union, from the supply system to the engine—the engine's aorta, if you like—had parted; and Bud had made it in the nick of time. Whether or not my good fortune in spotting the leak had been instrumental in saving Bud's life I don't know. If it had, I fear it was all in vain, for our great Canadian chum was to die in any event within four months.

We flew back to Wingfield, had lunch and refuelled. In mid-afternoon we returned to *Illustrious,* now round to False Bay, and landed on. The wind was so fierce that she had to reduce to six knots—just sufficient to give her steerage way—while we had to turn in to the deck when abreast of the bows instead of the stern, which was or usual pattern. We docked in Cape Town at 1700 and loaded our squadron ratings, bags and baggage and spares during that evening.

12

Now there were four of us

Soon after we left Cape Town *en route* for Ceylon, the weather worsened and our met officer, Norman 'Schooly' Jenkins, began to look thoughtful. It seemed that a typhoon lay ahead of us, astride the Equator. Its position was foxing, for he couldn't decide whether it would turn out to be a 'north' or a 'south'. They have different patterns, according to which side of the Equator they occur. We spent two days and nights trying to dodge it, but it won in the end and on October 26 it hit us with all the force of Nature gone stark, staring mad. It continued to hammer us for three days and I have no desire to experience another. Everything about it was terrifying. The sky, for one thing, was a dull, yellow blanket that covered us from one horizon to the other. The wind: we had 115 knots blowing down the flight-deck. The seas: from my cabin, down aft near the stern of the ship, the waves could be heard hitting the bows like the blows of a sledge-hammer. The ship's speed was pulled down to the minimum, just sufficient to keep her head into wind. We crawled along and took fearful punishment. The sailors up in the forepart were sick in their hundreds; and, as no one could possibly survive on the weather-decks, a breath of fresh air was out of the question. Our deck-park of 14 aircraft required continual vigilance and sailors were held by lifelines as they moved gingerly from the island on to the deck to fix and check extra lashings. The wind was actually turning the propellers of these aircraft—and that against the compression of 18 cylinders! Everyone had to use the starboard passage to reach the island and to stand on the compass platform was an awesome experience. Outside was a mad, mad world of elements gone crazy, where the noise of the wind was that of the endless high-pitched whistle of a steam locomotive.

On the evening of the third day the sky began to clear. Next morning we had sunshine, although the sea still retained its gigantic, terrifying swell. Two off-duty Petty Officers, sitting on the forward round-down in the agreeable sunshine after being so depressingly cooped up in the bowels of the ship, were swept away by a gigantic wave of 50 or 60 feet. One was never seen again. The other one, luckier, fetched up in the forward starboard gun turrets with broken ribs and limbs.

By the next day we were flying again and once more making good progress towards Ceylon which, after another short call at Addu Atoll, we reached on November 1. As we sailed into China Bay, we found the battleships *King George V* and *Howe* lying at anchor—and what an imposing spectacle they made! We refuelled and sailed again in the afternoon. *Illustrious* was sailing for Colombo and, as she rounded the southern coast of the island, my squadron flew off to land at an RAF station at Koggala, near Galle, there to learn fighter-bombing. It was a wild spot. Dense jungle covered the whole area apart from the clearings which accommodated the Station. About half a mile inland was a large lagoon, on which reposed a squadron of Sunderland flying-boats. The jungle, which came right up to the doors of the huts, harboured everything that flew or crawled; and the lagoon was the home of countless crocodiles of the extra large variety. A very homely spot!

There was one runway strip which stretched from the lagoon to the sea. The RAF squadron had no aircraft other than their big boats, so we were fortunate to have the exclusive use of the runway. Around the airstrip stood a collection of basha huts which housed the personnel.

Despite the primitive conditions under which the RAF lived and worked, they couldn't have been more friendly and hospitable. Group Captain Francis made us more than welcome and only once did I see his sangfroid slightly dented. Ronnie Hay (Lieutenant-Colonel R. C. Hay, Royal Marines, Air Group Co-ordinator in *Victorious*) must have been in a happy, care-free mood one morning. Francis and I were standing at the inland end of the runway, where he was regaling me with a short but friendly homily on the sins of low flying. (I was accumulating quite a collection of these!) Suddenly a Corsair appeared over the edge of the jungle, very low indeed and going like the clappers. He nipped down the runway, barely inches above the concrete, and disappeared out to sea, soon lost in the morning haze.

'Good God in heaven! Well, I'll be damned! That one of your boys, Hanson?'

'No, sir.' This was true.

'Any idea who it was?'

'No, sir.' This was a downright lie. 'I didn't get his number.' This was back to half-truth, for I *had* seen 'RCH' emblazoned loud and clear on the fuselage; and if Ronnie wanted to pay us a social call, it would have been extremely churlish on my part if I had let the cat out!

The livestock around the living quarters was hostile enough to persuade everybody to carry a stout stick when walking along the paths between the lush grass; and every officer additionally carried a

.38 revolver. Cobras, kraits and Russell's vipers were regarded as being especially inimical. Because of the intense heat, the whole station took a siesta from lunch until 3.30 or 4 pm and one day an RAF pilot pulled back the sheets, to be greeted with a most unfriendly hiss from a cobra which reared itself hurriedly and angrily at being disturbed. The rightful owner of the bed retreated two paces, drew his revolver and, miracle of miracles, shot it through its spread-out hood. Since it was hit at point-blank range, just about everybody got a piece. The .38 shell, too, passed through a fair number of living quarters before settling.

To learn fighter-bombing, we dropped 11½ lb practice bombs on specified targets out in the thick jungle. These were no more than a few minutes from Koggala, so the flights were of very short duration, with the boys maintaining a steady shuttle service. I had dropped only a few on the unsuspecting flora and fauna when I was whipped into hospital with foot trouble which was to plague me for the rest of my life. One evening as I lay upon my bed of pain, reading a nine-week-old *Daily Telegraph*, Keith Munnoch came in. He was wearing an expression which I knew was bringing bad tidings.

'Evening, Bash. Nice of you to drop in.'

'Er . . . ?'

'Who is it, Keith?'

'Jerry Morgan, Hans.'

I looked at him. 'Not . . . ?' I went through the motions with my hands.

'Just like that. Just like you said he would when we were at Cape Town.'

Rogers had returned from dropping a stick of bombs. While the armourers reloaded the racks, Morgan climbed into the cockpit with the engine still ticking over. Munnoch assured me that, although it sounded rather like a romantic novel, the truth was that, as Morgan left a ring of pilots to walk to the Corsair, he had turned to them with his parting shot:

'Just watch this for a wizard take-off!'

They were his last words on earth. He had held the aircraft on its brakes while opening up to full throttle and had then completed one of his suicidal take-offs, barely off the runway and out to sea. *This* time, during his steep turn, he had pulled on the stick that millimetre too much—and that's all it takes. He stalled and slid gracefully into the Indian Ocean.

I found it difficult to understand. Many pilots killed themselves in accidents, many of them foolhardy. Errors of judgment blossomed as the green bay tree, but to throw away one's life in a manoeuvre which was so patently a killer was something beyond my comprehension. If we meet again in the next world, Jerry might expound a little more lucidly.

It was good to be back aboard *Illustrious* after a few weeks—although I was not yet fit for general duties. The only excitement I seem to have missed was a spectacularly bad barrier crash by Reg Shaw. This lad was beginning to live dangerously!

Indomitable had arrived shortly before we left for South Africa and had been flagship, with Rear-Admiral Moody aboard, during our absence. Together with *Vic* she had undertaken some operations against the enemy-held Nicobar Islands, in the Bay of Bengal, and certain targets in Sumatra. Soon we would be joined by *Indefatigable*; then we would be four, the complete striking force of the new British Pacific Fleet, with Philip Vian of *Cossack* fame as RAA. He was already in Ceylon, waiting to take over his command.

Now our Barracudas left us for good, to be replaced by the Avengers of 854 Squadron; machines with a better top speed and a much greater range. The aircraft we wouldn't be sorry to lose, but their crews were a different matter. Fanny Forde and his boys were as integral a part of the ship as her rivets and their departure was an occasion for sadness.

Vian wasn't long in getting us down to work. We went to sea with him on exercise, when the new Avengers did a dummy strike on the ship for him. We, too, showed our paces, with an escort for the Avengers and some frighteningly realistic strafing attacks on all the ships in company, firing live ammunition just over their heads. News gravitated down the grapevine that the great man was pleased with us. I think our Captain, who by now had won all our hearts, was even more pleased to discover how pleased Vian was!

Three days later, in company with *Indomitable* as flagship and our usual friends, we sailed on an operation. The objective was Pangkalan Brandan, an oil refinery in north-eastern Sumatra, about eight miles inland from the Malacca Straits. Between us we provided 28 Avengers, 16 Hellcats and 12 Corsairs. Additionally we took along four Corsairs, each armed with two 500 lb bombs, if only to show that we hadn't been wasting our time at Kogalla.

It was five more shopping days to Christmas; and a lousy time of year for weather off the Asian coast. We took off at 0630 into weather in which no self-respecting householder would have put out the cat. Doc Stuart, *Indomitable*'s bomber wing leader and strike leader on this occasion, had the unenviable job of taking us there; and I wasn't the least bit surprised when we ended up by milling around in the clouds like London Transport buses in a thick fog. Not that I blamed Doc for one moment. No one without the aid of radar could have led us straight to that confounded oil refinery.

After some minutes of hanging around and the expenditure of some fruity language, Doc rightly decided that the coast might provide better weather. He accordingly pushed off the few miles to the east. He was right—though it wasn't much better. There was still a lot of cloud at varying levels, but sufficiently clear to see Belawan Deli, an oil outlet port, on which we duly vented our spleen. We strafed anything worth hitting and some of our fighters—either lost or frustrated—attacked the airfield at nearby Medan, with moderate success.

The operation had been singularly uninteresting, but the return more than compensated. I like to think that Doc knew what was going on, for I am sure that the rest of us hadn't a clue. The utter abandonment of all R/T discipline caused unbelievable confusion. I latched myself on to a group of Avengers which, I assured myself, I was now escorting. In reality, I was hoping that their navigators would lead me back to the Fleet, for there were moments when I began to wonder precisely how far from—or how near to!—Singapore we were! These lads immediately dived for the sea, taking me rather reluctantly with them. We burst through low cloud to sea level, where I was horrified to see the whole gaggle of the strike flying in circles in about 200 feet of air space. Eventually we set course to rejoin the Fleet to the north of Sumatra and, on instructions radioed by the Admiral's staff, sent in two flights to attack whatever they could find on Sabang airfield as we passed abeam of it.

It must have been about lunchtime on the following day before I realised what a field-day a handful of enterprising Jap fighters could have enjoyed in the midst of that mêlée!

Christmas came, with all the traditional naval trimmings. One of the ship's boys toured the mess-decks, adorned in Captain Lambe's cap and reefer jacket. We served Christmas dinner to the ratings of our squadron and sang a few carols with them. In the afternoon the Fleet held a regatta. The highlight which I recall most clearly was the officers' whaler race. *Victorious* was tipped to win, so something clearly had to be done about it. At the crucial moment, as the starter was raising his pistol to fire, Jack Parli very adroitly swam beneath the favourite's boat and dislodged the bung. The *Vic*'s officers started to pull away with water already surging round their ankles. Alas! It was too much of an anticlimax when the starter realised what had happened, stopped them in their tracks and ordered a re-start.

We had a good party in the evening with no end of entertainment. Our acting fraternity produced a one-act Noel Coward play. Churchill and Parli staged one of their sensational wrestling shows. And, of course, there were songs. Bob Eddison rose to the occasion with a new song—*Penelope Prang*—which brought the house down.

I'm Penelope Prang,
And I don't give a hang
What they do to me when I'm on the booster;
But they *still*
Get a thrill
From that joystick, my dear;
And caress it
And press it
Without any fear;
Till I'm really quite chokka
When *up* goes my rear!
Crash! Bang!
Penelope Prang!

Elsewhere, too, there were fun and games. Some high spirited character from *Victorious* swam down to *King George V* and removed all her boats from the booms to tow them quietly down to *Vic*. Later that evening *Vic*'s OOD, who had patently entered a shade too enthusiastically into the spirit of Christmas, was surprised to see a middle-aged gentleman in swimming trunks emerge from the Stygian darkness of China Bay on to his gang-plank and climb the ladder to the port gangway. Having shaken off most of the water like a great Labrador, he then addressed himself to the OOD—naturally RNVR!—with a polite request that his boats might be returned. The OOD countered with an alcoholic, peremptory 'And who the hell are you?'

The dripping gentleman retained his composure.

'The captain of *KG-V*.'

Not unexpectedly, this brought forth a great guffaw and the classic reply—'And I'm fucking Napoleon!'

When the bather quietly stuck to his guns, the OOD adjourned to the wardroom to find the Commander, who lost no time in reaching the gangway. There he stiffened to attention, tearing off a smart salute and 'Good evening, sir!' Seizing a moment, he turned to his unfortunate subordinate and hissed—'He *is*, too, you bloody fool!'

The Captain was thereupon made welcome, suitably dried off, refreshed and returned to his ship along with his boats. Whilst all this was going on, someone else had taken the opportunity to steal *Victorious*' boats, which was funnier still!

Indefatigable turned up at Christmas and a week later Vian led the Fleet to sea again, this time fully determined that the air strike should find and destroy Pangkalan Brandan. When we heard that the job was to be done by *Indomitable*, *Indefatigable* and *Victorious*—without *Illustrious*—our indignation knew no bounds. Quite unfairly, we wondered what Vian was doing, leaving at anchor the only carrier that knew its stuff? He was taking a gang of sprogs: Avengers who couldn't find their target, fighters with no discipline who abandoned their charges without the slightest compunction and aircrews who obviously found it impossible to maintain radio silence. And, mark you, we were talking about our *friends*! But on such lines did our conceit run. Some kind person—I cannot believe it was genuine—let go the buzz that RAA had decided to leave us behind 'because we were too good—it was the others who needed the experience'. True or not, it soothed gullible souls like me and removed most of the scowls.

As a matter of fact, the operation was a great success, thanks to much improved weather and a thundering good job done by the boys of the three air groups.

13

Palembang

With the British Pacific Fleet now in being, we were ready to sail for Australia. Their Lordships had looked forward to the Fleet's appearance in Australian waters on New Year's Day 1945 but the late arrival of several ships had rendered this impossible. The aim was now the end of January.

After some heart-searching, Their Lordships had decided that the Fleet would strike at Palembang *en route* for Sydney. This great complex of oil refineries, reputedly the greatest and most productive available to the enemy outside Japan itself, was a tough nut to crack; and there were those in Whitehall who thought the Fleet—and the carrier squadrons in particular—too green and not yet sufficiently practised to tackle it. The two great refineries—Pladjoe and Soengei Gerong—lay astride a river flowing into Banka Strait, on the east coast of Sumatra. The air strike would have to cross 150 miles of high mountain ranges and dense jungle to reach it. Fighter strength in Sumatra was by no means lacking, for it was known to be an important training ground for pilots whose instructors—experienced airmen from their carriers—would be sure to take the air against us. The inestimable value of the target to the Japanese was calculated to bring into action their full force of interceptors. Lack of oil, however, was now a major headache to the Japanese War Cabinet; and the destruction of Palembang, high on the list of priority targets, was finally deemed to be important enough to warrant all the risks involved.

We had time for one big dress rehearsal. On January 13 1945 we were steaming around the Indian Ocean to the east of Ceylon, carrying out day-long attacks on the island. Our four carriers worked like demons. Colombo and Trincomalee suffered heavy simulated attacks from Avengers and Fireflies, escorted by Corsairs and Hellcats; and every airfield in the island was subjected to ceaseless ground-strafing by swarms of fighters. The Navy's shore-based squadrons and RAF fighters were up in strength to do battle with us. The air was full of planes from dawn to dusk, yet miraculously there were no collisions. Each with three or four sorties under our belts, we were dog-tired by the end of the afternoon.

Around 1530 the Fleet stood in towards China Bay and by 1630 the last flights were landing on. Four flights of us collected in the area astern of the carrier, waiting for her to turn yet again into wind. Landing commenced. One or two Corsairs were safely on the deck when Graham-Cann approached the round-down. Normally a safe and dependable deck-lander, he made a bit of a mess of this one and drifted up the deck, failing to catch a wire. He hit the first barrier full on. His belly-tank unhooked with the sudden declaration, leapt forward and was cut in two by the propeller. A sheet of flame sprang out which, in a 30-knot wind, quickly engulfed the after part of the deck in a sea of blazing petrol. Tony got out of the cockpit, made as though to jump forward (which would have saved his life), changed his mind and jumped aft. He slipped on the deck—probably on oil leaking from the fractured main union—and fell on his back into the flaming petrol. He was on fire as we watched him pick himself up and walk down the deck, where he was swathed in blankets and rushed to sick bay. The doctors managed to keep him alive until the ship entered harbour, but the poor devil died as they carried him up the gangway of the hospital ship.

Nine or ten of us were still circling. As we were now running short of fuel, I spoke to our FDO, John Parry, to obtain permission to take the boys into China Bay, refuel and await further instructions. He came up on the radio a minute or two later to give me the go-ahead from Wings. The deck was in a hell of a mess and would have to be sorted out.

So we flew into Trinco, landed, parked our aircraft and started to refuel. As luck would have it, the station's petrol tanks had become contaminated with water because of monsoon rain and refuelling had to be carried out the hard way, through chamois leather—a long, weary process.

We lay on the grass away from the aircraft and smoked cigarettes. Shaw, Rogers and I were in a group. It was Rogers' birthday (it so happened it was *my* birthday, too). We were hot, filthy, unutterably tired and whiled away the minutes by describing to one another in great detail what we would do to the wardroom bar that evening

I had started the duty crew refuelling at the far end of the line. They had completed two or three when a despatch rider came over with a signal from the ship, telling me to resume landings as soon as possible. I sent out these already serviced and despatched the remainder, one by one, as soon as they were topped up. Eventually Rogers and I remained; then he went.

He got to his feet, looked down at me and gave me his usual grin.

'I'll have that drink waiting for you, boss.'

I looked at my watch. 1700. The bar would open in half an hour's time.

'OK, Rog. Do that. See you soon, provided they put more petrol than water in my cab.'

Fifteen minutes later I took off. It was a wonderful evening. The setting sun was spreading gorgeous colours over the sea, fading to dusk—or what goes for dusk in the tropics—out to the east. I felt better again after a rest and threw myself into a couple of snap rolls just to assure myself that I was still firing on all cylinders. My lovely Corsair, worked to death all day long, was still purring like a leopard and revelled in the throwing-about. As I came up to within three or four miles of the ship—now alone on a salmon-pink sea, serene and majestic—I saw a splash on her port quarter. Presumably one of the boys was ditching a belly-tank, or maybe it was an Avenger getting rid of a hooked-up depth-charge—yet weren't they all aboard by now?

I came in on Johnny's bats and landed comfortably on the third wire. As I walked back down the deck, Wings leaned over his bridge and beckoned me to go up. When I reached him:

'Hans, how many are there still to come?'

'None, sir. I'm the last.'

'What about Rogers?'

'Left just—well, ten or 15 minutes—before me, sir.'

'Then he's the one.'

'One what, sir?'

'The one who's just crashed. Went in on his approach turn.' (So that was the splash I had seen.)

He had lost flying speed on the final turn to the deck, stalled and spun in. Then they told me that Graham-Cann was in a bad way. Dear God! What was happening to us? Two good boys within an hour and not an enemy in sight! At that moment it seemed possible to me that there was a chance that not one of us would survive to see home again.

I went down to my cabin, undressed, put a towel round myself and trudged off for a shower. Later, as I dressed, I thought about Eric Rogers. He was a grand chap, young for his years—even on his 25th birthday—and still very much of a boy. He was one of the cheeriest characters we had. Whatever the circumstances, Eric's gaiety was something I had always been able to rely on. Now he was gone—gone forever. I can't honestly say that I felt over-sentimental about him, for by now we were in danger of forgetting what tears were for. More than anything, I felt unutterable sadness that I should never see a good friend again. I produced a deep sigh and plodded off to the wardroom. There I ran into Steve Starkey who, sensible as ever, had already made arrangements for an inventory of Rogers' gear to be taken.

Whatever one's feelings, the mundane things of life still had to be attended to. I joined an unnaturally quiet bunch of the lads for a drink. We hadn't much to say. What the hell *can* you say? In another corner were some 1830 boys, obviously talking about Graham-Cann's death, news of which had just reached the ship. My God! The atmosphere was like a morgue!

Then through the doorway came an old friend, Freddy Smallwood. He came over and we shook hands. Freddy had made a name for himself in earlier years by pranging a Walrus. Somebody said in a high-speed stall which, as Euclid had pointed out, was impossible. Now here he was, large as life. I knew *Ameer* was in harbour, but I didn't know he was her batsman. So we had a couple of drinks, then went in for supper, with a bottle of South African wine and a couple of Van der Hums to round off with. After that it was all right. The spirit of the wardroom rose again. The long-suffering piano was trundled across the passage into the wardroom and away we went. Wings kicked off with *My name is John Johnson* and *The wheel fell off the hearse* and we were launched on a session.

Later—much later—I pushed off to climb into pyjamas before going out to the quarter-deck. In my cabin I found Freddy Smallwood hard and fast asleep on the carpet, snoring away his alcohol. He looked as happy as a sandboy. I found a pillow, stuffed it under his head and left him to it.

A messenger found me just leaving the quarter-deck at 0700 next morning, with a signal from *Ameer* to say they were sending a boat at 0800 to recover what was left of Fred. I roused him to life, encouraged him to have a brisk wash and shave and eventually saw him away from the gangway, looking as though he would probably live.

I was grateful to him. He had soaked up for me all the trials and tribulations of yesterday. Today was another day and I felt—although somewhat shakily—confident that I, too, would get through it, despite the little men who were busily hammering a tunnel through the back of my skull. (After all, it *had* been my birthday!)

January 24 1945. A dark, unpleasant morning at 0600, with occasional light squalls of rain blowing over. I was strapped in my Corsair at the head of the range, cold and shivering with the usual butterflies doing circuits and bumps in my tummy. There was chatter all around me on the deck; ratings, manning the chocks, were calling to one another; Cunningham and Hastings, the two deck officers, moving around with Lucite torches, blue and theatrical, in their hands. I was nervous, like a racehorse ready to go.

My eye caught a hiccup of oily black smoke as it puffed from the funnel. The boys down in the boiler-rooms were flashing up more burners to increase speed. So it wouldn't be long. My aircraft

195

conveyed the vibration through to my backside. She really was opening the taps!

Wings came up on the Tannoys.

'Fighters start up!'

There was the usual brief pause while the lads moved to safety, away from the reach of those deadly propellers which would soon be thrashing the air, lethal and invisible. I was all set. All I had to do was to press the tit. The Koffmann starter coughed like an angry tiger and the prop, just visible now against the lightening sky to the east, disappeared from view in a wreath of blue smoke. The engine was running as sweet as sugar. Just stay like that all day, baby! Check, check and check again. Everything OK. The sweet, sickly taste of oxygen in my mouth tried to spoil what little breakfast I had eaten. Never mind! I'll have a real breakfast when I get back! All pressures up, temperatures normal. I was ready.

The sky was brightening by the second. A choppy sea, but nothing to worry about. Come on, Ian! Come *on*, let's *go*, for Chrissake!

He must have heard me, for the port oleo gave slightly—and the Corsair with it. We were turning to starboard into wind. Any second now! The ship was pushing on, turning on a sixpence with a great heel to port. I could feel the increasing wind speed over the deck.

I saw Colin wave away the chocks with a gesture from his torch. Then his torch came up, 'wound me up' and I was away.

The British Pacific Fleet was at sea off Enggano Island, to the west of Sumatra, and the greatest airborne task force of the Royal Navy was taking off for Palembang. Five minutes later, aircraft from the four carriers, carrying navigation lights, were milling around the Fleet virtually in darkness, trying to form up into one cohesive unit and, despite all the odds, managing to achieve it. There were surprisingly few non-starters. *Victorious* and *Indefatigable* had some trouble getting their Avengers away—and trouble with a few that didn't get away—but no lives were lost.

The bombers, 43 of them, were Avengers. To escort them, we had a Top Cover of 16 Corsairs led by Chris Tomkinson of *Victorious*; a Middle Cover of 16 Hellcats and eight Corsairs under the command of Tommy Harrington, the Fighter Wing Leader of *Indomitable*; a Bow Escort of 12 Fireflies, led by Major Cheeseman, RM, of *Indefatigable*; and as Stern Escort, myself with eight Corsairs. It was a powerful force. With each Avenger carrying 2,000 lb of bombs, its potential destructive power was considerable.

The Air Group Co-ordinator, boss of the whole shebang, was Lieutenant-Colonel Ronnie Hay, RM, Fighter Wing Leader of *Victorious*. Leading his own flight, he was responsible for directing the attack.

Three Avengers ran into problems on the climb and had to return to *Victorious*. The rest of us fought for altitude quickly, for we had a mountain range of something over 10,000 feet to cross shortly after reaching the coast of Sumatra. Palembang lay 100 miles beyond the mountains. In all, I suppose, we had a flight of well over 200 miles before us.

We were too busy on the climb to take much interest in the rest of the escort. The Avengers were clawing for altitude and their speed was accordingly pretty low. To weave our flights at a diabolically low speed and still keep in close company with them gave us a perspiring time. What was more, climbing steeply as we were, we just had to be on Jap radar. We could, therefore, expect to be jumped by their fighters at any time. I was sufficiently nervous about this to pull my eight Corsairs out of line, where we could open the taps and crack on more speed. There was no future at all in being jumped when we were floundering around at about 150 knots.

Once we levelled out on top, however, I was more than shattered to find that our eight Corsairs constituted the whole of Low Cover. Where the hell were the Fireflies? I hadn't the faintest idea what had happened to them and at this stage couldn't break radio silence to find out. We positioned ourselves over the centre of the bomber formation and hoped for miracles.

The country below us was impressive. As far as the eye could see—and that is quite some distance from 13,000 feet—stretched the rich green of the jungle, broken only by the wondrous range of mountains running, peak after peak, on both sides of us. Then quite suddenly there was no more time to goof at the scenery. Things began to happen. The Avengers opened the throttle and cracked on more speed. Our eyeballs were now rotating as though on swivels. I kept checking and re-checking oxygen pressure, gun switches, super-charger (Yes! It's on, you stupid bastard! Like it was the *last* time you looked!) And all the time searching, searching, searching for those black dots which would mean 'rats'—enemy fighters. Palembang appeared and, away in the distance, the Banka Strait gleamed in the sunshine with the river, glinting snake-like, winding through the green flat country to join it. There, astride the river, lay the massive refinery—God! What a size! A town in itself! I was still taking it all in when—

'RATS!! Eleven o'clock up!!'

Top Cover was shouting the odds and the battle was on. The air became alive with warning shouts, orders to close up and all the natter that excitement generates. And then I could see them. Over to the north, pinpricks were hurtling downhill from a great height and contrails streamed out across the azure sky as our fighters pulled tight .

corners to get at them. The Avengers were now deploying for their bombing run and their line was lengthening. Christ! I could do with 20 more Corsairs right now! Suddenly a Jap levelled out over on the port side, coming at us like a thunderbolt, making his run to take the bombers below us on the beam.

'Break left—GO!!' and the flight wheeled over on to its wingtips. We gave him a burst head-on and he ducked. Whether or not we hit him I don't know; but fire from 24 machine-guns of .5 calibre is enough to make the bravest put his head down. I hadn't turned the flight back to the Avengers before someone yelled 'Rats, three o'clock up!!' and there were two more, belting in at high speed. Churchill had already turned his flight at one of them. We took on the other. One of the four of us must have been a damned good shot, for bits and pieces of it flew around as it dived down, down. The pilot had forgotten all about the bombers now; we had given him something else to worry about! There was a great temptation to chase him; but our job wasn't to mount up scores. Our purpose in life was to keep them away from the bomber boys, whether we hit them or not. Now we turned back to the line of the attack. The Avengers were diving on their run to the target and were going like the clappers. The bloody great balloons were still up, floating between us and the earth like some fat, green reptiles with bright red spots. And I cursed the Fireflies. They were the great destroyers who were going to clear these ugly sausages out of the way for us; and as far as I knew their crews were still sitting in the wardroom with their feet up, reading *Lady Chatterley's Lover*. Where the bloody hell were they?

We were searching out ahead, weaving all the time like bastards, when tracer flew past us, fired from astern. There in my mirror was an Oscar—it looked as though it was sitting on my elevators—with guns flashing along its wings. I had time neither to shout nor to break before it dived beneath us, only to reappear in a split second, pulling up in front of us, the length of two cricket-pitches away. We all heaved back on our sticks and gave it the works; no need for gunsights. The silly bastard was half-stalled, sitting there like a broken-down old whore. Its port aileron took off and sailed over our heads. What looked like a section of flap fell away to our right. Someone must have hit the engine. The aircraft fell, smoking, down on the port side and Matt Barbour must have nearly flown through it. God knows how he missed it. I yelled and did an aerobatic turn to port where another fighter—a Tojo?—was boring in. No—it was another Oscar. We gave it a long burst, tearing chunks out of the back end of the fuselage and tail section, and it sheered off to starboard. Jesus! Business was brisk and we were tearing around like frustrated virgins!

I straightened up on the line of the last Avenger or two and had a quick shufti around to see how the boys were faring. Reggie Shaw and Matt Barbour—Nos 3 and 4—had vanished. I did a quick scan around the sky. Not a sign. How had they gone? Had that Oscar got them? Certainly not the one we had hammered up front. They had been with me then. What about that last desperate turn from the bombers? Had the speed of my turn taken them by surprise? When you lose a fast-flying formation, you can be miles away before you realise it. I just couldn't remember when I had last seen them. Whatever the reason, Jimmy Clark and I were alone. Winnie and his flight had disappeared—perhaps he was already on his way to the rendezvous on the far side of the target area. So we pushed off in that direction, diving to get up some more speed. Thick, black smoke was now obscuring a lot of the target and Ronnie Hay would be having a few words to say about that!

I was still worrying about Shaw and Barbour when a Nick rose out of an empty space—a sleek, two-engined fighter. It came up like a rocket on our starboard side, very close; and the aircrew hadn't seen us. I saw quite clearly the two Japs sitting side by side in the greenhouse. Jimmy was the nearer of the two of us and turned to give it a quick squirt. I lifted and horsed the stick over, firing over the top of Jimmy's Corsair. A rash of bullet-holes appeared on the Jap's port wingroots as he fell off to starboard, faster and ever faster, plummeting down to the chaos of the refinery below. Again for one fleeting moment I damn nearly followed him; but again I remembered what my job was—and it certainly wasn't that—and flew on to the rendezvous.

We came up to some Avengers, all of whom seemed reasonably relaxed and unworried. One of their pilots looked up and gave me a grin and a 'thumbs-up'. We formed over them and soon were joined by two more Corsairs—*Victorious* jobs. There were still a few calls for 'Rats'—probably some fighters loafing around upstairs waiting for easy pickings. One whipped in at the Avengers, and the *Victorious* boys, on the starboard side of the weave, sheered it away. There were Hellcats about 1,000 feet above in classic open formation. Things at our level remained a bit disorganised—no wonder!—and still someone was calling 'Rats!' A Jap scudded across in front of us—a Tojo, I thought. Looked a bit like a FW 190—way out of range. It was a full deflection shot and I hadn't more than one chance in 10,000 of hitting it. I let fly anyway, just for the hell of it. Then it was suddenly quiet—Oh! So unbelievably quiet!—and for the first time I saw that we were over the mountains again.

The blessed sea came up—safety! I felt like old Xenophon —'Thalassa! Thalassa!' I could have yelped with joy. We struck out towards the Fleet, keeping a wary eye above and behind us.

At last, beneath us, spread the pride of the Royal Navy. And how bloody marvellous they looked! Two great battlers in the centre; four carriers in square formation round them, spaced out with all the precision of guardsmen; and cruisers and destroyers as far as the eye could see. They were already into wind and we started to land on.

We sorted out our various carriers, waited a minute or two, then I led the flight (we had just been joined by a couple more of our Corsairs) up the starboard side of *Illustrious* and lowered hook and undercarriage. Undercart OK anyway; down and locked. About a mile up, then round to port in a great 180-degree turn. Down 20 degrees of flap. Ten degrees more. There was something wrong. What in God's name was the matter with the thing? The flaps just weren't taking the speed off it. I started to juggle, working out how to go about the business of landing and sailed on, well past the stern end of the ship. Eventually, somehow or other, I got it down to manageable speed and turned in towards the ship. I was low—too low. Down to about 350 feet—and a long, long way astern. Should I go round again? No—Bats was giving me 'Roger' so I pressed on and gave it a bit more throttle to get some extra height. I was in a bloody awful position, but he obviously thought I would make it OK. Then from the port side came a Corsair, in a steep turn, doing *its* approach to the deck; and was upon me before I saw it. I heard the roar from its engine above my own—God! It *was* close! And the pilot couldn't see me beneath his wing! I crashed the throttle wide open to clear out of its way and promptly stalled. I had collected all its slipstream.

My Corsair fell out of the sky like a stone, port wing down. I screamed. I knew, without a shadow of doubt, that I was done for. From 400 feet, in a six-ton aircraft, you don't stand a dog's chance. The stick was whipped out of my hand by the sudden stall and was far to the left, set as though in concrete. I took both hands to it—no good. I got my left knee behind it—still solid. The sea was coming up at me at a sickening speed. Any second now. Then the stick became free—I had regained flying speed. Thank God, I did the right things instinctively. I kicked the starboard rudder hard and she stopped spinning. I straightened up the wings and started to pull—gently, though. I didn't want to go into a reverse spin, which a Corsair would do without any trouble. For one wildly optimistic moment I thought I was safe. The sea was close, horribly close and I was going fast now. But I was pulling out of the dive—gently, gently!

Everything went black, as they say.

I never heard the bang. I came back to consciousness in a world of water, dark and frightening. I was drowning; hanging upside down, suspended in my harness. I moved to put my hand outside the cockpit, but there was no opening, only a jumble of levers which I didn't recognise. My head was bursting, air bubbles were rushing from my nose and mouth and my heart was pounding with a thumping ferocity that appalled me. I put my left hand above and behind my head and felt the perspex of the cockpit hood. Now forward—a gap! It was about a foot wide. I undid my safety harness and, somehow or other, clambered upwards, squeezing my body out. Blast it! I couldn't get my chute out! Back through the gap into the cockpit again. Off parachute harness; and I remembered to tear off my helmet with its restraining R/T and oxygen leads. Now I got through the gap again and looked up as I fought to rise, the whole of my body bursting for relief from this killing anguish. The water above me was pale green and the Corsair hung beside me, motionless, tapering upwards to the tail. I pulled the lever of the CO_2 bottle of my Mae West and urged myself to the surface.

I emerged into a grey, featureless world, and a nasty choppy sea. Four feet away was the Corsair's rudder, projecting three or four inches above the surface. As I watched, it sank. I had escaped in the nick of time.

But my heart was my chief concern. I could feel it—even more, I could hear it—banging away at the hell of a rate. My mouth was wide open and the mad, frantic rate of breathing was something I didn't believe could last. The lop of every wave hit me in the face and pushed more and more water inside me. I couldn't stop it. I had to try to breathe or die. In my bewilderment from having been knocked out cold, I hadn't the wit to release all the gear that pulled me down into the water—a revolver, 50 rounds of ammo, a jungle machete, heavy shoes. As the sea first lifted me, then dropped me back into the trough, I could see my belly tank floating high on the surface, some 20 to 30 feet away. If it had been 20 *inches* away, St Michael and all the angels couldn't have helped me to reach it. The ship had dropped a smoke float which I could see burning blackly—how far away? Perhaps a quarter of a mile. Beyond that, nothing. I was alone.

Neither the loneliness nor the hopelessness of my situation seemed to worry me. (Nor did the possibility of being attacked by sharks. Off Enggano Island they are in such numbers that one could walk on their backs!) Staying alive was the main, the only, thing and I couldn't see myself lasting much longer. I held back my head, trying to keep the water out of my mouth, but the padded collar of my Mae West didn't do a thing to help me in that direction. Then, wonderful to see, a destroyer came into view as I lifted on a big wave. She had seen the smoke float, then the belly tank—and thank God, she had decided to search the belly tank area. She must have also spotted my head rising and falling in the water. As she hove to, she started to lower away a whaler. I'm sure the lads were doing their best, but to my tired eyes it seemed that the bloody thing couldn't possibly reach me in time. I forced myself to turn away—I was going to die before they reached me.

My inability to breathe and the thumping of my heart were now infinitely worse. More than that, I now found to my horror—as much horror as I could muster—that I could neither see nor hear. I lay motionless in the water, my strength and the will to do anything fast ebbing away. Then someone grabbed the collar of my Mae West. Another bod, presumably, took a handful of the seat of my flying overalls and hoisted me inboard. They dropped me to the boards like a great fish and water surged from my mouth. I coughed, half-choking, and they lifted me up and sat me on a thwart.

The destroyer—*Wessex*, with Lieutenant-Commander R. Horn-castle, RN, in command—was at action stations. As soon as the whaler was out of the water, she was off again at a rate of knots. The whaler was swung inboard and the crew got out on to the iron deck. Now I could see somewhat vaguely and my hearing was returning. Fortunately for me, *Wessex* was big enough to carry a doctor and this young man was standing by, ready to give me a helping hand. He grasped my arm to help me on to the deck. From some hidden reserve—and I certainly hadn't much of *that* left!—I found the energy to wave him away. Something inside me said that I would die if I moved. I just sat there, feeling like Death himself. I put my head down in my agony and water gushed again and again from nose and mouth. Still my heart pounded against my overalls and the thumping of it in my head was a fast, maniacal drumbeat. I just couldn't understand how I stayed alive.

I sat there for the best part of an hour and the doc, bless him, stayed with me. He didn't interfere, nor did he say a word. At long last, I made an effort and rose, rockily, to my feet. He took my arm and led me, still unspeaking, to the sick bay. There he stripped and examined me. A lump on my head like a duck's egg; a rip on the inside of my left knee, where I had tried to force the joystick—and that was all. He wrapped a blanket round me and took a long look at me. Two minutes later he came to me with a glass.

'That's about all I can think of. I'm sure it won't do you any harm.' It was a half-tumbler of neat whisky and it tasted like nectar. He gave me a large enamel bowl and told me to take it easy. Every few minutes I put my head down and the salt water continued to burst from me like a siphon. Hell! I must be full of the stuff!

And then, suddenly, I was much better. Lunchtime arrived—12 o'clock. I had been picked up at 1005 and already I was getting back to normal. I had some lunch and a drink and felt even better. (I hasten to say that a drink was strictly for me! The ship's officers were at action stations and were 'on the wagon' for the time being.) In the afternoon I

joined the bridge party—Captain, No 1 and Officer of the Watch. I
thanked them with all my heart and repaid them, in some small way,
by helping in aircraft recognition.

I stayed the night aboard *Wessex*; her officers couldn't have been
kinder. Next morning I found the whaler's Coxwain to thank him,
too, and gave him my sheath knife as a memento. Soon after breakfast
there was a signal from *Illustrious* to say they intended to recover me
without delay. The Captain certainly wasn't wasting any time! We
cruised up her cliff-like side and took station on her, 20 to 30 feet away
from her starboard side, doing about 18 knots. Tricky work. *Illustrious*
expected it to be, too; the goofers were there in their hundreds! Out
swung the great crane, lowering a scrambling net to the bottom of
which were suspended three sacks of fresh bread; a commodity always
welcome to a destroyer. The crane driver made one pass at us and
damn nearly carried away the bridge. The First Lieutenant (Michael
Parker, later to serve HRH The Duke of Edinburgh as secretary)
turned to me and grinned:

'No chance there, old boy! After yesterday, we can't have you
written off by a sack of bread!'

His second sweep was better. This time the net hovered momentarily over the port side of the iron deck. As quick as a flash the lads
severed the cords attaching the sacks and at the same time I leapt for
the net, clawing for a handhold. My hands stuck. Before I could gain a
foothold I was swinging high over the gap of boiling sea, making for
the flight-deck. There were loud cheers and I was home and dry. The
Commander stood beside me on the deck. He grinned as he assured
me that it was the best deck-landing I had ever done. Then he led me
up to the Captain on the compass platform. Charles Lambe, bless
him, who I am sure felt for all of us as though we were his sons, took
my hands between his. 'Hans! My dear Hans!' was all he could say
before turning away.

When I went below to change out of my grimy overalls, there on my
desk, in solitary state, stood a glass, full of rum; and I knew that our
squadron ratings, too, were glad to see me home again. It was a great
feeling to be back with friends. It was good to be alive.

Later in the day Wings told me what had happened. As far as they
could see from a distance of about 600 yards, I had almost cleared the
sea in my recovery from the incipient spin. Then the undercarriage
had struck and the Corsair had whipped over on to its back. It had
stayed there for a matter of seconds before the nose had sunk. They
thought it was curtains; for whom, they didn't know until they
received a signal from *Wessex*.

I could figure out the rest. When I hit the water, the instantaneous
deceleration had sheared the locks of the hood, allowing it to rocket

forward and to knock me unconscious with its hard rubber rim. At the same time the locks of the seat, incorporating a sheet of armour-plating, had also sheared and the whole thing, with me still strapped into it by the safety harness, had rolled forward and down, my face only just missing the gunsight and instrument panel. When I recovered consciousness my head was 20 feet below the surface. I had been in the sea for 35 minutes before being rescued.

Whilst we had been leading the high life over Palembang, Michael Tritton had led a *Ramrod* of Corsairs over three enemy airfields on very successful strafing runs. They had destroyed 34 fighters. Had they not done so, I suppose we would *still* be fighting the battle of Palembang! The whole operation, in fact, had been successful, although a heavy price had been paid; the Fleet had lost six Corsairs, one Hellcat and two Avengers. *Illustrious* herself had paid dearly. Our two squadrons each lost two pilots—Sutton and Brown from 1830 and Shaw and Baxter from 1833.

Admiral Vian knew that, too. His signal to us is worth recording: 'The determination of your squadrons to hit the enemy to the full at whatever cost has involved *Illustrious* in important losses which we all deplore. I hope it may be satisfying to you that I have no doubt that it is upon the gallantry and resolution of such men as these that the great successes achieved at Palembang chiefly depended.'

My No 3, Reggie Shaw, as I have said, had become parted from us during our fast breaks over the target area. An Avenger pilot from another carrier had seen a Corsair, thought to be Shaw's, diving for ground level with a Tojo fighter hard on its heels. Evan Baxter had been hit when at considerable altitude and had been seen to bale out well away from Palembang.

A rendezvous had been arranged at a small lake—Lake Ranau—in Sumatra, not many miles from the western coast, whither our Walrus amphibian, piloted by Lieutenant (A) N. E. Walker, RNVR, flew on January 29, escorted by two fighters, to look for signs of any survivors who might have reached the meeting place. Nothing was seen, however, and Walker returned empty-handed.

At that time, five days probably seemed a not unreasonable lapse of time for healthy young men to walk anything up to 70 or 80 miles. Thirty years later, however, in the light of after-knowledge, we know that their task was not humanly possible. When one considers the odds stacked against them—the contours of the island, the thickness of the jungle vegetation, the presence of the enemy and those natives under his influence, the possibility of wounds or bodily damage sustained in 'arriving' on the surface of Sumatra—their task is seen to be just not on.

Walker himself, after his valiant attempt to find aircrew at Lake

Ranau, was unfortunately killed later in the same day when our ship suffered damage from the Fleet's gunfire.

It wasn't until after the war that we learned that both Baxter and Shaw, together with seven other aircrew, had been executed by the Japanese.

Bud Sutton and 'Tiddles' Brown, of 1830 Squadron, had been killed over airfields whilst ground-strafing. Bud was not seen again after completing a third strafing run over one of the fields attacked by Tritton's *Ramrod*. Brown had been hit fair and square by flak as he went into a strafing run and had cart-wheeled through a line of Jap fighters drawn up on the runway. The poor chap was probably stone-dead as he crashed through them at 300 knots.

We had lost more than four pilots. Four good friends had gone forever.

It had been the intention to hit Palembang again on the following morning, but monsoon weather intervened and it wasn't until five days later—January 29—that the strike force again climbed away from the decks, out to the coast and away over the mountain range. Each night as darkness fell the Fleet stood in towards the land through thick, murky weather. Each morning at 0100 the Tannoys announced that the operation was postponed for 24 hours.

During these days the maintenance crews worked non-stop to achieve maximum serviceability. The aircrews discussed the first operation and ways and means of bringing about improvements. During a refuelling session in mid-ocean *Indomitable*, Vian's flagship, was able to convene a Wing Leaders' conference at which most of the 'beefs' were argued. Various things had gone wrong on the way to and from Palembang. For one thing, all were agreed that there had been too much natter once radio silence had been broken. Too many men had asked too many damn silly questions, rendering it difficult to pass genuinely urgent messages. The absence of the Fireflies in the early part of the attack (they had, apparently, joined in halfway through the battle, although I hadn't seen them), which had produced such acrimonious thoughts over the target, had come about by a starter failure on the part of the aircraft leading their range, holding up take-off for an unconscionable time. There had been a lamentable failure to concentrate quickly and effectively over the rendezvous on the far side of the target, leaving too many Avengers vulnerable to attack before fighter cover became organised again.

The chief complaint seems to have been the lack of close escort over the bombers. The absence of the Fireflies, of course, had been one contributory factor; but it was also felt that Middle Cover might have given more assistance instead of bashing around—as the New Zealanders put it, 'like blue-arsed flies'—looking for Japs to kill. Finally, it was essential that the balloons should be hacked down before the Avengers bombed.

So the chat went, until the 29th at 0100 when the Tannoys said that it was 'on'. My friend Bob Ellison, examining me on my return to the ship, had declared me to be concussed slightly from the bang on the head; and 'physically and mentally buggered', to use his own medical terms, from the effort I had put in to escape from my aircraft. He stipulated two weeks on light duties—in other words, no flying. I felt sadly left out of things as the Corsairs took off. The unsettled weather made the form-up tricky, but eventually the strike disappeared into the morning drizzle. Soon afterwards Mike led his strafing force off the deck. I crossed my fingers for him. Twice on the same job, over the same airfields, was tempting fate with a vengeance.

For the first time I endured the agony of the long wait, but in the end it was all over. It was a great moment when we counted the Corsairs—not one missing! 854 Squadron, though, wasn't so fortunate. Two of their Avengers failed to return—that of their commanding officer, Charlie Mainprice; the other captained by R. S. Armstrong, a Carlisle boy. Both of them had struck balloon cables on their dive down to the refinery and all six crew members were killed. It was a sad loss for our bomber friends, for both crews were well thought of.

Mike returned, too; and he hadn't been back in the ship very long before there were air raid warnings of varying urgency. It was said that fighter patrols were busy. Then we were attacked. Seven 'Bettys'—two-engined aircraft—appeared from the direction of the coast, coming in fast and low, and made a determined attack on the carriers. All were shot down, most spectacularly, by Seafires from *Indefatigable* and by the Fleet's guns, but during the action we suffered heavy damage when *Euryalus,* our pivot cruiser, failed to check her fire when we came between her and her target. She slammed two 5.25-inch shells into us. Twelve men were killed and more than 20 wounded before the firing ceased and the danger was past.

And then we were heading south, away from Sumatra and away from Palembang. The big battle was over and we who were left were counting the cost. When the pulses had become normal again and the guns were quiet, we felt listless and tired. For the moment, our little war was over—until the next time.

John Winton, in his book *The Forgotten Fleet,* now regarded as a classic history of the operations of the British Pacific Fleet, counts the casualties suffered by the Fleet Air Arm in the two operations. Forty-one aircraft were lost from the four carriers: 16 in actual combat, 11 in ditchings near the Fleet and 14 from deck-landing crashes. As Winton says, this works out at roughly one aircraft for every ten sorties flown;

and he adds his own significant commentary: 'a casualty rate which would have made even Bomber Command flinch'.

Against these losses, it was estimated that we had destroyed 68 enemy aircraft—38 on the ground and 30 in the air, not taking into account several 'probables'. Palembang, whilst not completely destroyed, was effectively put out of the war for a long time to come.

14

To the Pacific Ocean

With the fury and excitement of the two battles of Palembang behind us, a couple of days' sailing on a southerly course brought us to Fremantle, Western Australia. We had buried our dead. Now we transferred ashore our wounded, refuelled, collected some mail and—blessed event!—took on board some fresh food. (A pint of milk at the door every morning is the most trivial of the day's events. But when you have subsisted for months on the powdered variety, the sight of a jug of the real stuff is a matter for universal rejoicing. Throw in some fresh eggs, lettuce, vegetables, fruit and meat—and you have firmly laid at least one of the foundations of a very happy ship!)

We were at cruising stations one lovely morning as we plodded southwards towards Australia. Our Major of Marines, David Mahoney, and I were standing on Wings' bridge, chatting idly, looking out across the flight-deck. *Illustrious* was back marker of the Fleet.

David gripped my arm.

'There's a man out there, Hans! *Look*!' As he spoke, his two fists hit the alarm buttons: one, 'Man overboard'; the other, a signal to a Marine on the quarter-deck to throw two lifebelts astern.

There was a man, too, sliding past at 18 knots. He was 50 yards from the ship's side. His mouth was open and one arm with hand outstretched was raised over his head. We rushed on to the compass platform, bursting in on the Captain and OOW to break the news. Captain Lambe brought a patrol of Corsairs down from 5,000 feet to search astern of the ship and a signal to *Indomitable* quickly brought a destroyer from the screen to the area behind the Fleet, where the smoke from the lifebelts' flares was already marking an approximate position.

They found nothing. What was more, no ship had reported man overboard. This was incredible! The flagship signalled 'Were we sure?' Yes—we were sure.

More questions. More stout affirmations from David and myself. Inevitably the Fleet was ordered to clear lower deck. Every ship mustered their crews.

No one was missing.

By now, destroyer and aircraft had been recalled. Again came questions from the flagship. Just *how* certain were we? Was there, surely, some mistake? Was it not gash thrown over the side that we had seen? Was the arm that we had seen not a broken spar floating in wreckage?

No. It was a man. We stuck to our guns. No matter how hard we were pressed, we knew we were right. It had been a man.

At 1150 came 'Up spirits'—the daily issue of rum. Then, and only then, did the tragedy unfold. The man we had seen, the man who had died that desperately lonely death as he watched the Fleet sail past him unheeding, was a Royal Marine from *Indomitable*. When last seen, he had been 'pulling through' his Bofors or Oerlikon cannon in the port nets. He had obviously taken one step backwards too many and had fallen 50 feet to the water. His shouts had gone unheard, lost in the beating of the propellers in the wake and the roar of the air intake fans.

Poor devil! What a lonely death to die.

The fortnight of light duties which followed the slight concussion I had suffered in the crash expired during the voyage round to Sydney and I now sought my friend Bob Ellison officially, for I was anxious to fly again. We met in sick bay where he could use his paraphernalia. He tested heart, lungs and reflexes. He examined eyes and ears. Then he said 'Mercury'.

The mercury test is one of the crucial items of a flyer's medical examination. The victim is confronted by a metal stand supporting a U-tube containing mercury—how much I don't know, but during the test one gets the impression that it amounts to a hundredweight or two! You are handed a rubber tube connected to one end of the U-tube. You take a deep breath and proceed to blow. The object is to raise the mercury to a required level and there to hold it steady, with as little oscillation as possible, for about 60 or 70 seconds.

It's murder. It had seemed pretty bad when I had undergone the test twice in the early days, but now it was hellish. Bob looked at me.

'Is that the best you can do, for Chrissake?'

'Give me another shot.' This was against all the rules and I knew it. But what are friends for?

This time it was better, but by no means as good as the book said it should be. There was a moment's silence.

'I suppose you really do want to fly again?'

'Of course! I'm damned if I'm going to sit around watching all the other guys! And for God's sake don't send me to sit on a bloody airfield for the rest of the war!'

He sighed. 'Go on then, you crazy bastard.' He moved to stow away all his gear. 'But don't fall in again, Hans. That last effort frightened me.' He grinned.

'Nowhere near as much as it frightened *me*! And thanks for the let-off with that fornicating apparatus.'

'You might have done better if I'd pushed the bloody tube somewhere else. Come on for a drink.'

As we approached Sydney Heads we flew off our aircraft and landed at Nowra, out in the sticks of New South Wales. This was the Navy's first Mobile Naval Air Station (MONAB), designed to be picked up, packed up and moved at the drop of a hat to God knows where. Commander Nunnerley, a friendly, charming little man with an elfish glint in his eyes, was in charge. He had a mixed bag under his command, some good, some bad—but it was 1945 and the scraping of the barrel for recruits was nearing the bottom.

We flew for a couple of days, then high-tailed it for Sydney for a short leave. We lived aboard the ship and were faintly surprised to find her high and dry in the fine new graving dock at Woollamalloo. Inspection of the ship had revealed that the centre propeller shaft had developed a wobble in its tunnel—caused through deterioration of the *lignum vitae* glands in the shaft tube—which had reached serious proportions. Time did not allow for lengthy repair work, so the propeller and its shaft were removed and the tunnel, from which the shaft emerged to the water, was sealed most effectively by an enormous, streamlined steel sheath. 'The biggest and toughest contraceptive in the world', as the boys named it.

In Sydney we went to one or two night-clubs and indulged in a bit of drinking. This was a bit erratic, for I don't think we ever really understood Australian licensing laws, infinitely madder than our own. So far as we could see, the pubs opened for about two hours between 5 and 7 pm, during which the entire male population of Sydney erupted from its offices, banks, warehouses or whatever and invaded the nearest hostelry, where bloody battles ensued, the weakest going to the wall, their thirst unassuaged.. Thirsts appeared to be phenomenal and to stand in the way of an Aussie making his tank-like advance upon a pint of beer was a hazardous blunder to make.

All too soon we were back at Nowra. We resumed our flying practice and made the most of the modest and restricted pastimes available to us. A few of the lads even found some girls—where from, God knows. All I could see in the district was sheep. The Nowra of those days was a drab little town in the middle of a great, dusty plain, comprising one very long, very dusty main street, lined with wooden-frame houses, shops and pubs. All had wooden rails on which to tie up one's horse—very Hollywood. Johnny Hastings, who had insisted on sharing our exile out in the backwoods, organised a concert—well, an entertainment!—for the local inhabitants. I must say it went like a bomb and we could have stayed there forever as far as they were concerned, starved as they were for live entertainment. Officers and ratings alike rallied round and put on a great show. During the singing of our sexier solos, I was gratified to see some of our sailors looking hungrily at 50-year-old farmers' wives. Apparently even our kind of music had charms!

The highest speed I ever achieved in a Corsair occurred at Nowra. I took a worn-out aircraft up to Bankstown, near Sydney, and returned with a new one. Flying the odd 80 miles back to Nowra, I saw from my watch that I would be hard put to it to arrive in time for lunch—and lunch in the mess was rather like the Sydney pubs; you had to be there when the 'Come and get it!' call went out, otherwise you missed out completely. I arrived over the field at 18,000 feet. Hungry and thirsty, I dropped her into a vertical dive, took off the supercharger and let her go for Mother Earth. I was doing a hell of a speed. My circuit of the field was almost aerobatic as I put down wheels and flaps and did a quick landing.

I reached the mess just in time and found myself sitting opposite Eddy Jess, leading navigator of our Avenger squadron. Eddy was a mathematician, obsessed with navigational problems, vectors and courses.

'Who was that coming downhill in a hurry just now, Hans?'

'Me,' I replied.

'You were going at a hell of a lick!' He fished from his pocket his small air computer. 'What height did you start your dive?'

I told him.

'Did you happen to notice your air speed indicator?'

Yes. I had seen exactly where the needle was during the fast drop to ground level. He muttered something about air temperature and did a bit of twiddling on the computer. He whistled through his teeth.

'Yes. You *were* moving. I reckon you were going about 535 mph. Quick, I would say!'

During our voyage to Sydney, I had been considerably impressed by the keenness of two of my young men, maintenance Petty Officers. A recent AFO had asked for volunteers from the ranks for flying training (no one yet knew of the atomic bomb and we all thought the war against Japan would go on for ever). These two boys had got wind of it and asked me to recommend them.

As I say, I was impressed. Not that they were in any way unsuitable; far from it, in fact. But I would have thought that the hammering the air groups had taken at Palembang might well have made them think twice! Anyway, here they were and I was prepared to back them to the hilt.

'Has either of you flown at all?'

They looked at one another.

'No, sir.'

'Well, to begin with. Are you sure you would like it? It isn't everybody's cup of tea, you know, and I would rather you didn't apply at all than volunteer and then find you hated it.'

I thought for a moment. I wasn't going to risk their lives with a 'first time off the deck' in an Avenger whilst at sea.

'Tell you what. When we reach Sydney I'll find some way or other of getting you airborne. Then we will see how you feel about it.'

We hadn't been at Nowra a day before they reminded me of my promise. That evening I asked Nunnerley if I might borrow a Tiger Moth on the following day to give these young men a short trip.

I summoned them next morning and had them fitted out with parachutes and Gosport helmets. They were straining at the leash.

Having given the first joy ride to the quieter boy, by the time I returned the other lad had worked up to a full head of steam. He almost *wished* the Tiger off the ground, so keen was he to become airborne. I levelled off at 3,000 feet and he immediately yelled down the voice-pipe.

'Will you do some stunts, sir?'

We certainly had a keen baby here!

'What sort of stunts?'

'Well—you know, sir. The lot! Will you, please?'

I told him to tighten his harness. Then I threw him around for a while—rolls, chandelles, wing-overs. No sooner was I straight and level again:

'You haven't done a loop yet, sir!'

Bloody little glutton!

'All right! Here goes!'

As we came out of the first one, he whooped in sheer ecstasy. So I went straight into a second. As we recovered from that:

'One more, sir—*please*!'

Throttle wide open, stick forward. Now back, back and more and more right rudder. Now we're on the top and the engine has cut out. Let her fall again, cut the throttle and left rudder.

The engine failed to cut in again. Height? 3,000 feet. No danger. Where to put her down? The airfield was on the port side, less than a mile away. OK.

In strictly conversational tones, I said to him:

'One of these days you might have to do a forced landing with no engine power. This is how you go about it.' As I glided and S-turned down to the downwind end of the runway, I described every move I made. The prop, which had been gently windmilling, stopped rotating as I slowed down on my final turn to the runway (the grass and sand on either side was an unknown quantity for landing) and stuck there like a bit of bloody firewood. Then I received the shock of my life. Just turning on to the downwind leg was a mob of Avengers spacing themselves out with practised precision for their landing—and here was I, about to flop down in the middle of the one and only runway.

I put the Moth on to the runway. In a flash I was out of my cockpit, undoing the boy's harness.

'Out! Quick! Come on, for God's sake! Now, get under that other tailplane and help me to push this bastard contraption on to the sand!' (You can see I *still* loved Tigers!)

As we dropped the tail-skid into the sand the first Avenger swept in, touching down abreast of us. We walked away to get out of the dust and the racket. The boy looked at me, uncomprehendingly.

'But why didn't you taxi in, sir?'

'No engine, son, no engine. It flaked out in that last loop.'

'So that was a real forced landing?'

'It was.'

When he had retrieved his lower jaw from the sand and had recovered his sang-froid, he became the squadron bore for a couple of days! I'm pretty certain that the squadron cooks, whose fascination with aircraft was about on a par with their interest in the sayings of Confucius, were left in no doubt at all that his very first flight had culminated in his very first forced landing!

I put recommendations for them through to the Captain, but I doubt very much if they ever saw another cockpit. For them, at least, the war would end too soon!

Michael Tritton had received as replacement for 'Tiddles' Brown, a new boy called Marritt; and one morning he asked me to take him out, mainly to run the rule over him in low flying. He was young, green, intelligent and mad keen. But he was no low flyer, as yet. Only practice would bring confidence and 'surefootedness'. When I took him below 30 feet, he shied like a young foal and bounced back up to 70 or 80 feet. He obviously had no affinity for Mother Earth.

I took him up to 300 feet and had a quiet chat with him. Whilst ten feet would probably see him safely home for lunch, 30 feet would undoubtedly get his head blown off. Close-range Jap gunners were hot stuff and aircraft flying at 30 to 60 feet above the ground were easy pickings. So let's try again.

It didn't work. He had his limit and that was that. As we buzzed along, rising and falling as we followed the contours of the sand-dunes, I tried to assure him that, provided he stayed two or three feet above my wingtip, he would come to no harm. I myself had no intention of burrowing my way through a sand-dune; and if I didn't, he wouldn't. Wasted words. I cajoled. I encouraged. I swore like a leading stoker. But it was no use. He certainly wouldn't kill his chums, but his own life expectancy, particularly if he tried low-flying, wasn't insurable.

For the last time we were summoned to Sydney, to be aboard by lunchtime. The Duke of Gloucester, Governor-General of Australia at that time, was to pay an official visit to his old friend Captain Lambe. The Duke circulated very cleverly, chatting for six or seven minutes with each small group. He had just left us after a short conversation, during which we had found him to be extremely well informed on naval aviation, when one of his party joined us.

For a week or two, our minds had been developing the idea that, when *Illustrious* sailed and we would join her outside Sydney Harbour, we would fly via Sydney in one beautiful, tight formation of 36 fighters and take the whole shebang under the famous Bridge. We hadn't got around to thinking about possible repercussions. We would worry about them if and when we ever returned from the Pacific. We had done a fair amount of practice and were agreed that it would be a piece of cake.

As I said, the Duke had just left us. An RAF Group-Captain, drink in hand, strolled up to us. With no preliminaries whatsoever, he growled:

'Don't you bloody do it!'

We looked at one another.

'Don't do what, sir?' said Michael with a pleasant smile. Groupie looked very hard.

'You know bloody well what I mean! Try it and I'll court martial all 36 of you! And that's no idle threat!'

He walked away. Who had talked?

Ah! Well! I had been too close for comfort to a court martial in South Africa to seek an encore; and Michael was far too sensible to fly in the face of fortune. But it would have been banner headline stuff!

We sailed on March 7 and the air group landed without mishap. We had looked very longingly at Sydney Bridge!

Flying was pretty limited as we drove north. During the next six or seven days we did one or two exercise strikes—not much, certainly, but sufficient to give us the feel of the deck again. Our course took us along the line of the Great Barrier Reef to the Coral Sea, thence northwards through the Louisiade Archipelago—a myriad of small, brilliant-green islands—skirting New Guinea. Then we broke out into the Bismarck Sea and eventually reached Manus, chief of the Admiralty Islands, about two degrees south of the Line. Here we rejoined the Fleet, most of which had arrived on the day we had left Sydney.

My God! It was hot! I took a bathing party ashore on the afternoon of our arrival. Not only was the sand unbearably hot on one's feet but the temperature of the water was such that to swim was almost an impossibility, so completely was one's energy sapped. When I heard that the carrier, a quarter of a mile from the shore, was registering her water intake for the boilers at 85 degrees Fahrenheit, I wasn't the least bit surprised.

Close to the beach we saw our hated enemies face-to-face for the first time. A barbed wire stockade stood within the palm trees. Inside this were hundreds of Japanese prisoners taken, presumably, during the recapture of this group of islands. Whilst we stood there, the Americans were unloading more of them across the open beach. They were taking no chances with these boys, either, for each Jap was securely shackled by chains, hand and foot, to ring-bolts set in the decks of the small vessels transporting them. Some wore khaki shorts, most of them loin-cloths. Only a few had shoes or sandals. All of them looked thin and their crew-cuts only served to stress their gaunt appearance. They stood in groups, inscrutable, silent and wholly impassive.

In the centre of a long, broad beach rose a great outcrop of rock, about 30 feet high and 30 feet square. A sickly, nauseating odour pervaded the whole area and it was only when we had climbed this rocky eminence and found, running across its centre, a deep crevice in whose darkness we could just discern upturned shoes or boots with the tell-tale detached big-toe compartment, that we realised we had discovered the source. Japanese soldiers had fallen into the crack when shot dead; and their putrefying corpses were rendering Paradise hideous with their disgusting gases.

Now we were back in the tropics, fresh water had to be rationed again. The intense heat drove us to showers and refreshing drinks and 1,800 men, thirsty for anything wet, soon overloaded the system. The two evaporators could produce 140 to 160 tons of fresh water a day, but that was insufficient when temperatures were running well over the 100 mark. Our squadron office, immediately below the flight-deck, regularly registered 127 degrees at mid-day.

After three days we sailed, heading for the Carolines, and on March 20 anchored in Ulithi, inside the great coral atoll. Someone said the atoll was well over 20 miles in length; and it seemed that every inch of it was occupied by ships of one kind or another—and mainly warships, both USN and RN. A 30-knot wind blew across it night and day. What a hell of a place! I thought of boyhood reading and R. M. Ballantyne's *The Coral Island*. It wasn't like this at all!

It was our last chance for a conference before we went into battle again. Aboard *Indomitable*, Vian's Chief of Staff, Captain Wright, conducted a meeting in the early part of a hot afternoon. After one hour precisely the door opened and Vian came in—tall, erect, slim-figured and with his pale-blue eyes alert and quick-silver. He strode smartly to the side of his Chief of Staff.

'All right, Wright,' he said, loud and clear. 'If we can't organise the thing in an hour, it's not worth doing.' There was a pause as those searching eyes, surmounted by heavy eyebrows, surveyed the officers who fairly filled the wardroom. 'Stand up the flying boys!'

The COs of the many squadrons rose to their feet.

'I've a short message—no. Don't bother taking notes. It's only four words—for you to take back to your aircrews. GET BLOODY STUCK IN! Any more questions? Right—and the best of luck to all of you!'

We were soon to learn that he was well worth 'getting bloody stuck in' for.

15

Kamikaze‼

On March 23 the British Pacific Fleet, in all its might and majesty, sailed from Ulithi for the new theatre of war. The bureaucratic side of the Navy which no doubt directed our destinies but, beyond that, appeared to our lowly eyes to leave us otherwise uninvolved, had been busy. The US Navy in Washington had never been over-anxious to see the Royal Navy in the Pacific Ocean. Moves and counter-moves had been made whilst we were chewing straws at Nowra, or swinging to buoys in Manus and Ulithi, and eventually the decision had been taken.

The US Navy's Pacific Fleet, under the command of Admiral Chester Nimitz and his deputy Admiral Raymond Spruance, was now poised to launch Operation *Iceberg*—the invasion of Okinawa, possession of which would give the US air forces airfields from which to attack the mainland of Japan itself. The direction in which the energies of the British Pacific Fleet should be channelled had long been the subject of controversy—at times acrimonious—between the US and British Governments. On March 14, however, the diplomatic skies cleared at last and the British Pacific Fleet received a signal directing it to report for duty to Admiral Nimitz.

So the Fleet, under the command of Vice-Admiral Sir H. B. Rawlings, now became Task Force 57, to work alongside the Americans' Fast Carrier Force (Admiral Mitscher), both under the direct command of Admiral Spruance. This officer ordained that the neutralisation of the three islands of the Sakishima Gunto—Miyako, Ishigaki and Iriomote—should be our responsibility. Their importance in the coming battle lay in the fact that all three possessed airfields. When the fury of the US Fleet's air attacks fell upon Okinawa, the enemy's hopes of replenishing their supply of aircraft would lie only in staging them from China, through Formosa and the Sakishima Islands group. It was hoped that our operations would render this impossible or, at the least, extremely hazardous and uncertain.

The Fleet Air Arm was now to embark upon a war of attrition in which, like all toe-to-toe slogging matches, there was to be neither glamour or spectacle. It was to be sheer drudgery, with a heavy price to be paid for a result which would never be assessed with even a moderate degree of accuracy.

The passage of 30 years has blunted for me many of the details of our part in that seemingly endless battle. Of the four carriers which took the fight to the enemy that day, *Illustrious* was the weary one, for we had endured life in the tropics longer than most and strain and tiredness were now to be seen in the faces of the aircrews. We were becoming worn and 'twitchy'. To seek an early night's sleep just didn't seem to work. One flew round the cabin, dodging the flak, practising a landing, for the first two hours; and if sleep eventually came, only three hours or so of fitful rest remained before a shake from the duty boy brought one reluctantly to the dark, cold beginning of another day. Breakfast had always been a cheering time with plenty of wise-cracking and laughter. Now it was a silent feast of too little food and too many cups of coffee and cigarettes—and a significant absence of chatter.

The losses and prangs we suffered now had a telling effect. Where our pilots in earlier days had produced resilience and courage, which seemed automatic, to recover quickly from their own accidents, or crashes or death involving their friends, the losses were now hard to bear and brought dejection and fretfulness. Their natural ebullience retreated and left them thoughtful and introspective. Tiredness brought lethargy and carelessness to their flying. Some of the landing approaches and landings themselves were hideous to behold and to watch them was a nightmare few could endure for more than minutes at a time.

Yet, through it all, youth and the rich instinct born of sound training could still find a crack to burst through, to express themselves in a bright flash of repartee and fun. And every day produced a fresh crop of incidents which, tragic or dangerous though some of them might be, at least sent the adrenalin pumping through, strongly and excitedly, and restored the boys, even briefly, to their old excellence and brilliance.

Despite the tiredness, Operation *Iceberg* brought out some of the best in us, even though the life we now led was something which, like a penetrating fluid, searched out, exposed and exploited that tiredness.

The Captain, Commander (Flying) and the Navigator rarely left the island during the whole operation. The day's work began at 0330 when aircrews, squadron ratings and flight-deck parties were roused. Between 0430 and 0500 the ship closed up to action stations in readiness for suicide attacks, for we were now in Kamikaze territory. All guns' crews closed up. All watertight doors were secured, which meant that for most of the officers their cabins were barred to them.

KAMIKAZE!!

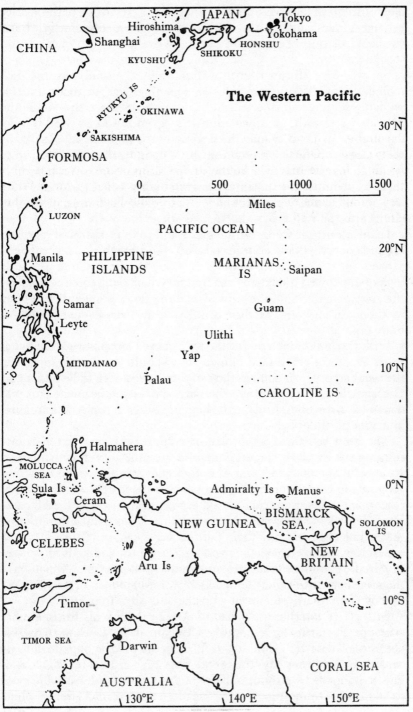

The Western Pacific

The ventilating fans were shut down, causing the inside of the ship to become airless and, as the day wore on, decidedly smelly! Food consisted of bully-beef sandwiches and endless tea—typical action stations rations.

So we were thrown out of our cabins, usually at the last moment—and, if you were unwise enough to snatch those last few precious minutes, unwashed and unshaven. Some chaps, in a fine 'Oh!-Sod-it!' spirit, shunned ablutions—even breakfast—and flew all day in their pyjamas against the Empire of the Rising Sun. Most of us went along for some sort of breakfast. Those on the early shift, so to speak, then made their way to the air operations room, some to remain there on standby, the remainder to grab their helmets and Mae Wests and go out to the flight-deck in the cold of a pre-dawn morning, to climb into their Corsairs and sit and shiver.

In the meantime Colin Cunningham and John Hastings were checking and spotting the aircraft for take-off, most of which duty had been carried out the previous evening. At 0600 the first standing patrols took off, followed quickly by the first mixed striking force of the day, the Avengers to bomb the runways on the three islands, the fighters to shoot up any aircraft they could find and stand guard over the bombers.

With the first launch out of the way, more Corsairs were ranged at readiness, to be scrambled immediately should the enemy appear on the radar screens. As soon as the early strike was seen to be returning, Corsairs flew off to continue the patrols over the islands. This was usually a three-hour stint, with the patrols being replaced at regular intervals until darkness fell.

The ship remained at a state of readiness throughout the day, conditioned by three stages of air-raid warnings—Yellow, Blue and Red—which demanded, for the fighters, standby, readiness and scramble in that order. So the day wore on; take-offs and landings at regular intervals, requiring the Fleet to turn into wind on each occasion. And how the destroyers loved this! It provided for them a refreshing change from their faithful zig-zagging and asdic watch which they pursued zealously and endlessly; for suddenly they were required to re-form their screen as quickly as possible, which gave them the chance to show their paces by romping through the Fleet at a rate of knots, with no end of panache and exhibitionism!

In the late afternoon a strike of Avengers took off for one more attack on the airfields, to pound once again all the landing strips just before darkness fell. This made it difficult for the Japs to do any repairs to them that day, thus rendering it hazardous for night landings to be made by aircraft hopeful of staging through from Formosa to Okinawa. On morning patrols we often saw crashed aircraft which had fallen foul of some crater, obviously having attempted to do just that. At dusk, when all our aircraft had returned, they were serviced, refuelled and re-armed against the next day's operations. Those which were unserviceable were set upon by the weary fitters and riggers who would work all the night through, if needs be, to get them back into fighting trim. We were, of course, still burdened with our deck park of 14 aircraft which could be neither refuelled nor re-armed until the next morning. In that condition they could not possibly be set on fire by a night suicide attack.

When the COs of the squadrons and their maintenance chiefs had finalised their 'Mayfly' lists—aircraft serviceable to fly on the morrow—the first take-off of the day was decided upon. Then the hangar parties set to work, ranging the allotted aircraft on to the lifts and up to the flight-deck, where the deck parties would spot the Avengers and Corsairs in the correct positions for the next morning's take-off. This chore could keep these grand chaps hard at work until nine or ten o'clock at night.

Blessed relief from action stations came with nightfall. Cabins were once again accessible and one could indulge in a shower and a change of clothing from the everlasting flying overalls, grimy and dank with perspiration. Full ventilation was resumed and at long last a substantial meal was available. A quick beer, then off to bed. These were no nights for sing-songs.

For three days on end this was our existence. Late on the third afternoon the Fleet turned away from the operational area and, after a hard night's steaming, rendezvoused next morning with the Fleet Train; a great supply fleet with its main base in Sydney and a forward one at Manus. For 40 hours we cruised together at low speed. Tankers were there to top up every ship. Aviation spirit tankers brought the life-blood for the aircraft. Escort carriers were there with replacement aircraft and pilots. And, for all of us, ammunition and supply ships with everything else we required—especially food and mail.

As far as possible, the Fleet relaxed and rested. Frigates and sloops of the Fleet Train maintained anti-submarine patrols. Fighters from the escort carriers patrolled all the hours of daylight over the vast conglomeration of ships.

On the evening of the second day we parted company. Again we steamed hard for the *Iceberg* area and by dawn we were once more fit and ready for the fray, for another three-day routine. This was the pattern of all our lives.

Our battles with the enemy on the Sakishima Gunto started on March 26 and for the first time we fell upon the airfields of Miyako, Ishigaki and Iriomote. The old firm of *Illustrious* and *Victorious* suffered disaster almost immediately. One of our Avengers was shot down with the loss of the three crewmen and *Vic*'s Chris Tomkinson, CO of 1836 Corsair Squadron, failed to return from the islands. Flak was the great leveller. It could send to a sudden, flashing death the experienced and the sprog alike; and Chris was regarded as a good, safe hand—a great pilot with many, many hours under his belt.

My log-book tells me that my flight was over Ishigaki next morning, where we destroyed a twin-engined aircraft. It also says that we were lucky enough to get in and out with a minimum of fuss. That type was what we all hoped to find! In the first attack of the following day our new Avenger CO, Freddie Nottingham from Johannesburg, was hit over the runway at Hirara, on the island of Miyako, setting on fire the starboard wing. He promptly dropped his bombs, turned in a flash and dived steeply out to sea, successfully extinguishing the fire. However, he had little or no time to congratulate himself on his success for, without the slightest warning, the starboard wing broke off at the roots and the Avenger, at no more than 2,000 to 3,000 feet, spiralled towards the sea. Freddie yelled to his crew to bale out, waited for a few seconds, then hit the silk himself. He landed safely in the water and was aboard his dinghy in quick time; but the 'escape-in-a-hurry' exit of the Avenger was not very easy, particularly when the aircraft was falling at one hell of an angle, and his navigator and air-gunner died with the aircraft. Nottingham saw them die and resigned himself to whatever fate awaited him.

An Avenger from *Indomitable,* on his way back from the same island, saw the dinghy and circled low, transmitting a continuous 'Mayday' signal. No one acknowledged his call, nor did anyone turn up to relieve him. Inevitably, running short of fuel, he had to leave the scene. What with landing-on, de-briefing and all the excitement that fairly bubbles over after an operational sortie, it wasn't until some time after 1100 that he remembered the dinghy. He rushed to his Commander (Operations) and reported it.

Despite the fact that the Fleet was now heading south, away from Sakishima and towards the rendezvous with the Fleet Train, Admiral Vian, ready as always to pull out all the stops to rescue one of his flyers, detached a destroyer to go back to search the estimated area. Not long afterwards an American air/sea rescue submarine—*Kingfish*—came up on the Admiral's wavelength. She had heard something of the exchange of signals; she wasn't too far from the reported position. Could she do anything to assist? She was given such information as was available—scanty enough—and thanked for her assistance.

Around 1330 the flagship signalled us to say that the submarine had been on the air again. According to her reckoning the dinghy must be somewhere nine or ten miles south of Miyako. As she had to search on the surface she would need fighter cover. It was our man in the drink, said the Admiral's staff, so it was from *Illustrious* that the fighters should be despatched.

At 1400 my flight took off and headed back towards Miyako. We hadn't gone far before I saw the destroyer which had been sent back. She was far away on my port side and on an entirely different course. (I had checked mine with Ian Steele, our navigator—and Ian was *never* wrong!) Was *Undine*—for that was the destroyer, commanded by Commander T. C. Robinson, DSC, RN, as I was to discover later—wrong? I rang her up and suggested she might be. Not surprisingly her reply was a bit terse. After all, the navigational capability of fighter pilots was as huge a joke to the Fleet as their ability to interpret the flashings of a signalling lamp! In measured, polite terms she said she would go her own way, thank you.

The destroyer never came within miles of Freddie, but she did nearly run down another dinghy. When they had rescued the inmate, they found him to be an American fighter pilot who had been shot down off Okinawa, some 40 to 50 miles further north, two or three days before. How lucky can you be?

Yet *I* was the one who was wrong and *Undine* right, for I had sadly misjudged her. Too late to be apologetic about it, I found later that there had been no cause to question her course, for she was on her way to pick up 'Doc' Stuart, *Indomitable*'s Bomber Wing Leader and his crew, who had also had the misfortune to ditch that morning. But I hadn't been told that a double rescue was afoot—and I have never been clever enough to refrain from interfering in other people's affairs!

Hours were to elapse before Freddie Nottingham was found. My thoughts were interrupted by an R/T call, so strong it nearly blew my helmet off. It was the *Kingfish* to tell me that she was over to port from me; and when I scanned carefully from 10,000 feet, there was her wake, five or six miles away. She was on the surface and going like a bomb. A big job, too—and she looked great.

As we went up to her to have a chat, the clouds were gathering over the Gunto and I didn't see much danger of an attack. My own estimate—with which she agreed—was that we were still some considerable distance west of the probable position and I said that we would fly searches ahead of her, a section at a time. Numbers 3 and 4 led off, while number 2 and myself remained around 7,000 feet to give us room for manoeuvre in the event of some Jap trying his hand. The boys came back in 20 minutes—no joy. So Jimmy and I set out.

Now we had to drop down, for dinghies are difficult to find from the air. It's even harder if you're looking for a head surrounded by a Mae West collar—and we had no guarantee that Freddie was still in his dinghy. We were scudding along at 50 feet, engaged in what I hoped was a fair imitation of a 'square search'—something at which navigators are expert but which to a fighter pilot is a closed book. Anyway, we roamed the empty seas for half an hour without success.

We toiled on through the long afternoon, running on a very lean mixture and coarse pitch to give us maximum endurance. We had long since exhausted our belly tanks. The submarine and I kept up a commentary until, about 1630, we decided we were well inside the area. Still nothing showed up and still we went on searching. The submarine was now engaged in some search pattern of her own and we were combing a pretty big area around her.

Around 1745 I started to have dreams of home. I hadn't the faintest idea where the Fleet would be, other than that they were somewhere to the south. As to how many miles away I couldn't even begin to guess—and it would be dark by 1900 to 1930. I didn't fancy a night landing for some of the new boys—or for myself. Corsairs could kill us quite effortlessly in broad daylight, without any assistance from the darkness.

So at 1800 I called up my American friend and told him I thought we should be heading south. A pity, he said; for he felt we were so near. Could I possibly stretch it to 1815? I looked around at my pilots—who were listening, of course—thinking of their lives and realising that they would automatically leave the whole thing to me. And then I thought of Freddie Nottingham, out there on the darkening sea.

'OK. 15 minutes. There's little danger of any interference now, so we'll send out three and I'll keep guard myself. Out!'

The boys tore off again into the gloom to the east. They were scarcely out of sight before I saw a red star rise from the water down to the south. The submarine saw it at the same time and her wake described a great arc of silver as she put her wheel hard a-starboard. I recalled the other pilots and, diving down to water level, flew past the dinghy at ten feet. Freddie was waving his little flag like a madman. Great stuff! We waited until the submarine came down to him, two ratings in swimming trunks already out on the outer casing. As she hove to with a frenzied flurry in her wake, they jumped, tied to the ends of life-lines, to help Nottingham on to the casing. After a minute or two the Commander came on the air.

'The pilot's name is Nottingham; I repeat, Nottingham.'

I can't remember now what I said. There was a burst of mutual thanking and metaphorical back-slapping. We wished each other God speed and went on our ways.

It must be said here that Nottingham had shown himself to be extremely cool and remarkably courageous. He had only three small rockets in his Mae West—little more than Roman candles—and, although he had watched us for more than a couple of hours, searching

224

to the north of him, he had withstood the temptation to fire them, knowing full well that we would be unlikely to see them whilst the light remained good. Only when dusk fell did he let go the first one—and we saw it. Freddie the Unflappable!

Now the rescue was achieved, it was 'Home, James!' We roared off to the south, climbing like dingbats for altitude in order to establish radio contact. We were up to 16,000 feet before I got a reply. Then *Indomitable*, with the best radio in the Fleet, came up loud and clear. She told me not to waste time giving her a fix, just to press on and await their call when we appeared on radar. Sometime later the FDO was back:

'Now we've got you. Eighty miles to go. Turn 10 degrees to port on to 175 degrees. Over.'

I thanked him. I was a lot happier now and could almost hear the boys whistling with good cheer. We were still up in the mellow light of an orange setting sun with the sea, far below us, as black as ink. The minutes ticked away.

'Twenty-five to go.' Time passed.

'We're down on your port side now. Can you see us? Over.'

I looked down, at an angle of some 45 degrees. Nothing.

'Not yet. Over.'

'Good God, man! You're looking down the bloody chimney! Look again! Over.'

Yes; they *were* there. When I had lost some altitude and done a couple of circuits to accustom myself to the comparative darkness, I now saw the faint white smudges which only delicately relieved the leaden gloom of the sea. We did the rounds of the carriers to find *Illustrious*, putting on navigation lights for the benefit of Colin Cunningham, who was doing the batting. In fact, by the time we had flown our pattern, we could see reasonably well and landing was no problem.

Nottingham was taken by his submarine to Saipan and in the course of a day or two Admiral Nimitz, USN C-in-C Pacific, had him flown to Leyte in the Philippines in his personal aircraft.

The suicide bombers came at us out of Formosa. Despite their fanatical courage and determination, the battle was by no means one-sided. On April 1 *Victorious* was attacked by one whose approach was spectacular, even if the end result was disappointing for him. This son of the Divine Wind passed over *Vic* at a considerable altitude, did a half-roll and then pulled into a vertical dive. Captain Denny judged matters to a nicety. When the Jap was fully committed to his dive, with his ailerons good and frozen, he gave a helm order to port and the horrible little man plunged into the Pacific only yards from the starboard bow.

225

Earlier in the day, two Kamikazes had been more successful. At first light, as we were out on the flight-deck supervising the first take-off, there was the scream of a diving aircraft passing over us. The hell of a bang followed as a suicider slammed into *Indefatigable*, sailing parallel to us about 300 yards on our starboard side. She took the blow in the worst possible place—in the angle between flight-deck and island—and casualties in dead, wounded and missing were heavy. The armour-plated deck protected the hangar from damage, but itself suffered a severe dent from the sheer impact. Ingenuity, however, is only one of the many arts of which a Royal Naval ship is mistress. Quick-drying cement was poured into the depression and levelled off. Within a few short hours *Indefat* was operating her aircraft as though she had experienced nothing more than a slight hiccup.

Ulster, one of our fine destroyers, took a Kamikaze on the same day, with tragic results. This little man must have heard about armoured decks on carriers and had decided to take on easier meat. He came steep and fast from the port beam and drove his aircraft—or his bomb; I never knew which—through *Ulster*'s iron deck into the port boiler room. Above the gaping hole leading into the inferno below sat a Bofors gunner who must have been a cool customer for within seconds of the explosion he shot down a second Kamikaze which was following the first. Poor *Ulster*! She was stopped in her tracks, sorely stricken but by no means lost. *Gambia* took her in tow and evacuated her safely from the danger area.

The days passed, patrol after patrol. Sometimes morning, sometimes afternoon or evening—often all three. We became tired, we lost appetites. There was no time for laundry to be done and our flying overalls became sweat-sodden and dirty. They were long, long flying days punctuated by brief, flashing moments of excitement, fear and heart-stopping flap. The enemy had a seemingly endless supply of flak ammunition and the more aircraft we flew over his islands, the better his practice became. We drove ourselves to attack him through all the hours of daylight and he never failed to greet us with his withering fire of deceptively slow-climbing balls of red and green as the flak rose to bracket us.

Apart from the ever-present menace of the enemy, we occasionally manufactured a few problems for ourselves. As we flew our landing pattern one afternoon, a panic call about Kamikazes in the vicinity of the Fleet alerted us. Right on its heels came an order to get the hell out of it and to give full bore on an interception course. I tucked up wheels and flaps, gave it the gun and went into a fast climb to the west, at the same time turning on my gun switches; six of them with a master switch, situated immediately below the windscreen. We must have been about 8,000 feet when the recall came; some Charlie had approached the Fleet not showing his IFF.

Coming in to land for the second time, I was clueless enough to forget to flick off the gun switches. Having taxied up to the forward round-down, switched off the engine and unharnessed myself, I heaved myself up to get out of the cockpit, pulling on the joystick with my right hand for a bit of assistance. My six guns roared out with a fine, uninhibited two-second burst. A destroyer keeping station on us two cables ahead promptly turned up the taps and proceeded to belt off at high speed in the general direction of Australia. I didn't blame her for one moment. A seemingly endless succession of chunks of armour-piercing steel, half an inch in diameter and about two inches long, scudding smartly above one's head is sufficient encouragement to push off for any destination—even Australia. I walked down the flight-deck wearing as nonchalant an expression as I could muster. But I couldn't fool Captain Lambe. As I passed close beneath the flying bridge, trying to avoid attention, I heard 'Hans!' in unusually soft tones. I looked up. His face bore the suspicion of a grin and his right index finger beckoned me. He listened to my feeble excuse without interruption. Then:

'I'm sure it's easily done, Hans—probably *too* easily on a day like this has been. But you know, you really shouldn't frighten people like that.'

I knew, as he did, that I could easily have killed some of 'our side'. But he knew that I knew—and he was great enough to resist delivering clichés.

One evening a young new pilot came into my cabin. He was just out from England and had come up with the Fleet Train. I had a chat with him and tried to make him feel at home; a pleasant kid, cheerful and as keen as mustard. As he turned to go, he hesitated for a moment and said:

'Did you say your name was Hanson, sir?'

I nodded.

'Did you by any chance go to Pensacola, sir?' Yes, I had trained there.

'Do you know they're still talking about you?'

'Well!' I said. 'That's very nice of them! As a matter of fact, I played the organ there for about six months and thoroughly enjoyed myself.'

'Oh! I didn't know about that. No. It's about the decompression chamber there. The Surgeon-Commander told us to be human—or natural. I can't remember which. But certainly not to behave like another Limey called Hanson who had done the job with maximum marks—the only one ever. Was that you, sir?' He grinned. 'He doesn't seem to have got over it!'

'It's true, for what it's worth. But I'm a bit surprised he still talks about it. If he's still there—and from what you say there's a fair chance that he is—I would have thought he would have learnt to do it himself! Anyway, the hell with history. Come on for a drink and I'll introduce you to the boys. You'll be flying in my flight.'

I have said that our long spell in the tropics was now beginning to take its toll. *Victorious*, our chummy ship, was much fresher. Where some months earlier we had been able to beat them decisively to the draw where launching and landing were concerned, they now had the edge on us. In an endeavour to show *Vic* that we were still a force to be reckoned with, Wings launched us one day a little prematurely, before the ship was fully turned into the wind. *Illustrious* was still wheeling quickly into wind, with starboard helm, when I rolled up the deck. As I passed the island and became exposed to the full force of the breeze blowing from the starboard side, it caught me completely unawares and carried me fiercely to port. The port wheel mounted the forward 4.5-inch turret, there was a big bang and I almost half-rolled into the sea. (The bang, I discovered later, was the impact of my port flaps on a stout metal stanchion standing about three feet high, at the very corner of the deck.) With the stick hard over to starboard, a lot of praying, sheer will-power and one hell of a lot of luck, I scraped the Corsair off the water leaving a wake like that of a motor-boat and struggled into the air. I was relieved when, having reached sufficient height to retract undercarriage and flaps, I found that she flew perfectly well.

For three solid hours, off and on, I worried about the landing to come. Half an hour before we were due to land on I handed over command of the flight to Johnny Baker and pushed off to a large cumulus cloud which was sailing serenely on its way to Hawaii. Using it as a flight-deck, I made my approach. Wheels down—OK. Flaps down—frightening. Again the aircraft rolled off to port. I looked down at the flaps as best I could. The inboard section was just below half-way down; the outward section was only very slightly down. With only partial lift on that side, the lift on the starboard side was too strong. So I went round again, this time using only half-flap. The effect was not nearly so scaring, but my landing speed had to be much higher. I put on full throttle to test the effect in case I had to take a wave-off. I went into an awkward, half-sideways roll that was violent enough to shake me rigid.

Just before we started the descent from 10,000 feet, I called Baker over.

'Johnny, I've got a problem. Come underneath me, stick your head in the wheel-well and tell me what the hell has gone.'

He came close beneath me—there weren't many pilots I would have allowed to come as close to me as that!—and after 30 seconds he emerged and came alongside.

'Is the undercarriage damaged, Johnny? I know the flaps are buggered.'

'Undercart OK. The jack on the port flaps is broken and you are losing all your fluid. The metal of the flaps is badly torn—clumsy sod, aren't you . . . sir?'(Big grin from the cockpit.) 'But your undercart is definitely OK. Tyres look fine, too—no sign of a burst.'

As we dropped down to the ship I called Johnny Hastings to the FDO's radio. I told him I had problems and had been trying some ADDLs on one of the local clouds. I would have to land fairly fast and straight—no screaming turn, for I couldn't take a wave-off. It would have to be a first-time effort.

While the other boys were landing on, the ship came on the R/T again. The Captain gave me three alternatives: a landing, bale-out or ditch; and I had to make up my mind quickly. I didn't hesitate; I would go for the landing. When the other aircraft were safely out of harm's way, the fire-hoses were run out on deck and I could see the firefighters donning their asbestos suits. I gulped once or twice—it was a daunting moment. Then:

'Right! Come on in!'

I went into my landing pattern. On the last turn towards the ship I tentatively tried the flaps—still that tendency to roll out of my hands. And my stall warning light flickered ominously. I'd gone in on this corner before and I wasn't keen to do an encore. I put on a bit more urge—88 knots—and kept it there. As I approached from something like 15 degrees from the fore-and-aft line, Johnny gave me 'You're fast!' Sod that, I thought; you'll just have to like it, John. He brought me down, down, down—still saying I was fast. Then he cut me and, with still a lot of right stick, I chopped the throttle. Christ! The wires were flying beneath me! A dirty great barrier looms up in front—so this is what it's like! Then my head was practically jerked from my neck. I had caught the last wire—for the very best of reasons known as the 'Jesus Christ'. Over the Tannoy I heard Wings say something at once friendly and pleasantly vulgar. Home again in one piece.

Two sections of flap and a new jack were replaced within a couple of hours. Certainly a damn sight faster than I recovered!

The appearance on the radar screens of suicide aircraft galvanised the whole Fleet into activity. Airborne fighters were vectored towards incoming enemy aircraft, and fighters at readiness were launched. Very good interceptions were made as far away as 20 to 30 miles from the Fleet. Invariably the enemy chose weather which was partially overcast. They were expert at 'cloud-dodging', an art which occasionally reduced the serious business of war to a game of cowboys and

Indians. There was one morning when two of our fighters caught a Jap on the hop, far away from the Fleet, who elected to seek safety inside a large cumulus. We posted boys all round the cloud—and above and below it—and awaited developments. The impatient Churchill, however, dashed into the cloud and in no time at all emerged on the far side, there to see his enemy only a matter of yards away from him. The Jap was quickly despatched.

Other moments, too, were reminiscent of Laurel and Hardy. Mike Tritton and I were on standby one sultry afternoon when a red warning came up. We hurtled down the ladder and out on to the after flight-deck, where we leapt into the first two Corsairs we reached. Other pilots were running behind us to clear the deck of aircraft. Mike took off very quickly indeed, closely followed by me. My choice didn't sound very happy; she was running very roughly and only just staggered off the deck. This was going to be a great flight! I could hear Mike being vectored towards the enemy as I pulled up the undercarriage and went into a tight turn to form up on him. As I put on the power, however, nothing happened apart from the hell of a lot of banging up front. It sounded as though the engine was about to leave its bearers. As Michael faded rapidly into the distance, I abandoned all hope of becoming an effective part of the defence and turned for the carrier, yelling at her as I did so to keep her into wind. I couldn't see this old cattle-truck staying airborne for much longer and I wanted an emergency landing—badly.

As I jumped to the deck after parking up forward, 'Wolf' Maddison, our Squadron Maintenance Chief, a wizard with aero engines if ever there was one, was waiting for me. He looked a bit sorrowful.

'You shouldn't have taken *that* one, you know, sir,' he said, in the manner of a kindly though somewhat morose farmer delivering a homily to a schoolboy caught in the act of stealing apples. 'She's waiting for a plug change and isn't fit to fly.' He scratched his ear and surveyed the deck with the look of a man who had been indulging in some heart-searching. 'It's been a bloody awful afternoon altogether, really. I tested the engine of this thing right after dinner—and we *still* haven't been able to use the lift to get her below. That's why she's still here.'

I stared at him, open-mouthed.

'Can't understand what you're bitching at, Chief! *I* can tell you she isn't safe! Not even to go shopping with! But if you *will* leave your rubbish lying around the deck . . . I didn't know she was unserviceable when I jumped into her. You want to be careful in these dangerous times, Wolf—you might have been shot off in the thing *yourself*. At least you could have done the plug change while you were at it!'

When the Japs came within range of the Fleet's guns, the atmosphere was like a Wembley Cup Final, with goofers on all sides urging the gunners to 'get the bastards, for Chrissake!' No one was under any delusion. Once a suicide attacker penetrated the patrols and reached a position five or six miles from the Fleet, there was only one end; he was coming in. Nothing, apart from being blown apart, would stop him now. The toiling crews of the 4.5-inch guns were execrated in appalling language when their shells burst wide of the mark. If the screaming Zeke were shot out of the sky, the cheering was ecstatic—a goal in any man's language. We had tragedies. Two Seafires from *Indefatigable*, hell bent on finishing off their prey, followed Zekes into the Fleet's field of fire and paid the awful penalty. It was psychologically difficult to break off when you had him cold in your sights. In an endeavour to avoid such unnecessary loss of life, orders were issued that aircraft returning to the Fleet while it was still 'trigger-happy' following an attack (and who shall blame them for being so?) should approach sedately in regular formation and with undercarriages lowered. One afternoon our flight returned in copy-book formation, wheels down, as though flying-past Buckingham Palace on a Sunday afternoon, when we were greeted with a salvo from *Howe*'s secondary armament of 5.25-inch guns. A fine welcome indeed! My language over the R/T was blistering and obscene. However, I was greatly mollified, first by the fact that their practice was poor and missed us by the length of Piccadilly and even more so when I received an immediate apology, couched in much more gentlemanly and decorous terms. The manners of the Dartmouth boys, even under heavy stress, were impeccable!

The flying was fast and furious. Two or three days later, whilst patrolling over the Fleet, we were given a vector to intercept which spoke volumes for the efficiency of the radar operators and fighter direction team, for we must have been 20 miles away when we saw them—four Zekes in straggling formation, heading straight for us and about 1,000 feet above. As we sounded the 'Tally-ho!' they broke formation and scattered to the four winds. Two of them, for some reason or other, headed south and I heard later that they had been intercepted and shot down by some of *Vic*'s Corsairs. The other two turned 180 degrees and opened up the taps for home. We gave chase—but they had at least a couple of miles' head-start; and even with our superior speed it would take some time to overhaul them. I bent the throttle lever and prayed that we would catch them before we had to land at Pekin to refuel! Suddenly Gerry Salmon came up. (Gerry was one of Michael's boys; we were flying a mixed flight on that trip.)

'Can we use the water injection, boss?'

Good God! Of course! The machine I was flying (not my own,

which was being serviced) was not equipped with water injection and the idea had never entered my thick head.

'Yes, Gerry! Bang it in and go get 'em!'

The three aircraft shot away from me as though I was going astern. I throttled back a little to ease my panting engine and watched the fun and games up ahead. Both enemy aircraft were quickly shot down.

By now we were enlarging our capabilities by attacking the enemy in the fighter-bomber role. Since the Japanese had been obliged to concentrate on suicide tactics, interference by interceptor fighters was non-existent and we could afford to increase our attacking tactics. The Corsair could carry quite comfortably two 500 lb bombs, attached to racks fitted to the centre section of the wings; and with these we helped the Avengers to devastate the runways. We also used napalm bombs which were frighteningly effective on airfield buildings and barrack blocks. Napalm 'cartridges', inserted into our overload belly tanks, were actuated from the cockpit a few minutes before dropping on the targets and the instantaneous carpet of fire which enveloped a large area as soon as the tank hit the earth was almost sickening to see from the air; a truly dreadful weapon. Our accuracy with the conventional bombs probably wasn't as professional as that of our Avenger friends; but if you can't hit a runway there's something seriously amiss with your eyesight!

Tiredness, probably the greatest enemy with which we had to contend, was now showing itself quite blatantly. Bruce Maclaren made a desperate attempt to land which was nothing less than a dive-bombing attack on the deck. Everything about it was wrong; he was too fast, too high and his approach had been diabolical. He thumped into the deck with his main wheels, bounced clean over both barriers and tried to stuff his nose down into the foredeck. Had he succeeded he would have destroyed himself and five or six aircraft parked in the bows. Fortunately for all of us his starboard wing clipped the boom of the mobile crane parked forward of the island, which slewed him round to starboard and shot him into the sea. He had the good sense to wait until he hit the water before releasing himself from the cockpit and was safely picked up by a destroyer. Certainly he never flew from the carrier again. Where deck-landing was concerned, Bruce had reached the pitch where Bob Ellison had to put his foot down.

That immaculate flyer Percy Cole was also tiring. In the course of three or four days he endured two very bad barrier crashes from both of which he was lucky to escape unhurt. In one of them, certainly, he admitted that he had 'forgotten' to close the throttle.

Jimmy James, my RN Lieutenant, stalled in the middle of his downwind leg run to the carrier. There was no good reason why he should have done so; his lack of attention, resulting from tiredness, allowed his aircraft to fall below flying speed. He crashed into the sea from 500 feet and escaped with a broken arm.

Most of us began to suffer from 'off' days; dreadful mornings when our normal relaxed attitude to flying was nowhere to be seen; days when the very thought of making low-flying attacks was positive anathema. I recall one morning when we were flying the first patrol of the day over Ishigaki, whose short-range flak was by now notorious for its deadly accuracy. From 10,000 feet, scanning the airfield through my binoculars, I saw three aircraft—or dummies. Even with an excellent pair of glasses it wasn't always possible to distinguish between them. Two were in revetments, the other on the grass 50 yards from the strip. Small boards, with a bulldog clip holding plans of the airfields, were strapped to our thighs; and I duly pencilled in the planes in their correct positions.

When we landed much later I went to see the IO and handed him the chart.

'Three there for you, my old cock-sparrow. You can put the bombers on to them.' He obviously hadn't heard or noticed the last sentence. He was busily writing up his cumulative report.

'Hans. Three aircraft. Ishigaki.' He looked up at me. 'Destroyed?'

'Not even scratched. As I said, put the bombers on to them.'

He stroked his chin with his pencil.

'But you had a go, surely?'

'Look,' I said impatiently. 'I don't have to explain to you what I did or why I did it. All I have to tell you is what I saw.'

'But why not, Hans?'

'Balls to explanations! I've given you the dope—now it's all yours!' I felt touchy and irritable; annoyed with myself for my gloomy premonitions and irritated by his persistence.

Two days later we were over the same field. Today was different. *I* was different. My Corsair was once again a part of me, not just a machine I was driving across the sky. I could have put her through the eye of a needle.

My binoculars showed me what could be a juicy Myrtle at the end of the runway. We came down from 10,000 feet and did a fast run across the field at about 5,000 feet. This was no dummy, for there was quite a gaggle of Japs buzzing about her. As we disappeared out to sea, I sized up the situation and turned to Baker. On a job like this he was invaluable; intelligent and courageous.

'You saw her, Johnny?' He nodded. 'Trouble is, the guns are right behind her. I want you to do a dummy attack from the east when I tell you. Make it look really good.' He knew what I wanted; he didn't even reply. When he had heard me out he gave me the 'zero' sign with finger

and thumb. I wheeled away from them and climbed out to the west.
When I had got myself organised I went on the R/T again.

'Tell me when you're all set, John. Start from about three miles
out.'

'OK. Wait.' Seconds passed. 'All set. Say when.'

I lined myself up on the runway from way out and took the compass
bearing.

'Now! GO!' I rocketed down from 10,000 feet, tearing a great strip
down the sky. As I crossed the coast I was low down, cracking along at
300 knots. I knew exactly where the Myrtle was. I was lined up on her,
well out of range, when I saw Johnny and his boys steaming down in a
great fast arc drawing, it seemed to me, all the flak north of the
Equator. Then I was there. I opened up at long range and saw tracer
going straight into the Myrtle. There were ladders up against the
engines—they were putting new props on her; she must have nosed
over on landing. Now I was really hitting her; men, ladders, chunks of
metal were flying all over the place. Something like a miniature
explosion blew up when the cone of my gun pattern hit her. There
were flashes from ricochetting tracer around me as I pulled over the
aircraft and dropped down again, to flat-hat out to sea.

They had been so engrossed with Johnny's attack that I doubt if
they knew I was there until it was all over.

We had been patrolling over the Fleet at 25,000 feet for two and a
half hours. Life was becoming a bit tedious and our rear ends were
beginning to notice what uncomfortable cushions parachutes provide.
We were looking forward to landing on in half an hour, at 1230.

At 1215 our FDO came on the air to ask my petrol state. I told him I
was OK; obviously much too cheerfully, for he promptly asked me to
'make it 1330, there's a good chap' and rang off before I could argue. It
was painfully obvious that the relieving flight was not yet ready to take
off.

We had a brand-new No 4 in the flight, freshly arrived via the Fleet
Train. He was just a boy. Now, over the wide watery wastes of the
north-west Pacific, his schoolboy voice piped up.

'I say, Johnny!' This to Baker, his No 3.

'Yeah.' Baker didn't waste words.

'What was that the CO said? 1330?'

'Right.'

'Well, I was thinking. That's half-past one, isn't it?'

'Right.'

'Well—what do we do for dinner?'

Before anyone could give him a suitable reply—and the suitability
would have been open to a lot of doubt!—an American beat us all to

the draw. From somewhere in the Okinawa area, anything up to 50 miles to the north, came a cheerful Bronx voice:

'They send your goddam dinner up to you! What else?'

In all the R/T chatter that filtered through the headset every day it was, I suppose, only natural that one should perk up a little when friends' voices were recognised, particularly when they came from other carriers.

A voice from nowhere—apparently young and naïve—came up on the R/T asking something which I would have thought to be self-evident and quite elementary. Our good friend Gammy Godson, CO of one of *Indomitable*'s Hellcat squadrons, appeared to be in agreement, for it was his voice which promptly told the youngster 'not to be such a bloody fool!' Always good advice!

A few days later we returned to the carrier on a dark, stormy evening, with plenty of pitch to the ship's stern and great, frothy bow-waves breaking down her side. The voice of *Indomitable*'s FDO came up, ordering her waiting flights to switch on navigation lights to assist the batsman.

'Wilco. Out,' came the reply from the senior Flight Commander and I was delighted to recognise the voice of my old friend Sammy Langdon. I was still thinking about him and of our good times together at St Merryn and in Egypt when one of his flight spoke to him. Funny how the youngsters could always be relied upon to provide the light relief; and this lad was no exception.

'I say, Sammy!'

'Yes! What is it?'

'Which *is* the switch for the navigation lights?' (Like us, the majority of the Hellcat boys were not night-flyers and, apart from those switches which we used daily, the vast expanse of the electrical switchboard down on the right-hand side of the cockpit was unknown territory to us.)

Sammy was a gentle, quiet creature with a voice which never rose above a subdued conversational tone.

'Buggered if *I* know, old son. Do what I've done—put the lot on and fuck the expense.'

I looked towards *Indom*. Sammy's aircraft, just turning in to the round-down, looked like a Christmas tree. Wingtip lights, formation lights, navigation lights, landing searchlights—all were blazing in magnificent illumination. He never changed!

A few days later both he and Gammy Godson were shot down. Two great pilots, two good friends. I had heard their voices for the last time.

It was inevitable that we should become the target for a Kamikaze attack and April 6 was the day.

I had sneaked into my cabin to freshen up after a hot, sticky day when everything happened. The 4.5-inch battery above me opened up and, as usual, everything took off. Books, shoes, glasses, photoframes—all showered down to the deck of my cabin in a hell of a mess. Something was really happening! I galloped down the passage to the nearest ladder, which I reached just before the Bofors started to crackle; and I was halfway up to the flight-deck when the whole ship jumped three feet in the water. Torpedoed!

It wasn't a torpedo. It was a Kamikaze; and the Jap who had expired in the last few seconds had come out of a cloud on the port beam in a fast, shallow dive. One of our Bofors gunners hit him with his first shell and continued to hit him all the way down. Seconds before the Zeke reached us, the whole tail assembly parted company and, having lost his rudder, the Jap slid off course. Instead of crashing into the angle of the island and the flight-deck, which had been his intention, he hit the front of the compass platform with the starboard wing and the plane, bomb and all, crashed into the sea 30 yards from the ship, where the whole lot blew up. The wind was from the starboard side and we were immediately inundated with a shower of crankshafts, pistons, sections of fuselage and assorted pieces of Mitsubishi manufacture. The pilot's dinghy, a gaudy red and yellow affair, flew lazily across the deck, inflating itself in transit, and fetched up on the port aerial mast. The pilot's own skull was the first object to land on the deck, to be gathered up quickly by the medical profession.

Perhaps the most macabre moment of the short action involved Bob Finlay, our piano-playing Captain's Secretary, who at action stations was the captain of a multiple pom-pom on the port side. When the Jap appeared from the clouds, Bob was ready and full of zeal, his eye glued to the gun's rubber eyepiece and his hands ready on the twist-grip controls. When the aircraft lined up on the ship, Bob sighted through the ring-sight further up the gun and let go, double *forte* and decidedly *con brio*. As the second Kamikaze—for there were two of them—made his dive, Bob opened up again, but had to cease fire momentarily to flick away, somewhat petulantly, something which partially obscured the ring-sight. He didn't feel very well two minutes later when he realised that what he had removed so peremptorily was a slender strip of Japanese flesh, about half a rasher. Things like that shouldn't happen to a Captain's Secretary!

One act of cold-blooded courage must be recorded. When the Kamikaze appeared, we had two Corsairs ranged on the centre line, all set for take-off. Churchill was leading, Parli astern of him, both with engines turning and ready to go. Suddenly the after 4.5-inch guns commenced to fire, simultaneously with a red warning over the Tannoys. The two pilots 'baled out' and, together with the mechanics who had been holding the chocks, ran to the island for cover. The steady, shattering thump of the 4.5s, ear-splitting in the painful explosions from their muzzles, and the whip-like crack of the Bofors and Oerlikons on all sides made incoherent all thought and speech.

Parli, on leaving his aircraft, had found time to pull the mixture control back to 'automatic cut-off' which stopped the engine instantly. Churchill hadn't lingered and the engine of his Corsair was still ticking over at about 300 revs. Now the engine's vibration, the tremor of the deck as the gunfire shook the ship and, finally, the ship's leap into the air as the suicider exploded—all these proved sufficient to dislodge the aircraft's chocks; and the Corsair slowly moved forward and slightly to port. In a matter of seconds it would reach the port nets and plunge over them into the sea. £75,000, apart from any injuries it might cause on its way.

There might be Kamikazes about, although I couldn't see any as I emerged on to the flight-deck. All I could see were shells exploding at a great height and a strung-out flight of Hellcats tearing upwards towards a bank of cumulus way up above us. A tug on my sleeve brought me back to ground level. From the door to the island, where he had sought shelter, came Demaine, our high-diving electrician, running swiftly towards the moving Corsair, completely disregarding Kamikaze and gunfire. He leapt on to the wing and climbed into the cockpit, where he managed to hit the foot-brakes in the nick of time, just as the wheels reached the three-inch deck-edge. He switched off the engine and sat there, cool as a cucumber, until two lads ran across with sets of chocks.

I tried in vain to get a DSM for him, for his was a deed of true bravery in the middle of an action. He was, however, mentioned in despatches which showed at least that his courage had been recognised by the hierarchy.

Finally, it should be recorded that only seven seconds had elapsed between the Kamikaze's first appearance through the overcast and his explosion in the water. It was, without a doubt, one of those occasions when seconds can stretch into eternity.

Back to Hirara as a change from Iriomote and Ishigaki. On this particular afternoon we were on a three-hour patrol, cruising in lazy circles over the island at 15,000 feet. We had searched the airfield—nothing. By now they were pretty wise to us and such aircraft as they were holding on the field were well hidden and out of harm's way. After two hours of this, one can become impatient and restless and one looks for action. Action, for God's sake, before we go mad!

'The hell with this, lads. Let's go down and see what we can find.'

We plastered the brickwork of a coastguard station on the northern-most corner of the island, but there was no sign of activity. Probably it had become a favourite target for the learners and the gentlemen of the coastguard service had decided that there were other and safer ways of spending an afternoon than sitting in a white box waiting to be shot at. I saw their point of view. That certainly didn't satisfy our lust. We beat up a small coaster—little more than a large fishing trawler—until I felt like a big bully and left them in peace to run into shallow water to beach what was left of her. We saw some Jap soldiers dash for shelter into a row of detached houses on the outskirts of the town. One run down the row was enough to bang some incendiaries into them. That was sufficient to make me feel a cheap little vandal and I slunk away, taking my three lads with me. We weren't winning the war playing around like this!

It must have been about 1630 as we crossed the town, flying at about 8,000 feet. Glory be! There was a parade ground! What was more, it was pretty full with all the licentious soldiery drawn up in serried ranks.

One of the Corsair's drawbacks as far as the enemy was concerned was that the exhaust roar from its 18 cylinders was all behind it. There was virtually no noise from the engine apparent until the aircraft was almost overhead. It was said that the Japanese called it the 'whispering death' for this reason. So when I decided to attack this juicy target, they broke formation only when it was too late for most of them to find cover.

There were three possible angles from which to attack, only one of which was dangerous. After an afternoon of sheer frustration, monu-mental stupidity born of weariness and a touch of 'twitch' chose for me the route which in normal and more carefree times would clearly have indicated—'A sticky death this way'. In my eagerness to get in amongst it without losing the invaluable element of surprise, I gave the boys no warning at all. I banged the stick over to the right and down, leaving them to follow as best they could. It was providential that I did so, for had I led them down in an orderly formation, at least two of them would have bought it. As it was, they had scarcely made their move to follow me down when they realised that I had made a hash of things, giving them time to alter their own approach to something much safer and more airmanlike.

Certainly I wrought a bit of death and destruction, there was no doubt about that. With that enhanced, falcon-like vision which fiercely pumped adrenalin produces at moments of high excitement, I could see soldiers fairly bouncing away from the sledgehammer impact of the .5 shells. It needed only a touch on the rudder-bar to cover square yards of the parade ground and there was a fair number of bodies lying motionless as I levelled out and pulled away. And then I saw it.

Rising sharply from the back of the military area was a sheer cliff-like eminence which I had completely missed in my haste to get to ground level. Now, as I approached it at 300 knots, it looked like the North Wall of the Eiger. Taking my life in my hands I pulled on the stick for all I was worth. I can only remember thick streamers springing from my wingtips before I blacked out good and true. The black-out hit me like pentothal—there was no greying-out, no fuzziness. I went out like a light.

When I recovered I was out at sea, climbing gently at about 150 knots, safe and sound. The others had formed up on me again and were gazing at me with uncomprehending eyes. Well they might. They had all been enthralled by the spectacle of their senior and most stupid bastard of an officer busily trying to kill himself. I hope my guardian angel put in for overtime for, by God, he had earned it!

April 7 started off in great style. We were over Miyako in the early morning and had a field day, with two aircraft destroyed and one damaged. Things were going well and the boys were on form. And then it just had to turn into one of those days.

Percy Cole took his flight to Hirara in his own particular style. His method—a good one, too—was to approach the island from the west, fly through the town at chimney-pot height, then drop down on to the airfield like the wrath of God.

He told me later that, as he was leaving the town and approaching the airfield boundary, short-range flak flashed from the gun emplacements on the field, prompting him to look across and up to Marritt. He was flying 40 feet above the rest of them and Percy screamed at him to get his head down. But young Marritt never heard him. As Percy pressed the R/T button on his throttle lever, he saw a shell blast through the windshield of the luckless Marritt's aircraft. The plane rolled on to its back and tore into the ground at 300 knots or more.

On the previous evening I had finished the flying orders for the following day and wandered along to the wardroom; there was time for a couple of drinks before going to bed. Winnie Churchill was the first man I bumped into.

'Winnie! Just the man I was looking for. I've put you on to Ishigaki for the first shift. OK?'

'Yes, sure, boss. My own boys?'

'Yes. As usual.' I paused for a moment. 'Now remember—no fooling.' He gave me an old-fashioned look. 'You know those bastards on Ishigaki as well as I do. Unless you damn well have to, no more than two runs.'

Now his look said, without a shadow of doubt—'Windy bastard!' I ignored it and pressed on.

'Look, don't be a bloody fool. You know they have the measure of you after two runs down that strip. I don't want those kids of yours to be killed because you want to be a hero. I just want new kids to be given a break.' (Johnny Lowder, his No 3, was a good, solid, experienced hand. It was the other two I feared for.)

So on April 7 Winnie went to Ishigaki. They came back with one of Mike's flights and I was standing with Wings on his bridge when they came down to the carrier. But there weren't eight—only seven.

The 1830 boys came on first; good, clever landings, the wires screaming out as they were arrested and the barriers clanging as they taxied up the deck in the old, efficient rhythm. There were four of them; so it was my flight that was one short. The three of them came on; again, good safe landings. The oxygen masks hid their faces but certainly Winnie wasn't there; I would have known *him*.

Johnny Lowder jumped from his cockpit at the front end and came running down the deck. He bounded up the ladder and joined me. He had a stammer which excitement and emotion were now exaggerating.

'It's Winnie, Hans. I'm awfully sorry, it's Winnie. He's gone.' There were tears in his eyes, running down in channels through the grime left by his goggles.

They had made a couple of runs up the airstrip, smacking one or two aircraft parked on one side. They then flew up and away, their job done. After a minute or so Winnie tapped his headphones, the top of his helmet and pointed to Lowder. This signified 'My radio is unserviceable. I am handing the lead over to you.' Winnie wheeled out of the formation and dived back to Ishigaki. Johnny turned the flight so that he could keep him in sight.

Lowder said he saw him tearing in from the west. He had no idea *why* he had gone back. They had seen nothing which called for another attack—but maybe Winnie *had*. He reached the eastern end of the runway, and of the island itself, when his aircraft seemed to falter; then it turned over very, very slowly and slid into the sea.

My immediate reaction was to be furiously angry. *Why* the hell did he have to be the clever bastard and refuse to listen? *Why* the hell did he think he was invulnerable where so many other pilots had fallen?

But I couldn't be angry any more when I saw Jack Parli's face. They had been inseparable buddies since they had joined up together in New Zealand. And Jack's face showed what it was going to mean to him to have to fight the rest of the war without his 'cobber'.

Churchill was as brave as a lion. He loved living and he loved fighting. Although I am convinced there was not the slightest need for him to return to that death-trap, I know, too, that one can rarely change human nature. If I could have brought him back to life that instant, given him a Corsair and told him to go back and belt hell out of Ishigaki, he wouldn't have hesitated. He wouldn't have had it any other way.

On April 11 the Staff decided that we should attack the Kamikazes on their home ground and strikes on Formosa were laid on. The weather intervened, however, and the operation was delayed for 24 hours.

The following morning we provided a strong escort of Corsairs for the Avengers as they made their way to Shinchiku airfield, on the north-western corner of the island. As we flew along the north coast, seven or eight miles from land, Jake Millard came up on the radio to report that his aircraft was failing quickly.

Jake, of 1830 Squadron, was a great fellow both in stature and in spirit. Prior to the war he had been on the Metropolitan Police Force and was renowned as a swimmer and a water-polo player. He was also a reliable pilot with a truly remarkable accident-free record.

I looked around to find him already losing speed and height through reduced power. We talked briefly and I realised that he had no alternative but to ditch. I looked at the coast, my watch and the compass and hoped I might be able to give something like a reasoned suggestion of his position. Then I told Baker to go down to see how Jake fared when he hit the drink. Johnny watched him glide into a moderate sea as I pumped out a Mayday signal. Johnny then saw him start to swim towards the shore; and we shall never know why he hadn't rescued his dinghy from the sinking aircraft. By this time the strike was well down the coast, so Johnny climbed back to a fair altitude to transmit another Mayday signal, confident that the air/sea rescue services in the area would pick him up. He then descended again—this time to sea level, but he was unable to find Jake again. As I have said earlier, it is extremely difficult to spot a man's head in the north-west Pacific.

By now we had reached Shinchiku. Cloud level was down to about 2,500 feet and visibility inland was poor. The Avengers went in to bomb the airfield and adjacent roads and railway lines. We did a quick pass round the airfield. There was little opposition, and nothing to hit. We made another circuit of the field. This time the short-range flak burst into life with a vengeance; fierce and persistently accurate. Eventually we rejoined the Avengers off the coast, feeling as though we had come on a wild-goose chase.

We had been back in the ship for only a short time when there was a flurry of excitement. We were summoned at the double to see Wings.

'Panic on, chaps! Maximum effort required. Get every damn thing that will fly refuelled and re-armed. The Admiral's calling for an all-out effort!'

Mike was the first to speak.

'What's the target, sir?'

'Shinchiku again. Get them cracking!'

I looked at Michael, then back to Wings.

'But there's damn-all there, sir! Hell! We've just come back! It's like Easter Sunday!'

'Hans! For God's sake don't argue! Get on with it! The Admiral says there's more than 300 aircraft there!'

Mike looked as bewildered as I felt. He tried again:

'So far as I'm concerned, there are 300 bomb craters there and nothing else. The Admiral has to be talking about somewhere else!'

By this time the discussion group—it was now 'war-by-committee'—had moved from the flying bridge to the compass platform. Now the Captain joined in.

'You're sure about this?' We nodded. 'You're sure you've been to Shinchiku?' Nods of assent again, unanimous and vigorous. 'And you say there's nothing there?'

'Absolutely nothing, sir.'

'Right. Leave it to me for five minutes. And don't pull out any stops until I say so.'

Within a few minutes he recalled us.

'The flap's off. It seems that a pilot from another carrier reported that there were "three or four aircraft". Some IO has apparently written down "Three *oh* four" and has reported it to the Staff as such.' He waited for explosions. None came. For once, we were tongue-tied. 'So the Admiral has called off the strike.' He grinned at Ian Sarel.

As we walked down the flight-deck, Mike said in his unemotional way:

'Now how the hell does anyone with any sense at all get around to accepting as Gospel a figure like 304?'

Gerry Connolly, a Southern Irishman whose famous uncle had been shot as a rebel by the British during the Easter Rising of 1916, and who accepted Englishmen with an easy-going tolerance, snorted and allowed a derisory grin to spread over his face.

'They must have worked it out that the pilot, whoever he was, counted 912 aircraft wheels and divided it by three. That's the English way, isn't it?'

Jake Millard never made it. The Mayday signals we had transmitted whistled up an American Martin Mariner flying boat, expert at its job of air/sea rescue. But, although they searched the area assiduously for hours, they had no luck. Jake had gone for ever.

16

Finished with engines

And then, like so many times over the past years, it was all over. For *Illustrious*, April 13 was the last day of Operation *Iceberg* and, after spending two days in the replenishment area with the Fleet Train, we sailed for the Philippines. Our anchoring in Leyte Gulf and the anticipation of the usual traffic between ships was clouded with sadness for me.

Johnny Baker's brother Sam was an Avenger pilot in *Indomitable*. In recent weeks we had seen him pull off a classic ditching alongside a destroyer when his undercarriage failed to extend. It was done so magnificently in a nasty, short sea with a vicious chop that Sam and his two crewmen had been rescued without difficulty. In fact, I doubt even if Sam got his hair wet.

So now Johnny took a boat across to *Indomitable* to see how Sam had fared in the Sakishima battles. He was frozen to the spot when her Officer of the Watch informed him on arrival at the gangway that his brother had been killed up in the islands.

I felt deeply for John. He was—and still is—a fine chap and in post-war years I was to be fortunate enough to become acquainted with all his family. To lose one's brother was bad enough; but to learn of it in such a manner was an even more bitter blow. I wondered then, as I do now, at the callousness of Sam's friends and senior officers who so lamentably found this to be their way of breaking such news. It could so easily have been done more delicately. A private signal to *Illustrious* would have enabled Captain Lambe to tell Johnny the bad tidings in his own very special way, with infinite kindness and sympathy.

There was, however, a more pleasant surprise awaiting us. There, across the great harbour, looking very smart and warlike, lay *Formidable*, third ship of our class, freshly arrived from the UK. She looked good and her Corsairs on deck brooded, as always, like menacing harbingers of death.

Michael Tritton was an old friend of 'Judy' Garland, one of her Corsairs' COs. With bitter memories of the toll that Sakishima Gunto had taken of our boys, he went across to *Formid* to put Judy wise as to what constituted life and death up in the islands. He would do it well, too, for there is nothing pedantic about him; quiet, reserved, pleasant and no 'fighter boy' nonsense. But Judy was in no mood to listen.

'Cut the shop, old boy. Get this drink down you!' Mike would have liked to say—'No Hendon Air Display tricks. Sneak up on them and hit them first time, for there won't be a second chance. Be a dirty fighter.'

No one wanted to listen. But then, who does? We all know very well how to do it and need no lectures. We all insist on learning it the hard way. When they went to Sakishima, Judy was killed on the first day, diving down to do a strafing run.

But we didn't go back. *Formidable* had three propellers, a fresh crew and a new, 'on-the-ball' air group. We had only two propellers and a crew and air group who were now very weary and firing on only three cylinders. Our time to depart had come.

Some of the young men who had joined us as replacements only during the last two or three months were transferred to other carriers to work out their stint—Johnny Lowder, Don Cameron, Syd Newton, young Hartshorn, Johnny Maybank. We sat in Leyte Gulf for a day or two, refuelled and took on supplies. Then one fine day we left the Philippines for ever. *Illustrious* was going home.

As we passed through the Bismarck Sea *en route* for Sydney, we heard the wonderful news that the war in Europe had ended—VE Day. About 1800 we told our attendant destroyers to sheer off out of range, then gave the Bismarck Sea a *feu de joie* with everything we possessed, from 4.5-inch guns to Very pistols. For 30 seconds there was one hell of a racket. The Captain said a few words to the ship's company, most of whom were on the flight-deck to watch the fireworks. He was followed by the Chaplain who asked us to join him in prayers. Then Captain Lambe came back to the microphone to announce 'Splice the mainbrace!' We descended to the wardroom and, for the one and only time during the commission, had a glass of rum.

Our voyage down the eastern coast of Australia passed remarkably quickly and more farewells were in the offing. When we reached Sydney, we would be parting with pilots who were heading directly for home instead of the United Kingdom—Johnny Baker and Mo Pawson to Canada; Mick Ritchie, Matt Barbour, Jimmy Clark and 'Pop' Quigg to New Zealand. We would be leaving Jimmy James in Sydney to give the doctors a chance to heal his broken arm. He wouldn't get very far with the nurses unless they were agile and extremely co-operative, for our docs had constructed one of those preposterous girder jobs on which the offending limb reposed at a great height.

As we approached Sydney Heads we flew our Corsairs off to Bankstown; and that was the last we saw of them. Strangely enough, I felt no twinge. I can only suppose I assumed without question that in a matter of months we would be back at Bankstown to pick up new ones!

We flitted round Sydney like a cloud of moths with no home to go to. Probably because we were tired, there was no great burning up of the town. There was an air of anticlimax mixed with a certain amount of relief. Certainly there was no hilarious rejoicing at our release from the chores and the daily hazards of Sakishima Gunto. Japan still had to be broken and if their defence of Iwo Jima, Saipan, Okinawa—yes, and Sakishima—was any criterion, to beat them on their home ground would be hell let loose. In our secret hearts we knew we would be back again. But all that was in the future. It would be a long time before we sailed again through Sydney Heads. So we lived for the day and wondered, in the vaguest possible way, what tomorrow—or next year—would bring.

At last we sailed; and it seemed strange to be passengers. The hangar was a great, echoing emptiness. The barriers and arrestor wires had been unshipped. There wasn't an aircraft in sight. And from Sydney Heads we saw not a ship until we sailed into Aden to refuel.

We stopped for 24 hours in Port Said, where Ian Sarel and I spent an hour or two at the Officers' Club. At midnight we strolled down to the quay to look for a boat to take us out to the carrier, anchored in the stream nearly half a mile away. There was a small rowing-boat tied up, with a couple of the usual unsavoury characters aboard.

'You want boat, Captain?' shouted one of them. We walked over to the steps and told them where we wanted to go. We were in a mellow, generous mood and didn't argue too vehemently about the fare. The oarsmen bent to their task as we settled ourselves in the stern-sheets.

Somewhere about halfway they stopped and rested on their oars.

'Come on! Igri! Igri!' I shouted, using one of my two words of Arabic.

'More money, Captain! We want more money!'

This is it, I thought. It's the old taxi racket all over again, but this time surrounded by water. I looked around for a weapon and was relieved to see that the tiller could be unshipped; but there was nothing for Ian. Strangely enough, for a man with no experience at all of the wiles of the Egyptians, he looked remarkably calm. He was still very composed as he produced a .38 revolver from his trouser waistband.

'Just carry on rowing and no funny business'—with a menacing wave of that thing in his right hand. Needless to say, we reached *Illustrious* in record time.

The Port Said of those days abounded in touts of every description, probably exceeded only by those of Cairo. Hawkers roamed the streets with anything from hair-combs to 'feelthy pictures' and small boys of unbelievable precocity touted for the girls, usually 'My sister! You come see my sister! Pink inside, just like white girl!' The story was told of a ship's Captain who, landing at one of the quays and striding purposefully for the administrative offices, was waylaid in such a manner by a scruffy little urchin.

'Run away, little boy!' said the Captain, testily. 'It's the harbour-master I want!'

'OK, Captain!' was the unabashed retort. 'OK! Come, please! Can arrange!'

Some of our young men had learnt a little about it even in 12 short hours. When Ian and I went down to the wardroom, we were lucky enough to find that some kind souls had kept a couple of drinks for us, for the bar had now been closed for more than an hour. A few of the subbies were saying hard things about the local inhabitants for, despite warnings from old 'desert types', they had nevertheless fallen for one of the oldest tricks under the Pyramids.

'You want dirty pictures, Captain?' was the opening gambit, with a quick flourish of a photograph, postcard size, of an Edwardian gentleman clad in black socks, sporting a large handlebar moustache, on the point of bestriding a buxom middle-aged old sport in black stockings and fancy garters.

'Packet of 12, Captain! *Very* dirty! *Ve-ry* exciting! Only 50 piastres!'

The boys fell for it like a gluttonous salmon going for a fly. While the high-pressure salesman was running like a hare down some unmentionable side-street, our young men were avidly inspecting their purchase: one nauseating shot of grotesque copulation, ten rather pleasant views of Cairo Mosque, the Pyramids and the de Lesseps statue and a dreadful portrait of the even more dreadful King Farouk.

After leaving Port Said, we organised evening concerts on the flight-deck, even at the risk of damaging our precious piano by bringing it up on the after lift. We had endless deck hockey tournaments. The highlight for most of us was a reversion to peacetime routine when at 1200 every day it was 'Hands to bathe'. The ship hove to and for half an hour anything up to 1,000 men cavorted in the blue water, miles from land.

Gibraltar; and another 24 hours' stop. We took on board the entire crew of a U-boat which had recently sailed in to surrender. The Captain was a nasty, flaxen-haired Teuton, full to the eyebrows of National Socialism who, contrary to the attitude of his more reasonably minded officers, appeared to possess a desire to continue the war on a private basis. He had to be strictly isolated from them. When he proved to be thoroughly intransigent, he was confined permanently to his cabin. We applauded to a man the orders of the Commander to the Marine sentry posted at his door with rifle and fixed bayonet, that he should not hesitate to run through this Nazi should he attempt to leave his cabin. I spent quite a lot of time hanging around that particular flat in the fervent hope that the Marine would be given his chance!

The U-boat's crew were a fine bunch of lads who readily joined our own ship's company in the task of chipping paintwork, in readiness for the forthcoming refit. The gusto and thoroughness with which they went about their work should have told us that Germany wouldn't be too long in recovering from the destruction of their country.

At 18 knots we plugged through the Bay of Biscay and were now within reach of home. The minefields down the east coast of Britain were still to be cleared and, at the height of a lovely summer, we cruised at a leisurely 13 or 14 knots through the Western Isles, sitting on deck and admiring the magnificent scenery as it was unfolded before us.

What awaited us when we reached port? I don't suppose many of us gave it a thought. So far as we knew, *Illustrious* would undergo a pretty thorough refit. We would probably find ourselves in some less exacting jobs for a spell—and then? Back to the Pacific without a doubt, for the subjugation of Japan itself promised to be another Thirty Years' War. (The destruction of Hiroshima, however, to astound the world within a few short weeks, would resolve all our problems. It would also pose a bagful of new ones.)

So we turned the corner and cruised southwards to Rosyth, happy and contented in our serene, blissful ignorance. We didn't know that never again would we have to face the fearful flak over Ishigaki. Never again would our heads spin round at the cry of 'Rats!! Three o'clock up!' No more would the Corsairs screech to a stop as they pulled out the screaming arrestor wires. The basha huts of Trincomalee, the crocodiles in the estuary, the incredible green of the Sumatran jungle and the wide, limitless expanse of the great oceans—we had seen them all for the last time.

Our war was over—and we didn't know it.

And what of our fine squadrons? The Canadians and most of the New Zealanders had already gone home. Those of us who were still in the ship would be scattered to the four winds as soon as we reached port. Only a handful of us would ever meet again.

Joe Vickers, Bud Sutton, Winnie Churchill and a host of others were dead. We had left them in America, in Sumatra, in Ceylon and in the great wastes of the oceans. When the tumult and the shouting had died we would remember them, for the ties of the Branch are strong and the comradeship, the courage, the fun, the heroism and the heartache of the war would never be forgotten by those of us who lived.

And then at last the saga was over. We steamed up the Forth, the first ship to return from the Pacific war. Every vessel in the estuary manned ship in our honour and their cheers floated down to us in turn as we passed them. There is something akin to a lump in my throat, even after all these years, as I hear the distant bugles sounding the 'Still' as our great Old Lady swept majestically up to the dockyard. She was *my* ship, the only ship to which I had truly belonged. My pride in her was still unabated. Her magic name has ever since been part of my life.

Appendix A

Pilots of the 15th Naval Fighter Wing

Wing Leader—Lieutenant-Commander (A) R. J. Cork, DSO, DSC, RN (killed April 1944)

1830 Squadron
Quonset Point, Rhode Island, USA. June 1943
Lieutenant-Commander D. B. M. Fiddes, DSO, RN (killed December 1943)
Lieutenant (A) D. F. Hadman, DSC, RNVR
Lieutenant (A) L. H. E. Retallick, RNVR*
Lieutenant (A) E. H. Gaunt, RCNVR (killed June 1943)
Lieutenant (A) A. W. C. Sutton, RCNVR* (killed January 1945)
Sub-Lieutenant (A) A. Harris, RNVR (killed June 1943)
Sub-Lieutenant (A) C. R. Facer, RNVR
Sub-Lieutenant (A) A. H. Millard, RNVR (missing, presumed drowned, April 1945)
Sub-Lieutenant (A) B. R. Guy, RNVR (missing, presumed killed, May 1944)
Sub-Lieutenant (A) A. H. Brown, RNVR (killed January 1945)
Sub-Lieutenant (A) A. Graham-Cann, RNVR (killed January 1945)
Sub-Lieutenant (A) G. McHardy, RNVR (posthumous GM, killed March 1944)
Sub-Lieutenant (A) D. Morgan, RNVR (killed June 1943)

Ex-1831 Squadron. October 1943
Lieutenant (A) P. S. Cole, DSC, RNVR (later RN, killed post-war flying)
Sub-Lieutenant (A) R. A. Quigg, RNZNVR
Sub-Lieutenant (A) B. Maclaren, RNVR
Sub-Lieutenant (A) J. Fullerton, RNVR

Ex-1838 Squadron. September 1944
Lieutenant (A) G. S. P. Salmon, RNVR*
Sub-Lieutenant (A) H. G. Scott, RNVR

Sub-Lieutenant (A) J. A. Roberts, RNVR
Sub-Lieutenant (A) W. Christie, RNVR

Replacements
Lieutenant-Commander (A) A. M. Tritton, DSC and two bars, RNVR (succeeded Lieutenant-Commander Cork as Wing Leader after the latter's death)
Sub-Lieutenant (A) M. J. Pawson, RCNVR
Sub-Lieutenant (A) H. Whelpton, RNVR
Sub-Lieutenant (A) S. Newton, RNVR (killed from *Victorious*, August 1945)
Sub-Lieutenant (A) H. Marritt, RNVR (killed April 1945)
Sub-Lieutenant (A) J. Maybank, RNZNVR

1833 Squadron
Quonset Point, Rhode Island, USA. August 1943
Lieutenant-Commander H. A. Monk, DSM and bar, RN (transferred March 1944)
Lieutenant-Commander (A) N. S. Hanson, DSC, RNVR*
Lieutenant (A) W. K. Munnoch, RNVR
Lieutenant (A) J. R. Baker, DSC, RCNVR
Sub-Lieutenant (A) F. C. Starkey, RNVR
Sub-Lieutenant (A) K. L. Boddington, RNVR (killed August 1943)
Sub-Lieutenant (A) R. J. Shaw, RNVR (killed January 1945)
Sub-Lieutenant (A) P. S. Builder, RNVR (transferred September 1943)
Sub-Lieutenant (A) G. Aitken, RNVR
Sub-Lieutenant (A) N. Brynildsen, RNZNVR (transferred August 1944)

Ex-1831 Squadron. October 1943.
Sub-Lieutenant (A) A. S. Booth, RNVR*
Sub-Lieutenant (A) K. Seebeck, RNZNR (transferred August 1944)
Sub-Lieutenant (A) D. Monteith, RNVR (killed January 1944)
Sub-Lieutenant (A) A. S. Vickers, RNVR (killed March 1944)
Sub-Lieutenant (A) S. Buchan, RNVR

Ex-1838 Squadron. September 1944.
Lieutenant (A) J. A. Parli, DSC, RNZNVR
Lieutenant (A) A. H. Churchill, RNZNVR* (posthumous) (killed April 1945)
Lieutenant (A) J. Morgan, RCNVR (killed October 1944)
Lieutenant H. James, RN

Sub-Lieutenant (A) J. W. Lee, RNVR
Sub-Lieutenant (A) E. J. Baxter, RNZNVR (killed January 1945)
Sub-Lieutenant (A) B. Heffer, DSC, RNZNVR
Sub-Lieutenant (A) R. Ayrton, RNVR

Replacements
Lieutenant (A) D. Cameron, RNVR
Sub-Lieutenant (A) E. Rogers, RNVR (killed January 1945)
Sub-Lieutenant (A) M. Barbour, RNZNVR
Sub-Lieutenant (A) M. A. Ritchie, RNZNVR
Sub-Lieutenant (A) J. Clark, RNZNVR
Sub-Lieutenant (A) J. Lowder, RNVR
Sub-Lieutenant (A) D. Hartshorn, RNZNVR

* Mentioned in despatches.
Ranks shown are those held at the end of the commission. (A) denotes
the Air Branch of the Royal Naval Volunteer Reserve.

Appendix B

Corsair and Avenger data

Corsair (F4U)
Built by Chance Vought, Stratford, Connecticut, USA. Single-engined, single-seat fighter. Engine: Pratt & Whitney 18-cylinder R.2800, 2,000 hp with two-stage supercharger. Wing span 41 feet, length 33 feet 4 inches. Take-off weight 11,093 lb. Operating height 36,900 feet. Maximum speed 417 mph at 19,900 feet. Armament: Six Browning .5-inch machine-guns, three in each wing. Later adapted to carry two 500 lb bombs on racks beneath wing roots.

Avenger (TBF)
Built by Grumman Aircraft Corporation, Long Island, New York, USA. Torpedo bomber, crew of three—pilot, navigator, air-gunner. Engine: Wright Cyclone 2800, 1,900 hp. Wing span 54 feet, length 40 feet. Take-off weight 18,250 lb. Operating height 23,000 feet. Maximum speed 267 mph. Armament: Two fixed Browning .5-inch machine-guns in wings; dorsal turret with one similar gun. One .30-inch machine-gun firing through propeller and one similar gun in ventral turret. Carried one 21-inch torpedo or four 500 lb bombs in enclosed bay.

Glossary

ADDLs Assisted Dummy Deck-Landings.
AEO Air Engineer Officer.
AFO Admiralty Fleet Order.
AGO Air Gunnery Officer.
Aileron A hinged section situated at the rear wingtip end of each wing which, together with the rudder, enables the aircraft to bank in a turn. Operated by sideways movement of the joystick or control column.
Aircraft (Allied) *Brewster Buffalo*: An American single-engined, single-seat fighter, obsolescent in 1942. *Chance Vought F4U Corsair:* See Appendix B. *Fairey Fulmar:* A single-engined, twin-seat fighter, obsolescent in the Royal Navy in 1941. *Gloster Gladiator:* A single-engined, single-seat fighter, biplane, obsolescent at the outbreak of war. *Grumman F3F:* An American single-engined, single-seat fighter, biplane, obsolescent in 1941. *Grumman F4F Martlet or Wildcat:* An American single-engined, single-seat fighter. Not so powerful, fast or heavily armed as the Grumman F6F. *Grumman F6F Hellcat:* Grumman's equivalent of the Corsair. Single-engined, single-seat fighter, with 2,000 hp engine and six .5-inch machine guns. *Grumman Avenger* TBF: See Appendix B.
Aircraft (Axis) *Junkers Ju 88:* German twin-engined all-purpose fighter-bomber. Generally considered to be one of the most successful aircraft of World War 2. *Oscar, Tojo, Zeke and Zero:* Code-names for Japanese single-engined, single-seat fighters. *Myrtle:* Japanese twin-engined, two-seater fighter. *Betty* and *Sally:* Japanese all-purpose, but mainly bomber/torpedo bomber aircraft.
Aldis Lamp A small, hand-held signalling lamp, operated by batteries.
Altimeter An aircraft instrument connected to an aneroid barometer showing height in feet above sea- or ground-level.
AOR Air Operations Room.
A/S Anti-Submarine.
Asdic Underwater submarine detecting device, used by submarines and their hunters—destroyers, frigates, sloops, corvettes, etc.

Bats The 'paddles' held by the batsman on an aircraft carrier. Made usually of fluorescent material.
Batsman The deck-landing signals officer; invariably an ex-pilot.
CFI Chief Flying Instructor.
CPO Chief Petty Officer.
Dartmouth Royal Naval College situated at Dartmouth, Devon.
DSC Distinguished Service Cross.
DSM Distinguished Service Medal.
FDO Fighter Direction Officer.
Flap A rear extension of the aircraft wing which can be lowered by degrees to achieve greater 'lift' at critically lower speeds.
Flight A formation of four aircraft, comprising two sections of two, flying in 'finger' formation. Led by a Flight Commander. (Earlier in the war, a formation of three aircraft in V formation.)
G force Force of gravity.
Gobs Enlisted men (ratings) of the United States Navy.
GOC General Officer Commanding.
Goofer An onlooker, often morbid.
IFF A transmitter carried by Allied aircraft which identified itself as such on a radar screen. Called 'Identification—friend or foe'.
IO Intelligence Officer.
Iron deck The main deck of a destroyer.
Irvine jacket A leather flying jacket, thickly lined with lamb's-wool.
MP Military Policeman.
NA2SL Naval Assistant to the Second Sea Lord.
OOD Officer of the Day.
OOW Officer of the Watch.
PMO Principal Medical Officer.
PO Petty Officer.
RAA Rear Admiral Aircraft Carriers.
Rattle To be 'in the rattle' is to be the subject of a disciplinary charge.
RFA Royal Fleet Auxiliary.
Rigger Naval rating—CPO downwards—whose responsibility was the airframe of an aircraft. Embraced virtually everything except engine, guns and electrics.
Robinson's Patent Disengaging Gear A device for 'slipping' into the sea, on an even keel, a whaler or cutter from the crane of a warship.
R/T Radio/Telephone. The VHF (very high frequency) radio equipment which was the fighter pilot's only communication with his carrier or shore station. TBR aircraft were similarly equipped but additionally had W/T (Wireless/Telegraphy).
Section A formation of two aircraft.

Senior Pilot Second-in-command of a naval air squadron. He was also in charge of aircraft maintenance.

Stall A dangerous attitude in flying, brought about by a loss of flying speed.

TBR Torpedo, Bombing, Reconnaissance.

Turn-and-bank indicator An instrument which shows the rate of turn being made by the aircraft; and which indicates if the turn is correctly balanced without yawing or skidding.

Whale Island HMS *Excellent*, Portsmouth. The Royal Navy's Gunnery School.